William Wetmore Story

Fine arts

William Wetmore Story

Fine arts

ISBN/EAN: 9783337311018

Printed in Europe, USA, Canada, Australia, Japan

Cover: Foto ©Thomas Meinert / pixelio.de

More available books at **www.hansebooks.com**

FINE ARTS.

WILLIAM W. STORY.

REPORT

ON

THE FINE ARTS.

Mr. Edward M. Gallaudet, in his report on the Vienna International Exhibition of 1873 and "The Governmental Patronage of Art," after regretting that no part of the appropriation made by Congress to enable "the people of the United States to participate in the advantages of the Exposition at Vienna could be expended in the purchase of a portion at least of the rich art treasures there exhibited," concludes by "expressing the hope that no such opportunity in the future will be neglected by the government." Reference to Vienna Exposition of 1873.

This hope has not been gratified. For the recent International Exposition at Paris not only was no fund specially appropriated to enrich our country with treasures of art, but the small sum of $150,000 actually appropriated to cover all expenses of every kind was not only so insufficient in itself, but was so tardily given as to render it impossible for America to make an exhibition worthy of a great country, not only in the department of the fine arts, but even in those of industry, commerce, machinery, manufactures, natural products, and mechanical arts.* Inadequacy of the sum voted by the United States Government for Paris Exposition of 1878.

Both money and time were wanting, and, as the limitation of time necessarily added to the expenses, the sum appropriated, small as it was, was by this circumstance practically diminished. The consequence has been an injury, not only to the reputation of the country, but even more to its material interests. Insufficient time for preparation.

"*Noblesse oblige*" is a motto which is unknown to or rejected by our country. We wish to take among nations the high place to which we are justly entitled, but we grudge the necessary outlay. Our penurious grants of money for great public objects retard the development of the country; our inefficient salaries to public officers of trust offer a

---

* This sum was in fact found to be so utterly inadequate that subsequently, after the Exposition was open, and it was too late to retrieve the past, an additional sum of $40,000 was granted to cover necessary expenses.

temptation to fraud, or exclude from them all who have not private means to sustain worthily their position and independence. The laborer is not considered worthy of his hire. The cry of retrenchment suffices to stop a proper and even necessary expenditure. We expect to secure great public services for inadequate pay, and that which would be recognized as folly in the administration of private affairs is thought to be quite satisfactory in the conduct of public and national interests.

Cry of "retrenchment."

The Paris Exposition of 1878 America's opportunity.

At this International Exposition at Paris a great opportunity was offered to America to lift itself in the estimation of the world, and to increase the market for all its material products. Whether or not we care what is thought of us abroad, we are at least susceptible to our interests, and these have been undoubtedly affected to a serious extent by the incomplete exhibition of ourselves which the government forced upon the country by its unwise economy and delay.

It may be quite satisfactory to those who opposed and delayed the grant of the insufficient sum which Congress finally gave to this Exposition, to be able to declare to their constituents that by their earnest efforts for "retrenchment," and by their tender care of the "people's money," they have saved the country the sum of several thousands of dollars; but it is not quite so satisfactory to find that for every thousand dollars thus saved it is the firm belief of those who have ample opportunity to know, that at least a hundred thousand dollars have been lost to the country by this parsimony. Nor is it quite satisfactory to feel assured that we have also made an incomplete exhibition of ourselves before the world, and, were we to be judged by this Exposition, would fail to take our proper rank.*

Penny wise, pound foolish.

Imperfect exhibition in our fine arts section.

If this be the case in the departments of industry and the mechanic arts, how much more so is it in that of the fine arts, where we were so sparsely and imperfectly represented. We have been accustomed to boast that in sculpture our country

* I desire here to bear my testimony to the spirit, energy, and efficiency shown by our chief commissioner, Governor McCormick, in arranging and directing the various departments and administering the fund appropriated to this Exposition. All that was possible to be done with the means at his disposal was promptly and admirably done. Whatever deficiencies there were were due to the necessities of the case, and not to any lack of administrative ability or earnest good will on his part. It was, for instance, to his efforts, in conjunction with those of Mr. Philbrick, that the educational section, which reflected great honor on our country and awakened a world-wide interest; owed its existence.

could at least take rank with that of any in Europe, but in this Exposition American sculpture had no place and no representative. It was necessarily excluded. There was neither money nor time to render such an exhibition possible. No space was assigned to it in the portion of the building allotted to the United States. Not only was no sculptor requested to send any of his works, but he was forbidden to do so. The grant was too small to enable the Commissioner-General to assume the necessary expenses of transmission or placing, or arrangement of a proper room, and the time was too short either to obtain such a room or to do what was absolutely necessary. Sculpture was therefore excluded. The expenses and risks incident to an exhibition of sculpture are of course far greater than those which are required for an exhibition of paintings, and, had such an exhibition been determined upon, these would have fallen solely upon the sculptors themselves, some of whom were unable and some unwilling to bear them. Those whose reputations were already established had little desire to assume such burdens, with nothing to gain and everything to risk, while others who properly had a right to be represented had not the means.

No exhibition of sculpture from the United States.

Sculpture excluded by the insufficient appropriation.

Small consideration has ever been paid by America to her own achievements in the fine arts in any international exhibition, but this is the first in which our country has formally excluded sculpture. With most nations, the department of the fine arts has ever been looked upon as the flower of their exhibition. No pains have been spared to render it attractive; no expense refused to give it importance and completeness. It is here that the highest laurels have been won, and in the success and distinction of their artists all other nations have felt the warmest interest and pride. We alone have treated art with indifference, if not contempt—wholly neglected its claims, and sternly refused any outlay of money to advance its interests. What we have done has been incompletely done and grudgingly done.

Fine arts the flower of all international exhibitions.

At the International Exhibition of London, in 1862, the Papal Government assumed all the risk and expenses of works of art to and from the exhibition, insuring the safe carriage and return of any work. Nor did it exclude from this generous plan the artists of other nations working at Rome, but extended to them the same privileges and rights it gave to its own subjects. It took care, at its own expense, and by its own expert commissioners, that the rooms allotted to the arts should be handsomely decorated and arranged. Its generosity was well rewarded. The Roman court was

Action of the Papal Government at the London Exhibition of 1862.

one of the chief features of interest in the Exhibition, and gave distinction not only to the artists but to Rome.

Duty of government towards artists.

But, without entering here into details, it may be said in general that there is no government in Europe which has considered itself absolved from all duties toward artists, and none which has not acknowledged the claims of art, and shown a generous and liberal spirit in advancing its interests. Not only the first-class powers of France, England, Germany, Austria, and Italy, but all the smaller countries, without exception, have equally felt it to be their duty, their interest, and their pride to develop national art, encourage national artists, establish museums and academies, and gather together, for the study and delight of all, collections of works of the past and present by the ablest masters in sculpture and painting and the sister arts. America is the only nation which, as a nation, has done nothing.

National museums and art academies.

Earnest efforts have undoubtedly been made in some of the principal cities of the United States to encourage and develop the fine arts, and various academies, museums, and schools of art have been founded by private munificence and association, which, as far as their funds will allow, are endeavoring to supply the absence of all action by the nation. These are well administered, and great credit is due to the founders and officers for their public spirit and energy. Among these may be mentioned the museums and academies at Boston, New York, Philadelphia, and the gallery at Washington, created and given to the city by Mr. Corcoran and sustained by his generosity. But these are all private and local in their character and their funds. They are not national institutions.

Private munificence in the United States a substitute for national encouragement.

Corcoran Gallery, Washington, D. C.

We have no national collections or schools of art.

We have no national collections; no national museums, academies, or schools of art. We have no national rewards for merit; no diplomas or medals for success; no recognition save that of public and general estimation for the works of distinguished artists. The medals, diplomas, and decorations which they have obtained have been conferred upon them by foreign countries. It is true that in the International Exhibition at Philadelphia, medals were assigned as well to the products of art as of industry; but the list of medallists was so extended as to detract from the value and significance of the medals given. The medals had all the same value, and no distinction of merit one above another.

Centennial medals were all of one grade and were not national.

But even these were not conferred by the nation, which neither gave its authority nor its purse to this Exhibition. It did, indeed, temporarily lend some money to further the enterprise, which was of a private character purely, but it strictly exacted the repayment of the sum. A government vessel was also sent abroad to transport free of freight the works of Americans, and especially of artists. The sum expended in this way, had it been differently administered, by an intelligent commission, would have gone far toward defraying the general expenses of the American exhibitors abroad. As it was, it was wasted in merely relieving them from the payment of freights—for which a quarter of the sum would have sufficed to transport the works in the ordinary way. Freight, however, was but the smallest of the expenses to which any artist, and particularly any sculptor, was subjected. All other expenses and risks were thrown upon his shoulders. If his picture or statue was damaged, broken, or lost, he had no remedy; if, as really occurred, the cases in which his works had been packed were destroyed by fire in the storage sheds, without his fault, he alone sustained the loss.

Government aid in transporting works of art from abroad to Philadelphia.

As a nation, we do not profess to look down upon art; at least, we utterly neglect it. It forms no portion of our education, and in the public representative bodies of our country a lamentable ignorance prevails. There is neither knowledge nor good taste in the patronage of the government. No great national academy or museum of art exists to confer honors and rewards, to educate students, or to improve the public taste; all the academies and museums that exist are private and local in their character, limited in their means, and unsupported by the nation. The American artist, therefore, having but restricted opportunities to educate himself in his own country, is forced to expatriate himself for the purpose of study. After he has to a certain extent accomplished himself in his art, if he returns to his own country he meets at every turn but obstacles and disappointments. The patronage of the government is for the most part in the hands of the ignorant, and it is but too often the prize of successful lobbying, from which the true artist withdraws in shame.

National neglect of art.

Americans forced to study abroad.

If we are a great country, as justly we claim to be, let us behave like a great country. Is it creditable for us, with all our wealth and prosperity, to be without a great national museum and academy of art—such as is to be found in every great capital in Europe? How can we expect to take rank in art with the great nations of Europe, when neither our nation itself nor any State or city in the Union possesses a gallery of art of which any second-rate government of Europe would not be ashamed? While we have nothing, can we without mortification look at the magnificent collections abroad and consider the munificent manner in which

Should not a national academy and museum of art be founded in the United States?

they are supported and constantly enriched by public grants? In England, besides the treasures of private collections, there is the National Gallery, rich in the most splendid works of the greatest painters; the British Museum, adorned with the noblest relics of antique sculpture, vases, gems, terra-cotta ornaments, bronzes, not to speak of the incomparable library and other departments in the museum; the Kensington Museum, a store-house of treasures of the mediæval world and of the *Renaissance*. Costly as these collections are, they are constantly enlarged by munificent grants from Parliament. Not a year passes that conspicuous sums are not paid to secure still additional treasures. It suffices that England knows that anything of real value and excellence is to be procured, and her purse-strings are liberally opened to obtain it. Not only this, large sums of money are constantly granted to explore the soil of ancient Greece, and to unearth the master-pieces of antique sculpture and architecture. There is no corner of the world where she is not prying, regardless of cost, to discover valuable relics of the ancient world of art. Under her auspices the soil of Halicarnassus yielded up the lost sculpture of the famous Mausoleum. The Parthenon conceded to her its glorious but defaced works. To her liberality, enterprise, and determination we owe it that we still have the remains of Lycian art, the massive sculpture and cuneiform inscriptions of Nineveh—the Phigalean marbles. Besides these great museums, it was under her patronage that the Royal Academy was founded and still lives, and is regarded as a national institution.

ENGLAND. National Gallery. British Museum. Kensington Museum. Grants by Parliament. British success in unearthing and securing antiquities. Halicarnassus. Parthenon. Lycian art. Nineveh. Phigalean marbles. Royal Academy.

Nor far behind her is France, with her magnificent national galleries of sculpture and painting, covering acres of ground, and illustrated with the noblest works of the ancient and modern world, with her academies of art, science, and literature, whose hard-won honors are coveted throughout the world, with her annual prizes to those who distinguish themselves in art. Her golden medals of merit, her "*Prix de Rome*," her encouraging hands are ready to help and cheer the artist. In no grudging spirit she expends from the public purse large annual sums to add to her already rich collections of art; and in celebration of this international gathering, has built the great palace of the Trocadero as a permanent gallery of retrospective art. Here are gathered together, in chronological series, the artistic relics of the past from the earliest ages—a mere description of which would involve the history of art itself. This she

FRANCE. "*Prix de Rome*." Trocadero Gallery of Retrospective Art.

has done to show to the world that the Republic does not intend to be behind the Empire in the liberal fostering of art. FRANCE. European galleries embrace the present as well as the past.

Nor can it be said that all the galleries of Europe are the accumulations of the past only, and that it would be impossible for us even to attempt a rivalship in this regard with the nations of Europe. The Kensington Museum and this very palace of the Trocadero, among others, are a proof of the contrary; and still more have we an example in Munich of what a large and generous spirit can do in our own day. Munich. It is within our own recent memory that King Louis founded the Glyptothek and Pinacothek there, and created and developed a new school of art. Glyptothek. Pinacothek. This, at least, is certain, that we never shall make any progress towards having a great national museum, or academy, or school of art, until we begin in earnest. Up to the present day, we have not begun. How, then, can we expect to have a national character in our art? But the unfortunate fact is that the very proposition in Congress to appropriate even an inadequate sum for such a purpose would probably arouse the strongest opposition, and afford an opportunity for much blatant talk about the necessity of retrenchment and the duty of keeping "the people's money."

As it is, art is heavily handicapped in America. Our government declines the responsibility of encouraging art. The notion of our government is that it must manage for itself, without means and opportunities of study and culture, depend for its support upon private patronage solely, and develop itself as it may in the cold shadow of neglect. One might as well expect the highest literary culture without libraries and schools, or the rarest exotic without a shelter from the chill of winter.

One could not but be struck, even in the most cursory glance at the Exposition, by the fact that the sharp division of schools which once characterized the different nations of Europe has become very much obliterated. Former divisions of "Schools of Art" becoming obliterated. The modern facilities of travel have tended to draw them all together into one great nationality of art. Formerly the artists of each country remained at home, seeking their subjects in the life and nature by which they were surrounded, and developing a national character and style. Not only was this evident in the schools of various nations in the past, when the Dutch and Flemish schools, for instance, were so widely separated in all their characteristics from those of Italy, but it was also seen in the various schools of the same country, those of Venice, Tuscany, and Bologna being clearly distinguished from each other. In the present day, however, these national

Centers of art draw students of every nationality.

characteristics are far less discriminated. The great centers of art draw to them students of every nation, who carry back methods there learned to their own country, and thus it happens that the French school has distinguished representatives throughout Germany, Italy, Hungary, and in like manner the German schools have their representatives in France and America, and the Spanish school in Italy and elsewhere. Besides this, many artists permanently reside and practice their art in foreign lands and cities, and are scarcely to be distinguished in style and method from the native artists. If this be observable to a certain extent among all nations, more or less, nowhere was it more strongly marked than in the American department of painting in this Exposition. Here there was no nationality, no peculiarity of method, style, or thought, distinguishing the works of America from those of the rest of the world.

American artists follow European methods.

Our artists have been driven abroad to study by the utter absence of any materials for study at home, and the natural consequence is that they have taken up the style and method of their masters, both in subject and in treatment. The aptness with which they have caught these characteristic features shows susceptibility, but, as Michel Angelo said, he who follows must go behind. We have many clever scholars, but, as yet, no masters.

American art imitative rather than original.

This tendency to imitation in American art, and this absence of bold originality, is specially to be wondered at in a nation which in other departments has shown so much independence of thought and character. What is still more remarkable is that the paintings which are claimed to be most American are least characterized by vigor of design, fine quality of workmanship, or originality of conception. Despite the talent which is often shown, there is, for the most part, a lack of culture, a lack of training, and a lack of ideas.

Individual exceptions.

In making these remarks I am only speaking of general characteristics and tendencies, to which individual exceptions are undoubtedly to be made. Some of the American pictures at Paris showed capacity of no mean order, but in few cases can it be said to have emancipated itself from the trammels of imitation, or boldly made its own path, or had anything special to say. In a word, there is little strong creative power, even where there is considerable mechanical accomplishment.

Art's excuse or being.

But if works of art are animated by no high poetic sense, and are neither original in conception nor admirable in execution, they have but little excuse for existing at all. Mere verses, however carefully written with all the requirements of rhythm and rhyme, are not poems.

AMERICA.

American pictures in Paris Exposition.

In the recent Exposition the comparatively few works of art which hung on the walls of the American department were well exhibited. The arrangement of the single room which contained them all compared favorably with that of any other nation. It is impossible, however, not to regret the absence of many of our most distinguished painters. In some cases undoubtedly this was occasioned by a misapprehension as to the period within which the pictures must have been painted in order to render them admissible, and also by an unfounded belief that only the works of living artists could be sent. In other cases, in consequence of the exceedingly limited space, pictures were rejected which ought to have been received. In other cases, the owners of some of the best pictures by American artists refused to incur the risk and expense of sending them without any guaranty of their safe restoration. In other cases, the painters had no sufficient notice to enable them to send their works. The time between the appropriation by Congress and its determination to participate at all in the Exposition on the one hand, and the opening of the Exposition on the other, was too short to enable the Commissioner to give proper notice. Everything necessarily was done in a hurry, and what is done in a hurry is seldom well done. Again, there were no committees appointed in the great centers of art—Italy, Germany, England, or France—to give proper information to the artists or to secure their co-operation. The result was that such artists as William Hunt, Cropsey, Tilton, Bierstadt, Haseltine, for instance, and many others who have attained distinction at home and abroad, were not represented at all; and those who did exhibit were restricted almost invariably to one picture, and that, in many cases, was selected, not because it was the best or most important one offered, but because of its size. Under such circumstances it is impossible to consider the paintings exhibited to be a fair representation of American art.

Reasons for incomplete display:

Misunderstanding of conditions of reception.

Want of notice.

Short time.

Some able artists not represented.

Number of pictures, etc., exhibited by— United States, 165.

England, 726.

France, 2,071.

Italy, 644.

The total number of pictures exhibited by the United States, in oil and water colors, was 143, and 19 engravings, etc. There was no sculpture. England exhibited 448 paintings and 46 works in sculpture and bas relief, 26 designs, 170 architectural designs, and 36 engravings, making a total of 726. France exhibited 1,065 paintings and 389 works in sculpture and bas relief, 388 architectural designs, 228 engravings and lithographs, making a total of 2,071. Italy exhibited 421 paintings, 180 works of sculpture, 30 architectural designs, and 13 engravings, making a total of 644.

PAINTING.

FRANCE.

FRANCE.

France, not only by the number of its works but by their quality and character, is entitled to the first rank and deserves to be first considered. The influence of its school of painting has been felt over all the world, and in its technical works it takes the lead of all. Some of the most admirable works of artists of other nations have been achieved under its influence and by the adoption of its methods; and its own achievements are generally in technical respects, and at times in poetic feeling, worthy of great praise. The drawing is for the most part admirable, showing that its artists have been carefully trained in those true principles which are the basis of all fine and intelligent work. They also are masters in their methods of using color, and their works, as painting, are vigorous, free, and rich in *impasto*. They understand the values of color, so that the different parts of their pictures take their place justly without confusion, and are properly subordinated in tone and effect. This, indeed, is the most essential technical quality of good painting. Without it there may fairly be said to be no good painting, whatever other merits a picture may have. It is this subordination of the unessential and unimportant to the main and important masses, alike in tone, color, and *chiaro-oscuro* which shows the training of the true artist. The intelligent understanding of the use of color and of its values, to use a technical phrase, is a marked characteristic of the French school, in which it is surpassed by no other school.

Influence of its school of painting.

Its great qualities: Feeling, Drawing,

Color.

Knowledge of color and its values, the test of the true artist.

One could not but be struck by the great and various talent which was everywhere displayed upon the walls of the French department of the fine arts. Among the thousand pictures exhibited there were few which, technically speaking, are positively bad; there were many that are admirable; there were a few that are masterpieces.

Technical execution may, however, become the master.

But, on the other hand, it is this very skill of technical execution by which French art is betrayed. Instead of being the subordinate and servant, it becomes the master. The mode of doing and saying has got to be of more consequence than the thing to be done and said. Execution has triumphed over ideas. A clever painting has got to be of more value than a poetic conception. Unworthy subjects are treated with masterly skill. The language has been thoroughly learned, but there seems to be little to say which is worth saying, and much that is said would be far better unsaid. There are almost no great conceptions, few poetic ideas, and little pure sentiment.* Among these many are purely *demi-monde* in character, or directly inspired by the model, and essentially studies from the nude. Naked women abound—standing, sitting, reclining—for no other apparent purpose than the display of technical skill in drawing and color. There are admirable reports of nature and landscape, but they are but too often mere studies, mere clever imitations of actual facts, without feeling or poetic charm. Any thing is good enough upon which the artist can exhibit his technical skill. There are many interiors of windows filled with *bric-à-brac* and furniture and vases and glasses, in which is seen a lady looking at herself in a mirror, putting on her gloves, plucking a flower, in which all the objects are rendered with admirable imitative skill, the folds and breaks of the satin dresses perfectly imitated, but which, after all, mean little, and are in themselves mere *bric-à-brac*. The greatest care is shown in painting all the details, and they are so well done, and so realistic, as to be almost, if not quite, as uninteresting as the reality thereof would be.

FRANCE.

Over-abundance of studies from the nude.

Studies, such as *bric-à-brac*, involving technical skill.

In a word, the attempt in all these pictures is to be realistic, not poetic; to demand applause for technical skill of execution, not to interest the heart and mind of the spectator by touches of passion, feeling, and sentiment.

Realistic, not poetic.

The desire to attract notice takes also two other phases, one to paint pictures so small that a *loupe* is required to see their finish of detail, one to cover great canvases with representations of incidents so brutal as to shock and startle the spectator. Thus art oscillates between the insignificant and the terrible. The same realism is carried into both. Blood and wounds are painted with a ghastly and horrible truth, as if the artist had a morbid relish for what is offensive and disgusting.

Microscopic minuteness of execution.

Startling brutality.

After these come the pictures of a debauched imagination, filled with innuendo and suggestion, corrupt in sentiment, and having nothing to recommend them but the technical cleverness with which they are done—the eternal nude model that the painter has painted from mere emptiness of mind, or for a worse reason, and which he tries to make poetic by the title of his canvas, but who only wakens in us the wish that she would put on her dress and go home.

Innuendo.

Pruriency.

In all this there is not only a singular absence of original

* The school of *genre* predominates and a large proportion of the paintings are devoted to anecdote and trivial incident.

FRANCE.

ideas, but a total want of recognition of what is the true end and object of art. One cannot but feel, on looking over this exhibition of erring talent, with Hamlet—that "there is something rotten in the state of [France]"; one cannot but regret that the great skill manifest everywhere should be so utterly wasted or dedicated to such unworthy ends.

A purer feeling reviving.

Fortunately, to this general tendency of French art, which is but the spawn of the last Empire, there are eminent exceptions, and it is plain that even now the current is beginning to set against it among artists and the public. The taste which had been so sadly debauched is beginning to revive in sentiment, and there are indications of a *Rennaissance* of a newer and purer school. It is to be hoped that this Exposition will have a beneficial influence, for here were collected some of the best pictures of other schools which appeal to a different standard. It is also to be feared that the search for novelty may lead them astray in another direction, and induce them to imitate examples which should be avoided in the future.

Absence of definite direction of art. Academic school departed. School of *genre* on the wane.

What strikes one at present is the absence of all definite direction of art. The academic school which so long triumphed in France has gone. The school of *genre*, which of late days has been in vogue, already begins to wane. Each artist seems in the general anarchy to be seeking blindly some new method—on one side, towards literal realism; on the other, towards sensational and vague impressions without detail or completeness; on another, towards extravagance; on still another, towards violence and brutality.

Little discipline, much individuality.

There is little discipline, but much individuality, and this in itself is good. Only one could wish that this individuality had its expression in better ways, and directed itself to nobler ends; that it were not so self-conscious and ready to sacrifice anything in order to attract attention, and that it acknowledged some distinct faith and some sincere purpose. However, we are now at a moment of indeterminateness between ebb and flow. The corrupt influence of the Empire has scarcely passed away; the tide has not yet decidedly set in a new direction.

Hopeful outlook.

But there is much to hope, and with their mastery of methods and their capacity of technical expression, we now wait to see if France has any great conceptions to express. Thus far there seems to be little indication of a powerful creative energy, of a lofty imagination, of a noble poetic feeling. The artists of to-day have thoroughly mastered their instruments, but, instead of symphonies and pure creations of music, we have scarcely anything

FRANCE.

else than trivial waltzes or the rubbishy jingle of "*La Grande Duchesse.*"

But it is not alone in painting and sculpture that this infidelity to truth and beauty is seen. In poetry, in romance, in the drama, in music, it is quite as clearly manifested, and exhausted sensuality strives to excite the jaded senses by new and extravagant irritations.

Public craving for novelty.

Undoubtedly the false taste of the public and its insane craving for mere novelty has much to do with this result. The public influences art quite as much, if not more, than art influences the public. Where there is a demand there will be a supply, and happy talent is but too often seduced by high rewards and gains to abandon its better genius. A higher public morality, more certain ethics, a calmer political condition, less luxury and extravagance of life, would soon beget a new spirit in art. But the violent contentions for wealth, the fatal excess of speculation, the excitements of politics, the worry and irritation of the world, the frivolities of society, depress and enervate art, and it becomes the plaything of the *virtuoso* and the *dilettante*. The influence of France in art is greater than that of any other nation. It inoculates all the world with its disease, but nowhere is its contagion so deeply felt as in the United States.

Causes of the debauched tastes.

Conditions necessary for improvement in artistic aims.

When society shall become more serious in its spirit and in its conduct, art will become more serious and manly in its aims, and not till then. What in America we have specially to guard against is the contagion of manners and morals averse from the natural spirit of a free republic, and degrading to life and to art, to which we offer ourselves as willing victims, rejoicing in the corruption we covet.

Let us now leave these general considerations and proceed to a review of some of the pictures of the French department.

Loss to art in decease of eminent French painters since Expositions of 1855 and 1867.

Since the International Expositions at Paris in 1855 and 1867, some of the most eminent painters who then illustrated its art have passed away. Belonging to a previous generation, whose principles and practice had not been forced in the hot-bed of the Empire, they still maintained a certain seriousness of attitude worthy of admiration. Among those who are no more may be mentioned the conspicuous names of Ingres, Delacroix, Descamps, Rousseau, Millet, Daubigny, and Troyon, each in his line a master, showing boldness, poetic feeling, originality, seriousness, and reserve in their works, qualities which but too often are wanting in their successors.

Millet, in the Exposition of 1861.

No lover of art can fail to remember with delight the remarkable pictures exhibited in 1867 by Millet. These, among others, were the powerful and intense "*La Mort et le Bucheron*," animated with the truest spirit of tragedy, "*Les Glaneuses*," "*Le Parc au Moutons*," "*Clair de Lune*," perfect in its depth of sentiment, and the "*Angelus du Soir*," profoundly touching in its pure religious sentiment. No one ever expressed as Millet did the simple poetry of peasant life. As themes, his pictures are at times almost nothing, but the pathos, sentiment, intensity of feeling, and profound simplicity with which they were felt and rendered are unsurpassed. There was nothing affected in them; they had no conscious graces to attract attention; no over-insistence of detail to show the cleverness of the artist. Homely, direct, and true to life, they went to the heart; in technical qualities they were masterly, broad, and firm; in drawing, deep and restrained; in color, penetrated by a delicate and exquisite feeling. One of his pictures may be seen in a private gallery of Philadelphia, which may serve as a lesson for all earnest artists. It is merely a shepherd leading home his flock after sundown. The delicate gleam of fading twilight lingers in the sky. The landscape is vague and dark with the coming on of night; the shepherd is but a *silhouette* in the foreground, and his sheep are densely clustered together so that you have to peer into them to see what they are, as you would in nature; nothing is overdone, nothing cries out to be seen. There is complete stillness and repose. The day is done; a tender regret, as for that which is gone, broods over the scene. The weary shepherd is going home, unconscious that we see him. Tenderness, refinement, and simplicity can scarcely go further.

Millet, Rousseau, absent in 1878.

Unfortunately for art, there were none of Millet's pictures in the recent Exposition, nor were there any of Rousseau's noble landscapes, which illuminated the walls in 1867. Of Corot's poetic but somewhat vague and blurred landscapes there were several, but they were not of his best. His delicate and refined talent has been largely appreciated in France, but it was not a robust and powerful talent, and his pictures are but too generally mere suggestions, monotonous in character, and with little vigor of sentiment or execution; on the other hand, they are quiet, unobtrusive, and refined, which, among the many noisy, impudent, and vulgar pictures of the present day, is in itself a virtue and a grace for which we must be thankful.

Corot,

Daubigny.

Several of Daubigny's landscapes adorned the walls of the Exposition, but they were for the most part ill-hung. One of them, perhaps the most beautiful of all, was a "*Lever de Lune, à Anvers*". The full, warm summer's moon has just risen, spreading a faint, purplish light about its yellow disk. A deep and delicate shadow hangs over the dim and quiet landscape; all is subdued, peaceful, and serene. Two figures may be seen sitting on a slope near the foreground. There is also another *Lever de Lune*, much the same in character and sentiment, with peasants driving cows home, and one kissing the other. Both these pictures are admirably painted, quiet in tone, and full of feeling. Besides these there are "*Le Tonnelier*," "*La Maison de la Mère Bazot*," "*Le Printemps*," all vigorous and striking pictures. The one which is least worthy of Daubigny is "*La Neige*," a snowy landscape with black leafless trunks, around which crows are flying, against a cold sunset sky, with gleams of bright color. This is effective when seen at a distance, but is of the impressionist school, painted rudely with the palette knife, and is a pretentious exhibition of technical talent of which we should hardly have thought this artist would have been guilty. Daubigny.

Of Henri Régnault there were only five pictures, but these were of a character and promise, as well as of performance, which make us only more deeply lament the untimely end of this young and gifted artist. Almost the last shot in the German attack on Paris struck him with death, and French art could scarcely have suffered a greater loss. In the few pictures he painted, he showed a surprising vigor and originality. They are very powerful in color, without being violent, neat in tone and quality, and admirable in drawing and composition. Nothing could exceed the refinement and delicacy of color, sentiment and character, of the portrait of "*Madame de Barck en Espagnole*", her head covered with a mantilla; and the "*Sortie du Pacha à Tangier*", which he left unfinished to go to his death, is a marvel of exquisite and splendid color as well as of composition. There are portions of his picture which leave scarcely anything to be desired in harmony of colors and tone. His equestrian portrait of Prim is also striking, and the head is particularly strong and serious. The black charger on which the General is mounted is excessive, and occupies too much the eye and the canvas. "*Execution sans Jugement, sous les Rois Maures de Grenade*," painful and disagreeable as it is, shows a wonderful mastery and artistic power. It is terrible and ghastly in its realism, but it shows a force of conception and treatment which in so young a man are marvellous. Régnault.

In the "*Sortie du Pacha*," the scene is in the court-yard

FRANCE.

Régnault.

of the palace. The walls are white, and pierced with Arab windows. The Pacha, on a white horse, clothed in a white *bournous*, is coming from the gate-way, accompanied by his mounted suite. In the center of the court is a group of horses and men with purple and green standards. In the foreground is a raised terrace looking down into the court-yard and thronged by spectators who are merely sketched in. Nothing could surpass the delicate splendor and harmony of color of the Pacha and his suite, or of the central group of horses and attendants; and the manner in which the white horse is retained against the white wall is a triumph of art. The key is high, but nothing is glaring, and the general tone is worthy of the greatest master. Nothing is hard or crude, but, brilliant as the picture is, it is subdued in tone, and full of air as well as light. The figures are scarcely more than two inches in height, yet nothing is niggled or little in their execution—nothing overdone or overstated.

If power such as is exhibited in these pictures could have been devoted to great conceptions, what might not the artist have achieved!

Genre.

Genre.

Meissonier.

Let us contrast with this picture the small panels of Meissonier. These, sixteen in number, were all arranged in a line upon the same wall. This was, perhaps, unfortunate, as it brought one too closely to a certain rigid monotony of effect which would not have been as evident had they been separated. Meissonier has a great reputation, particularly in our country, and his pictures have there brought enormous prices. There can be no question of his talent. He is an admirable draftsman. His works are finished with exceeding elaboration and pains. His attitudes and movements are correct, his minuteness of finish and study of detail are surprising, his precision of touch admirable, but all his work bears the mark of over-study and effort. There is a want of freedom and happiness in it all. It is very well done, but it leaves us cold. It is monotonous in tone, rigid and hard in feeling, and not agreeable in color. His figures are as hard as tin. His dresses have no texture and quality, his landscapes and skies no air. Everything has a look of pre-determination and not of accident. It is what it is, because the artist has chosen to have it so, and not because it happened to be so. Nothing is like the real thing, though it is wonderfully copied in all its details. The charm of a work that is finished more through happiness than pains is entirely lost—one feels the labor. One of his principal pictures, for instance, represents himself and his son riding along the shore near Antibes. There are the sea and the mountains, and the sky, and the road, and the figures of the horsemen—all of them have the same quality, the same definiteness and rigidity. The sea is not watery, the sky has no atmosphere, the mountains no haze of air. The drawing is correct, save always the preposterous little figure on the edge of the sea, which is totally out in perspective and is only as large, relatively, as a fly, but the whole has a preciousness of look. Take again the portrait of Alexander Dumas, *fils*. Elaboration can go no further—only every thing has the same value. The boots are as good as the head, the accessories as much insisted on as the essentials. There is all that makes up Monsieur Dumas and his study, part by part, but there is no whole and no reality of person. The "*Peintre d' Enseigne*," and the "*Portrait du Sergent*," contain the largest figures, but the latter is, perhaps, the thinnest of all in painting—one does not feel that they have any other side, they so stick to the background. "*Moreau et son Chef d'État-Major Dessoles, avant Hohenlinden*," is one of the best, if not the best. The drawing is good—the incident interesting—the story well told, and the subject lends itself to his peculiar style. The wind which blows the naked branches of the trees, the tails of the horses, the skirts of the dresses, the dreary coldness reigning over all, the two officers standing apart and studying the country through their glasses, the horses shivering in the bleak air—are all admirably expressed and composed—but there are still the same defects of color and tone. So too the long line of the "*cuirassiers*," stretching out in a wedge, is undoubtedly clever in all the details of the figures. Their attitudes are good, and they are most carefully drawn—but they are rigid in color and character as a line of Nuremberg tin soldiers. Details are painted which in nature would be beyond the sight, and the sky and landscape are vague, cold, and uncertain. Perhaps the very cleverest of all, as far as mere cleverness goes, is the smallest—for his extreme precision then has a value, which in the larger figures is lost—ordinarily there is no looseness of texture—no happiness of touch—no freedom of spirit. Yet despite all these drawbacks, there is no doubt of the great talent of Meissonier—and his honesty and patience of labor, his conscientiousness and faithfulness as an artist, his general skill in drawing and composition, are deserving of the highest praise. But he is not a colorist;

FRANCE.
Meissonier.

FRANCE.

Meissonier.

and one gets quite as good, perhaps even a better, impression from engravings of his works than from the original paintings.

Meissonier, jr.

His son, who follows in the footsteps of his father and imitates his style, had four pictures which are quite worthy of his master.

Gérôme.

Another distinguished painter of *genre* pictures is M. Gérôme, who exhibited ten pictures. The first by which he attracted the attention of the public were very large and crowded with figures, and had for subjects episodes or incidents of ancient Rome. Of late, however, he has devoted his talent to small cabinet pictures, ordinarily of a less ambitious character. These are elaborated to the utmost, and so labored in every detail as almost to be painful exhibitions of patience. The subjects are often drawn from Eastern life, but fail to reproduce the Eastern character studied. Clever as they are, they are wholly wanting in reality, and have a hard metallic quality of color and tone. Perhaps the best of the specimens he has here collected is "*L'Eminence Grise*," which is cleverly composed and drawn. Crowds of elaborately dressed courtiers are ascending the palace stairs and profoundly saluting His Eminence, who is descending, dressed in his monkish robes, and intent on reading his missal. Well as this is painted, and patient as are the care and elaboration shown in its details, it misses its point and fails to touch us with the sense of reality. The picture is clear and polished as steel, the dresses new and precise, the attitudes a little exaggerated, and all a little too exact. Compared with the picture by Zamacois in the Spanish department, representing the self-important Court Dwarf descending the court stairs accompanied by a great dog and saluted by smiling courtiers, by which this picture of Gérôme was plainly inspired, one cannot but feel the great inferiority of the French painter to the Spanish as a colorist or a delineator of character. Not only is the picture by Zamacois warm and rich in tone, and free in execution, but it exhibits a remarkable sense of restrained humor.

The paintings of oriental scenes represent "The Arab and his courser," "Women at the Bath," "Santon at the Gate of the Mosque," "Turkish Bath," "*Bachi-Bouzouks Dansant*," a "Lion," "*Café Rue de Caire*." These have a certain kind of interest, but they all have the same defects and the same merits. We have had quite enough of women at the bath, and these two are more than enough. They have no interest save that of nudity, and one of them is absolutely vulgar.

"Santon at the Gate of the Mosque" is an ugly Arab standing at a door which is surrounded by a mass of shoes and slippers—all very carefully done. The Arab and his dead horse in the desert is cold, hard, and antipathetic. There is no air and no feeling of desert and solitude, and the figures are finished to death. "St. Jerome and the Lion" is artificial in sentiment, and nothing is freely felt: the green eyes in the lion are scarcely worthy, in their exaggeration, of an artist like Gérôme. All these pictures are characterized by the same hard metallic quality of color; all are elaborated with the greatest patience—too much elaborated, in fact. The extreme pains has killed life and feeling. But, on the other hand, there is undoubted talent and capacity to seize upon characteristic subjects, careful drawing, artistic skill, and conscientious work. FRANCE.

Beside these pictures by Gérôme are those by Berne-Bellecour, in the same school, but rendered with more freedom and truth. One of these, "*Un Officier de Mobiles*," represents a soldier lighting a cigarette, with a cold, gray, brumy landscape behind him. This is very clever, free though careful in execution, and touched with much spirit. But his "*Coup de Canon*" is a work of much more power and character. It represents a group of cannoniers and officers firing a cannon over a rampart of earth-works. It is early morning. The sky is cold and gray, and the group is relieved darkly against the breast-high ramparts. The scene is represented with great truth and sentiment, the drawing and character are admirable, and the color is subdued. Berne-Bellecour

In the same room are seven *genre* pictures by Vibert, much in the same school, and, though very clever, sinning on the side of hardness and over-elaboration. Of these, perhaps the most interesting, alike in story, humor, and execution, is "*La Cigale et la Fourmi*." This represents a fat, well-fed Capucin carrying over his shoulder a basket laden with game and poultry, who, on a hill-side of cold snow, meets a slim, starving lutanist clad in green, with his long lute slung on his back. The poor, shivering lute-player craves alms. The fat, warmly-clad monk utterly rejects his demand. Both the figures are very cleverly painted, especially the strolling lutanist, and the picture is full of humor and character. Even more clever and spirited in character, drawing, and execution is the admirable portrait of Coqueter in the *rôle* of Mascarille in the "*Précieuses Ridicules*" of Molière. Of the others, "The Serenade" is a little confused and overcharged in details, and not so satisfactorily expressed. The "*Départ des Mariés*" is clever in composition and drawing, Vibert.

FRANCE.

as is also "*La Toilette de la Madone,*" but they have neither of them the excellence of the two first mentioned.

Worms.

In the school of *genre* the seven pictures by Worms are entitled to a high rank. They are, like all the other small pictures of this class, a little hard and over-careful, but they show a good deal of humor and character. "*Le Départ pour la Revue*" is admirable. A tall guardsman in full dress stands in the center of the picture drawing on his gloves before a mirror with its inevitable French clock, while his wife stands before him with clasped hands in mute admiration. The *raide* self-sufficiency of the one, and the *naïve* delight and approbation of the other, are very humorously rendered. Perhaps even better is "*La Fleur Préférée.*" This is a scene in a garden. A young girl is sitting sewing under a porch. The old father has taken away a young Spaniard to show him his flowers. He is holding up one in a pot, and pointing out its wonderful merits, but the young man, in a short Spanish jacket, whose back is turned to us, instead of examining the flowers, turns his head aside to gaze at the girl. The whole story is told with delicacy and sentiment, and the humor of the incident is not forced in any point. As far as mere painting goes the best is "*Le Compliment,*" which, besides being very spirited and characteristic, is in execution the freest of all the series. It represents a "*Bonhomme endimanché*" in a brown coat with a favor in his button-hole, his hands in over-large gloves and spread at his side, who, with an elaborate smile on his face, has just uttered his compliment, which he evidently thinks he has done very well.

Among the cabinet pictures of *genre* are also to be noted, as showing spirit and cleverness, the "*Voyage de Noces,*" by

Goubie.

Goubie, in which an old-fashioned chaise and postillion, with the new-married couple, are represented coming down a steep and deep-rutted hill, drawn by a black and white horse, while a storm is rising behind, and also "*Une Ci-Di-*

Goupil.

vant," by Goupil, which is delicate in color and pleasing in

Toulmouche.

character. Toulmouche also sends three pictures, "*Le Coin du Feu,*" "*Le Miroir,*" and "*L'Été.*" The last is a lady gathering roses. She is dressed in yellow-striped silk, with a blue sash tied behind, a blue parasol, and a red flower in her hand. "*Le Coin du Feu*" is the pendant. It is a lady in pink satin in a boudoir warming her hands at the fire. "*Le Miroir*" is another lady, or the same in blue satin, holding a mirror. In these pictures the silks, the satins, the stuffs, the furniture are all painted with the greatest care, but the sentiment is *fade* and affected, and it seems a pity to waste so much skill of execution on such weak and trivial subjects. Beaumont sends two pictures, "*La Fin d'une Chanson*" and "*Ou diable l'Amour va-t-il se nicher!*" The first represents a lover who, while serenading his mistress, has been killed under her window. She is weeping over his body. The faint light of morning is beginning to dawn. The story is well told, and the scene, though a little theatric, well rendered. "*Un Duel sans Témoins*," by Leleau, represents a girl in red woolen corsage with a dusting-brush, who is seated in a flowered *cretonne* chair hunting for a flea in her bosom. The picture is well painted; but what a subject! It makes one sad to think that talent should be so frivolously wasted on such unworthy themes. The title certainly is witty.

Beaumont.

Leleau.

Could such pictures as these be painted if the public taste were not corrupted?

Some very clever *genre* pictures must also be noted by Comte, one of which, "*Récréation de Louis XI*," represents the old monarch in his bed watching with amused interest two pigs that, dressed in green and red, with swords at their sides, are made to dance on the floor, while two Capucins are kneeling before the fire, pretending to be praying, but glancing aside at the pigs. The old king in the bed is quite in shadow. His attendants are at his side and at the foot of the bed. This picture is remarkably well painted, and exhibits great humor and sense of character.

Comte.

Leloir's pictures, five in number, must not be omitted in this connection. "*Un Baptême*" is very clever in character and design, painted with great care, but without niggling or hard elaboration or over-voyant colors. So also is the "*Pêcheurs du Tréport*," which is very quiet in tone, and represents two figures under an arch, one lighting a pipe, one with a turbot and basket. "*Le Repos*" is a delicate picture, of very pale grays and yellows, of a young girl lying on a couch tickling a cockatoo. "*Tentation*" represents Saint Anthony clinging to a low breaking cross planted in the ground, while two naked girls lie against him and fondle him. The picture is clever, and shows decided ability; but if it is sad to see talent devoted to trivial subjects like those we have mentioned, how much more sad to see art dragged into the mire of sensuality, and driven to such base uses.

Leloir.

And here, perhaps, it may be as well to give a glance at a series of pictures which have no other reason to be at all, save to gratify sensual or brutal appetites, but to which great talent has been devoted. Of the former class is particularly to be remarked "*La Sultane Favorite*" of M. Garnier, illustrative of some verses of Victor Hugo, and the

Garnier.

FRANCE.

picture is quite as exaggerated as the verses. The scene is in a seraglio. On the edge of a bath sprawls the nakedest of courtesans. The Sultan, a coarse and languid voluptuary, is seated cross-legged and leering at her, and behind him enters a slave bearing the decapitated head of a woman, a previous favorite, on a salver. There is a combination of the brutal and the sensual, which out-Herods Herod. The Sultan is asking whether it is necessary that for every *coup* of her fan there should follow a *coup* of the axe. The great vulgar courtesan does not seem to answer, but is quite satisfied with being utterly naked, as if that were an excuse for everything.

Garnier.

Overstress of the realistic, a revolt against the vague idealistic.

The over-stress of the realistic school on the common, brutal, and even ugly, is of course the revolt against the artificially tawdry sentiment and effeminate feebleness of the vague idealistic school. It is quite natural that a person of strong feelings, in disgust at the affected prettiness of the enameled dolls and characterless conceptions of nameless idealists, should even affect brutality and coarseness, as at least giving play to life and energy where before there was mere asphyxia, and prefer even the awkward and common to simpering affectation and platitude. But, like all revolts, this goes too far, and conducts the artist but too often to an opposite excess, and thus misses the true aim of art, which is to delight and not to disgust, to charm and not to repel. It is not everything in nature that is fit for art, nor is the mere plea of truth to fact a sufficient excuse for a work that simply repels the spectator.

Glaize.

One of the largest canvases in the exhibition represents "A Conspiracy in the Early Days of Rome," by Glaize. There is decided talent, but the conception is brutal and disgusting. It is an illustration of a passage in Plutarch (Publicola), and represents a group of men half-naked around a bleeding corpse. They have filled a cup with his blood, which one conspirator is holding up while the others make oath to some common crime. All the horrors of such a scene are emphasized even to exaggeration, as if the artist delighted to shock our sensibilities; and, acknowledging the talent, we can only regret that it should be devoted to so loathsome a subject. The taste of M. Glaize, however, seems to be in this direction. Another of his large canvases represents fugitives let down by a rope over the steep walls of a fortified place. Here again, the incident is over-told, and the painful character exaggerated. Still another canvas represents "*Le premier Duel,*" where a naked woman lying on a cliff watches with interest the death-struggles of two naked men, each striving to force the other over a precipice. This is the cleverest and least brutal of the three in conception and execution, and, painful as it is, does awaken one's interest, which the others do not. FRANCE.

Delaunay also, in his "Ixion," has gone farther in the delineation of the loathsome. His Ixion is the contorted, tortured shape of a human being torn upon a wheel, rent with wounds and bleeding. It is a picture from which every one must turn with horror. His "*La Peste à Rome*" is also painful in character, but there is a certain reserve in it which there is not in "Ixion," and it shows undoubted power. Dead bodies are lying on the pavement, while a good angel directs an evil angel, armed with a bar, to beat at the door of a house, where, according to the legend it illustrates, there will be as many dead as there are blows. There is over-emphasis of action in these two principal figures, but the picture shows strength. His "Diana," on the contrary, is merely the naked model executed with skill, though the action of the figure is not clearly or happily conceived, but far more like *Elise* or *Henriette*, who posed for it, than the goddess of the silver bow; so, too, his "*David Triumphant*" is a Paris *gamin* with his legs spread wide apart, armed with a gigantic sword and a sling, and screaming. Delaunay.

In such ideal subjects as these last two, nothing is so fatal as to attempt to embody them by careful imitation from particular models. The model should be but the dictionary or grammar of the artist, and not accepted as the true representation of his ideal. Into this error painters are far more apt to fall than sculptors, and in this Exposition we everywhere saw naked female figures plainly inspired by some actual model figuring under the name of a classic divinity or nymph, or representing some ideal virtue. For instance, Lefebvre's "*La Vérité*" is plainly merely a naked model, holding up a mirror. His "*Femme couchée*" has no pretense to be other than a study from a particular nude. It is drawn and painted with great ability, and as a study deserves very high praise, and, in fact, is far the best of all his nude women. His "*La Rêve*" is a nude model whitely and thinly painted on a cloud which hangs low above the surface of water, on which are lilies and leaves, and not particularly graceful in the pose. That is the dream. His "*Madeleine*" is also a nude woman, and evidently copied from a model. In like manner in "*Le Jugement de Pâris*," by Parrot, the three goddesses are merely naked models. Nothing ideal in character or feeling is even attempted; and this is still more striking in his "*Galatée*," which pre- Implicit copying of models. Lefebvre. Parrot.

FRANCE.

tends to be nothing but a naked model on an actual modeling-stand. Why he calls it "*Galatée*" it is difficult to see. There are several "Davids" also, which are all Paris *gamins*. All this is very tiresome and disappointing, and all the more so because of the technical skill displayed. What is wanting in the treatment of all such subjects is the creative power, the imaginative sense, the poetic sensibility, and in the realism of the present day these have little chance. The artist is too subordinated to his facts to pay heed to his ideas and inspirations. He becomes a painful copier and imitator of nature and fact, instead of a creator and coactor with nature. She rules him with a rod of iron. She does not inspire him.

Lack of imagination.

In the higher range of subjects this lack of imagination is fatal to all real success. In *genre* subjects it is less fatal, because imitation is more legitimate in these; the material things exist to be copied, and taste and skill, humor, and a sense of character supply its place. The subjects are to be seen by the real eye, and not to be divined and created, or at least not to such an extent. Whatever may be the explanation, the fact is certain, that while so many succeed in *genre*, so few succeed in the higher range of purely ideal work. We see many naked women, but no figure like "*La Source*," by Ingres, which was a sentiment and a creation, ideal in character, and perfectly pure in feeling.

Brutal pictures.

But to return to the series of what may be called brutal pictures, wherein the scope of the artist has been to be powerful at the expense of being disagreeable. An eminent example of this may be found in Becker's "*Rizpah protecting the Bodies of her Sons against the Birds of Prey.*" Here undoubtedly a remarkable talent is shown, but is it legitimately employed? Here is imagination, if you will, but is it governed by good taste, by happy selection, by proper restraint, by the sense of beauty, by the true sentiment of the subject? Is there any profound feeling in it? Read the story as told in the Old Testament, and see if this in any way represents it. Six ghastly naked dead figures are hung in a line upon crosses against the sky. Below at their feet is an enormous virago, one hand straight up, and the other swinging a club to drive away an eagle, which is swooping down on her. Where is the pathos, the solemn sorrow of the desolate mother, watching at night over her dead sons? This is but a theatrical display of horror and violence.

Becker.

There were other pictures, generally of large size, which are of a similar character, showing a total want of a true imaginative sense; but it is needless to enumerate them. In

Scripture subjects specially there is generally wanting all true sentiment. The incidents are forced, the attitudes exaggerated; there is almost invariably too much action. On the other hand, some of the religious pictures are academically sentimental and languidly weak. For instance, in the latter category are to be placed the three paintings of Bouguereau, representing "*La Vierge, l'Enfant Jésus, et St. Jean Baptiste*," the "*Pieta*," "*La Vierge consolatrice*." They are placed in line side by side, and are monotonously like in character, feature, and color. The surface is smooth as enamel. They are carefully drawn and worked out with extreme elaboration. In a word, they are fatally pretty and purely sentimental. This is the characteristic quality of all the paintings by Bouguereau which are there exhibited. "*La Charité*" is even weaker than those already mentioned. The most pleasing of all—and this has too much of an album prettiness—is "*La Grande Sœur*," which represents a sister pulling on the stocking of a little one on her lap. The subject of some of his pictures will clearly indicate the character—"*Âme au Ciel*," "*Nymphée*," "*La Jeunesse et L'Amour*." Bouguereau.

One other picture of the brutal school must not be passed over. It represents "*St. Sébastian et L'Empereur Maximien Hercule*." The ghastly figure of the saint is seen descending the steps before Maximien and his companions. He raises his white drapery so as to expose his corpse-like body covered with wounds and stabs. The emperor and his attendants start back in dismay, as well they may. Nothing can be more repulsive. The saint is well drawn from the model, but he is no saint—only a murdered man covered with wounds. The other figures are grotesque in their attitudes and purely academic, and the picture is an offense to good taste.

Moreau also exhibited six pictures of a purely imaginative class.—"*Hercule et L'Hydre*," "*Salomé*," "*Jacob et L'Ange*," "*David*," "*Moïse exposée sur le Nil*," "*Le Sphinx diviné*"—all kaleidoscopic in color, and of a strange bizarre character. There is undoubtedly a certain fancy and grotesqueness of imagination displayed in these paintings. They avoid at once the *academic* and the real; but they are neither of the earth nor the air, nor the waters under the earth. They are wild phantasies like opium dreams. Moreau.

Le Roux has also sent several pictures of imaginative subjects, partially historical, partially ideal. One represents the "*Danaïdes*," two vague lines of damsels, stretching far into the distance, the one bringing jars of water to pour into a well in the foreground, the other disappointed Le Roux.

FRANCE. going away. There is a certain poetic feeling in this picture, but it is pale, and vague of color and of form. Another picture by him is "*La Vestale Tuccia*" carrying water in an uplifted sieve; and still another, "*Un Miracle chez la Bonne Déesse*," is a group of vestal virgins all in white seated in a hall, while a sister virgin in black implores the aid of the goddess to relume the sacred fire. There is an idea in all these, and a refinement of sentiment, but they are pallid, weak in color, and want grasp and vigor.

Historical Paintings.

Historical. From these it may be well to turn to some of the purely historical paintings, and among these the most forcible and well conceived and expressed were those of Laurens. They were twelve in number, all vigorous in color and drawing, and all historical in their character. The least good were those which are taken from the New Testament, such as "*Jésus chassé de la Synagogue*" and "*La Piscine de Bethzaïda*." Far more satisfactory is he in such subjects as "*Le Pape Formose et Etienne VII*," which, though a little black and harsh in its shadows, is a powerful and well conceived picture, without exaggeration or confusion of figures. "*L'Etat Major Autrichien devant le Corps de Marceau*" is also an admirable picture. It is simply treated without that exaggeration and gesticulation which so often supplies the place of true action. The general tone is gray and subdued, the heads expressive, and the grouping good. The body of Marceau is lying on a couch, and the Austrian staff is passing into the room to pay its last tribute of respect. "*L'Excommunication de Robert le Pieux*," "*Funérailles de Guillaume le Conquérant*," and "*L'Interdit*" have all serious qualities, a true historical character, and simplicity as well as power. The last mentioned is especially marked by sentiment. We mark in M. Laurens, the evidence of a return to the older traditions and the more serious schools of art.

Laurens.

Robert-Fleury. Robert-Fleury also sent two large pictures one "*Le Dernier Jour de Corinth*," and one "*Pinel, Médecin en Chef de la Salpétrière, en* 1795." Of these, by far the best is the latter. It represents Pinel entering the court of a mad-house to carry out his reforms in the treatment of the insane. There is a good deal of character in this picture, and a good deal of expression.

Cabanel. Cabanel also exhibited four pictures of this class, one the "*Mort de Francesca da Rimini et de Paolo de Malatesta*," one "*Thamar et Absalom*." In neither of these has he been able, with all his talent, to rise to the dignity of history or the tragedy of his subjects. Both are forcibly feeble, exaggerated in action, and falsely conceived. It is impossible to recognize Thamar in the half naked woman in Absalom's lap, and it is equally difficult to recognize Absalom in the modern, violent, scowling, and overdressed Oriental who is clutching the air in so impotent a rage. There is nothing Biblical in the sentiment, the character, or the facts of this picture. It is rather like a modern harem. It shows talent as a painting, but not as a conception. These are not the sort of subjects in which this artist succeeds. The larger his canvas the weaker his work. His "*Peste Florentin*" was charming, and herein he showed his special talent. The enormous paintings in three divisions for the Church of Saint Geneviève still more bear out this opinion. They are feeble, flat, and characterless.

Lecompte du Nouy.

M. Lecompte du Nouy had a series of pictures, historic and semi-historic, displaying a very considerable talent, and of the school of Gérôme. The "*Homère Mendicant*" is well composed and interesting, but too enameled in surface. In "*Les Porteurs des Mauvaises Nouvelles*" Pharaoh lies on a couch looking out and anxiously awaiting messengers with tidings. Those who have already arrived with bad news lie slain at the foot of the couch. This picture is clever, but disagreeable in subject and hard in color. It has the defect so common in France of excess and over-statement in action, as if convulsion and attitudinizing could alone express deep passion and emotion.

There were many other large historic pictures, but time and space are wanting to go over all of them. Those already mentioned are the most prominent, and convey a fair idea of the character of this kind of work in France. There is in all of them ability. One cannot deny the talent or the artistic knowledge displayed; but it is *displayed*, and this is its defect. The heart of the mystery is not plucked. There is much realism and capital painting, but little evidence of high dramatic purpose, serious sentiment, or power of conception. It is perhaps worth remarking that in almost all the pictures, as well as statues, of figures in action, the toes are in *crispation* beyond all reason in nature.

Luminais.

M. Luminais' "*Le Roi Morvan*" and "*Brunehaut*" should not be overlooked. In the former particularly, M. Luminais has given evidence, not only of a strong sense of color, but also of discrimination of character. The composition is not very satisfactory, but the figure and expression of the queen, who is seeking by her wiles and caresses to deter the king from acceding to the terms of peace offered by

FRANCE.

the Abbé Witchar, are subtle and striking. Other pictures by M. Luminais also show talent and force, as the "*Éclaireurs Gaulois,*" two figures crouched to the earth and listening to distant steps, and the "*Retour de Chasse dans les Gaules,*" where four figures are carrying a wild boar on poles, while another on horseback, with shield and spear, accompanied by two dogs, is at their side. These pictures are low in tone and painted with much vigor.

Gustave Doré.

"*Les Martyrs Chrétiens,*" by Gustave Doré, has all his faults and some of his merits. It represents an amphitheater strewn with bodies, among which lions are walking, while a circle of bluish smoky angels are descending through the air. It will touch the sentimental side of many minds, but as a work of art it is poor and thin. "*Le Néophyte,*" by him, is a much better picture, and represents a young priest sitting among a line of old ones. The latter are sunken in the ruts of mechanical religious duties. To him comes regret for the past and dissatisfaction with the present. The theme is good, but the execution is weak and unsatisfactory. M. Doré has great fertility of talent, but no concentration of purpose or intensity of feeling. He is at times admirable, and he has great variety of fancy and facility of composition, but these large and ambitious subjects only bring into stronger relief his innate weakness as well as his flimsiness of execution.

Portraits.

Portraits.

Bonnat.

In portraiture there were many notable works. Those of M. Bonnat showed vigor of design and firmness of drawing and *impasto*, and as likenesses are evidently good. They have a metallic quality, particularly in their shadows, which is not quite agreeable, and the backgrounds are not pleasant in color, but there is great sincerity of work. That of M. Thiers is perhaps the most characteristic. But far beyond all is his portrait of M. Robert-Fleury. This is admirable, freely painted, loose in texture, and without the rigidity which is the defect of the others. The character and expression and pose are all good. All his portraits are on a dark background, generally of a hard maroon tone, on which the figure and face are cut out or almost modeled out in light, so that they affect one a little like embossed photographs. But, with all his defects, there is strength and manliness and firm intention, without weakness or sentimentality.

M. Bonnat also exhibited other pictures which are quite as noteworthy as his portraits. Of these specially is to

FRANCE.

be noted "*Une Rue à Jérusalem*," figures coming through a dark archway, on the right of which three women are seated. These figures are very cleverly executed, particularly those of the women, and the whole picture is effective. Another is a "*Barbier Nègre, à Suez*," which is also clever.

Lefebvre.

M. Lefebvre exhibited several portraits which are among the best of his works, particularly that of "M. Léonce Raynaud." Carolus Duran had several large portraits, in which there is distinction and character; among the best, "*La Dame au Gant*," a full length; the portrait of "Madame F." and of "Mad'lle Carolus Duran," which last is, specially of all, pleasing in effect, though careless. His "*L'Enfant Bleu*" is *criard* in color and far from successful in achieving the task he set before himself; but the best of all are those of "M. Émile de Girardin," and of "M. Pasdeloup," particularly the last, which is frank, robust, and full of life and character.

Carolus Duran.

Paul Dubois.

M. Paul Dubois, who has won his reputatlonas a sculptor, had on the walls three portraits in which there were sincerity and simplicity. The tones are gray and dull, but the eminent sculptor is scarcely a colorist. There is, however, considerable character and delicacy.

Delaunay.

Mr. Delaunay sent eight portraits, all clever. His portraits of ladies have, however, too much consciousness and pose. They are too sure you are looking at them. This, however, is the defect of nearly all the portraits of women in France. There is scarcely one which is simple and unconscious. Of all his portraits, the best is that of "M. Legouvé," which is full of character and spirit.

Cabanel

Cabanel sent five portraits in which this self-consciousness and posing aspect quite robs them of all charm.

Henner.

The portraits by M. Henner are very distinguished in light color and individuality, and were certainly among the most remarkable in the Exposition. They are faithful, simple, characteristic, and more like the old portraits of the best time than those which we see at the present day. Besides his portraits, M. Henner also sent a number of pictures representing various subjects, such as "*Bibli's Changée en Source*," "*Le Christ mort*," "*Les Naïades*," "*La Femme au Divan Noir*." But in all his pictures the subject is of little consequence. He does not attempt to be dramatic, or specially to enter the domain of the imagination. His aim in all is to produce an effect of light in flesh tints. Everything is sacrificed to this one end. All of his pictures have one or more nude figures, to which everything is subordinated. Nor does he fail in this aim. He is heart and soul a colorist,

FRANCE.

Henner.

though his scale is limited and his harmonies nearly always the same. Beside his flesh all the other pictures in the room look pale and thin. They are full of light and they glow upon the wall. He perfectly understands the values of his tones, and his pictures are always harmonious and remind one in the distance of Georgione in their masses and illumination; as for details, there are absolutely none. The outlines of everything are wanting. There is only the mass, so that on a near examination there is nothing to satisfy us. His *impasto* in the lights is thick, and in the tints the hairs of the brushes are left. His shadows are merely washed in. This is all of malice prepense, of course, but it is greatly to be regretted that with such power as a colorist he should leave his work so utterly incomplete.

Renard.

M. E. Renard sent only one work, a small "*Portrait de la Grand' mère*," but this is a very remarkable work. It has all the detail and minuteness of execution without the mechanical map-like character of Donner. It is a simple head of an old woman, studied in every particular with extraordinary faithfulness and love for the subject. The color is delicate, the tones refined, the expression simple, the pose natural, and the detail stupendous. Yet all these details are subordinated to the main general effect, and nothing cries out or is over-insisted upon. It is a very remarkable study from nature.

Gaillard.

Among the other noteworthy portraits were to be remarked a portrait of "Monsigneur Rogerson," by M. C. F. Gaillard, which is simple, full of character, and well painted;

Robert-Fleury.

a portrait of "Madame R.-F.," by M. Robert-Fleury, careful, pleasing and lady-like and without posing.

Bastien-Lepage.

But, perhaps, the most remarkable portraits for the expression of character were those of M. Bastien-Lepage. For individuality and personality, the portrait of "M. Hayem" could scarcely be surpassed. The hands, the pose, the movement of features, and specially the expression of the mouth are evidently of the person himself. The very trousers are expressive. All go together to make the individual. There is no attempt to flatter, and certainly the portrait is not flattering; but it is better than flattering; it is the person himself, as understood and felt in every particular by the artist. "*Le Portrait de mon Grand père*" is equally strking, and for the same qualities.

Landscapes.

Landscapes.

In the French department of landscape there was much talent and more study. In fact, many of the large landscapes

FRANCE.

Landscapes.

were mere studies from nature, very cleverly executed, careful and true to nature, full of facts vigorously rendered, but inspired by little sentiment or feeling. What I mean will clearly appear if most of them are compared with the exquisite works of Claude, in which nature is all subdued to sentiment. There is no reason why the two should be divorced. There are, however, remarkable exceptions to this general rule; and first of all, in combination of figure and landscape, are to be mentioned the remarkable pictures of Jules Breton, on which it is a pleasure to look. He sent nine pictures, every one of which is worthy of a great artist. It would be difficult, in the whole range of landscape and figure, to find a more exquisite picture than "*La Sieste*"—one more masterly in drawing, more perfect in tone, more simple and true in its sentiment, more admirable in its ideas. It represents a party of hay-makers, who are taking their *siesta* under the shadow of a great tree. The sunlight falls behind on the fields and haycocks, which are bounded by a line of foliage, and, peering through the great tree, flecks with spots of light one of the figures. A woman is seated and suckling her baby. An old man is smoking his pipe. The rest are stretched carelessly on the ground enjoying the luxury of the shadow and rest. One of these figures, a girl lying flat on her back straight in and out of the picture, is marvellously foreshortened. There is no air of effort about the execution; it is free, but mellow and clear. There is a little carelessness here and there in the landscape, but the figures are beautifully finished, low in tone, but transparently luminous and solid. Here is the very soul of sentiment; the feeling of summer; the languor and repose of noon. It is a delightful picture, which it is pleasant to see and to praise.

Jules Breton

Of an entirely different character, but almost equally animated with a true sense of the scene, is "*Les Pêcheurs de la Mediterranée.*" The scene represents a curving beach of pebbles stretching far round the bay, on which are two groups drawing in their nets. The sky is pure and bright. The blue sea gleams and sparkles in the sun as it rolls gladly in. One can almost feel the breeze and hear the hiss of the sea raking over the shingle. The figures are doing their work unconscious that we are observing them, and their sharp shadows are thrown upon the beach. The whole effect is of bright sunlight. If it have a defect, it is in a little excess of brightness, but this time will tame and sober.

Another of his pictures, "*Les Amies,*" is a little idyll. Three girls interlaced are walking through a cornfield

FRANCE.

Breton.

breast-high with poppies. It is twilight. They are going home. The sentiment of this picture is charming.

"*La Fontaine*" is also a masterly picture, with the same characteristics of simplicity, low tone of color, and sentiment. The figures are peasant girls come to draw water at a fountain, but they have a dignity of bearing, and an unconsciousness of posing, and a laziness of style that elevates the subject into the ideal. The same remark may be made of the large single figure "*La Glaneuse*," which has something statuesque and heroic in its pose and treatment.

Bernier.

The three landscapes by M. C. Bernier, "*Janvier*," "*Une Ferme en Bannalee*," and "*Sabotiers dans le Bois de Quimerc'h*," have all remarkable qualities. The first represents a farmer with a white and roan horse plowing. These form the main ground-light. Behind are farm-houses and almost leafless trees, with a few brown leaves on some, dark against a marble-gray sky. The second is a sunset scene in a farmyard. Here all is in tender shadow, except the sky where the sunset gleams. Cows are drinking; a pool in the center reflects the light of the sky; the farmer and his horses are going in; dark trees rear themselves on either side. The sentiment of the hour is most happily rendered. The tone is charming, and the soft growing shadow which involves the chief part of the scene is delicate and transparent. The third above mentioned is a very remarkable landscape, representing woods without underbrush and flecked with mottled light and dark, in which is a *sabotier's* cabin with a pointed roof, from which smoke is rising, while the *sabotier* and his wife are at work near by. Here there is a rare feeling of open air, a simplicity and truth to nature, united to breadth and freedom of execution, which made this one of the most striking landscapes in the whole Exposition.

Français.

The landscapes by M. Français are not characterized by strength and vigor of execution, and they are somewhat academical and sentimental. The best of those exhibited was "*Daphnis et Chloé*," which is a deep wooded landscape well composed, with two nude figures at a pool in the center.

Hanoteau.

M. H. Hanoteau sent a very vivid and brilliant picture representing an old mill, "*Le Moulin.*" A large tree, growing on a sloping bank beside the road, throws its shadow over the chief part of the foreground, and some pigs are coming down the bank. The road strikes across the picture over a bridge, passing the old mill, which is partially in shadow; and a house beyond in full blaze of sunlight. The picture is admirably composed in light and shade, very carefully studied in all its details, free of execution, and very brilliant in effect. The technical qualities of this work are remarkable. FRANCE.

There was also a bright and spirited picture by M. J. Masure, "*Rivage du Golfe Juan*," of blue sea, which a fresh breeze is rippling in to the shore. Masure.

M. J. C. Meissonier, fils, had also three little pictures after the manner of his father, representing "*Une Chemin aux Environs de Nice*," "*Plage aux Environs de Nice*," and "*Le Matin sur la Plage, aux Environs d'Antibes*," all worthy of his father in truth and character. Meissonier, *fils*.

The landscapes by M. L. G. Pelouse were very clever, but they have rather too much the look and character of studies from nature. "*Une Coupe de Bois*" represents a wood, with wood-cutters, with bright sunset clouds sloping toward the horizon behind the tall trees. This is perhaps the most effective of all, and is executed with spirit and talent. Pelouse.

M. A. Segé exhibited rather a remarkable picture of "*Les Chaumes*." It is just afternoon, and the shadows are beginning to slope. A shepherd and dog stand in a broad, flat plain with a crowd of sheep in shade with their backs touched with light. In the distance rises a village all in shadow, and beyond on the level a delicate horizon. The effect is very brilliant, the perspective of the flat plain is exceedingly well rendered, and there is a considerable novelty of effect and distinction in the picture. One regrets, however, the monotonous slaty color of the whole village, in which roof and walls are of the same hue and tone. The birds flying through the clear air are peculiarly rendered; the bodies are dark, the wings vague, dim, and fluttering in effect. Segé.

M. E. Van Marcke sent a very vigorous picture of cows drinking in a pool. A white cow forms the principal light, while dark trees and foliage cover the main upper part of the picture, leaving only a corner of clouded sky. This is very strongly painted and well composed. It is of the school of Troyon, and well worthy of that master. Van Marcke.

M. F. de Mesgrigny's "*Bateaux-Lavoirs sur la Seine*" is also an admirable picture. It represents a broad, still river with wash-houses on one side and ducks swimming down the stream in which trees beyond are reflected. The key is very light, and the effect clear and pleasing; the water and the reflections very transparent. Mesgrigny.

"*Un Marché à Grenade*," by M. A. Moreau, represents a street in Grenada on market-day. Half the street with its portico is a shadow. Two great oxen with yellow frontlets, and drawing a huge cart out of which rises a tall, coarse, gray net supported on poles, occupy the center of the picture, Moreau.

FRANCE.

Moreau. and around this are groups in costume coming and going, and, behind, the sun flashes on white walls of houses. Here is Spain in full blaze, yet without over-statement and noise of color, and without confusion of parts. The shadow side is transparent and cool, and gives a brilliant effect to the subdued colors around and the flashing walls beyond. I wish here to mark this picture particularly as admirable for its composed and effective treatment of many figures and brilliant light without confusion, and as an expression of Spain. I shall have occasion to refer to it in contrasting it with pictures of the Spanish school.

Girard. Among other pictures not coming exactly under these classes, several should be noted. M. Girard sent a small picture of "*Les Fiancés*," representing a party in very brilliant costumes coming through an alley of trees strewn with dead leaves. Some of the figures are a little too *voyant* in color, particularly those in the shadow, but the shadow itself is capital, the figures very carefully and elaborately executed, and the dead leaves admirably rendered.

Jacqueti. M. J. G. Jacqueti's "*Rêverie*" has something distinguished in character. It represents a girl in a red dress sitting a little affectedly in a chair and glancing out of the picture. If she is in a reverie she knows we are looking at her, and has a rather shy sense of it.

Hébert. M. Hébert exhibited four pictures, of which the best are the two representing "*La Pastorella*" and "*La Tricoteuse*," both of which are refined in sentiment and quiet in execution, and have a tender melancholy which is attractive.

Lambert. L. E. Lambert had a humorous and spirited picture called "*Installation Provisoire*," representing kittens which have got into a chest of drawers—the chest of drawers itself admirably painted.

Desgoffe. M. Desgoffe had some remarkable representations of still life, some of which for technical qualities and imitation deserve very high praise.

Vollon. The "*Curiosités*" and "*Coin du Halle*" of M. A. Vollon, uninteresting enough in themselves, are extraordinarily well painted. His "*Femme du Pollet*," a large figure of a peasant with a basket on her arm, has attempted to follow in the footsteps of Millet, but his work, though clear, has a coarseness of quality and character which is never seen in Millet.

Aquarelles.

Aquarelles.

In *aquarelles* the French have distinguished themselves of late. In this branch of art the names of Messrs. Detaille and Neuville should be noticed, though they exhibited no

FRANCE.

specimens of their talent here. To these should be added among others the names of Messrs. Harpignies, Berne-Bellecour, Bida, Berchère, Bruneau, Galbrund (*en pastel*), Régnault, Veyvassat, Worms, Saunier, and, especially, M. M. Leloir and Maréchal. M. Leloir sent six *aquarelles*, which, for splendor and brilliancy of color, were perhaps the most remarkable works in the whole Exposition. The subjects are "*Le Repos*," "*Les Souris Branches*," "*Danseuse*," "*Joueuse de Flûte*," "*L'Oiseau bleu*," "*Nonchalance*." The color, which is like melted gems for force, is not glaring or confused in tints, the composition is good, the values well rendered, and altogether this is a remarkable series of pictures. M. Maréchal's works are in *pastel* and are rich and low in tone, but strongly treated, almost as if they were oils. M. Worms' *aquarelles*, "*Après la Revue*" and "*La Toilette d'une Ballerine*," are of the same kind as his oil pictures, and admirably rendered. M. Régnault's "*Intérieur de Harem*" is brilliant, but too kaleidoscopic in colors, and too much inspired by the Spanish school. Baroness Rothschild also sent some very spirited and interesting aquarelles of different views, "*À Scafati, environs de Naples*," "*À Vitré*," and "*À Chartres*"; M. Berchère, several clever Egyptian scenes; Madame Becq de Fouquières a *pastel* of a "*Jeune Fille de Kerfuntun*," which is very pleasing in sentiment and character; M. Bruneau several admirable studies of fruit and small animals; M. Chaigneau a clever *pastel* of "*Les Rochers du Jean-de-Paris*"; M. Brunet-Debaines a capital view of "*St. Galmier*"; M. Galbrund a spirited portrait in *pastel*. Among the *aquarelles* should also be specially noted a street scene with old houses on a canal, by M. Saunier; and two bright, clear, and well-drawn pictures by M. Veyvassat, of "*Le Goûter des Moissoneurs*," and "*Une Charette*."

Harpignies, Berne-Bellecour, Bida, *et al.*

Leloir.

Maréchal.

Worms.

Régnault.

Baroness Rothschild.

Berchère.

Mad. Becq de Fouquières.

Bruneau.

Chaigneau.

Brunet-Debaines.

Galbrund.

Saunier.

Veyvassat.

ENGLAND.

ENGLAND.

Having now examined the French school, let us turn to that of England. Here, we are in an entirely different world. There are perhaps no two countries in which the technical methods, the subjects chosen, and the spirit in which they are rendered are so opposed or diverse. The characteristic excellence, as we have seen, of the French school is *technique* But this *technique* has been so over-insisted upon in France as finally to have become in the eyes of many of its cleverest artists the one thing to be aimed at, the one thing above all to be desired, and to this the higher claims of art have been subordinated.

Diversity of character in French and English painting.

On the contrary, in passing from the French school into

ENGLAND. the English, one is at once struck with the feebleness of the *technique*. The pictures are for the most part flat and comparatively feeble in execution. The grammar of painting in oil as distinguished from painting in water-color has not here been learned. The first impression is that all of the oil pictures are *aquarelles*, so little body and vigor of touch, so little depth of *impasto*, so feeble a perception of light and dark do they show. Some of them under glass we are forced closely to examine before we can believe that they are not in water-colors. There is no true sense of what is technically termed "values" of color. All the parts are comparatively of the same value. The foreground figures are no more vigorous and decided than those which are in the middle distance. There is little representation of perspective beyond what is expressed by drawing. The figures for the most part, as far as color and light and detail are concerned, are all in the same plane. There is a general monotony of color, a remarkable absence of shadows, and an equal insistance on all parts. Another peculiarity which is very striking is the lantern-like illumination of all the faces. No matter whether the light falls upon them or is behind them, or whether there is any intelligible light coming from anywhere, the faces all are self-illuminated, and, in many of the landscapes with figures, they glow mysteriously, whether turned against the moon or the sun or turned to them. What is also curious is that, though these faces are so illuminated, scarcely a figure casts a shadow. Much of this peculiarity probably arises from the fact that in England there is little brilliancy of sun, the prevalent atmosphere being gray and dim, and the counterpoises of light and dark little seen, so that the shadows are vague and feeble, and the effects misty. But whatever be the reason, the fact is evident. But on the other hand there is much delicacy of sentiment, and great refinement of feeling. The subjects are always pure in character, and if there be no great force of execution there is simplicity and sweetness, and an absence of violence and brutality of subject and of treatment. This sometimes errs on the side of sentimentality and almost of triviality, but there is never anything to shock the sensibilities, and in all there is a pure purpose.

Pictures feeble in *technique*, and *impasto*. No true sense of values of color. Monotony. Peculiar illumination of faces. Absence of shadows. Delicacy of sentiment. Purity of feeling.

Lack of draftsmanship. In draftsmanship there is much to be desired. The best of the English painters can scarcely be said to reach the higher average of the French. In figures, and particularly in the nude, their works show not only a lack of firmness and decision of outline, but an absence of careful

ENGLAND.

training, and of style in their drawing. Of the landscapes, some are carefully, almost painfully, studied after nature, but the detail is in many cases so over-emphasized that the mass is sacrificed to the parts. They do not seem to understand that a multitude of particulars do not constitute a whole. On the contrary, with some at least, their idea seems to be that unless everything is said nothing is said.

Over-emphasis of details.

English art seems to drift in various currents, without any clear and definite course, and to subdivide itself into various degrees rather than schools. Mr. Burne-Jones represents one direction, for instance, towards the romantic and vaguely ideal. Mr. Tritt another, towards the literal. Mr. Watts another, towards the mythological and heroic. Mr. Leslie another, towards the idyllic of common life. Mr. Armitage another, towards the antique and historic. Their methods and manners differ as much as their subjects. They have no style of workmanship in common; each, as it were, is striving blindly, as far as *technique* is concerned, to find a way for himself, and it must be confessed that in some of these efforts there is not a little affectation of originality, and, as it were, an euphuistic attempt at novelty, both in subject and in treatment. On the other hand, there are some who are truly earnest and capable, having ideas and sentiment, but wanting the mastery of the grammar and language by which to express them. There is, in consequence, a good deal of wasted power. The result is not equal to the effort. Still, in coming from the French department of the Exposition into that of England, one cannot but feel that he has entered into a serener atmosphere of simpler manners, and higher morals, and purer sentiments, the absence of which cannot be compensated for by any technical merits however great.

English art drifting in various directions.

Romantic and ideal.

Literal.

Heroic.

Idyllic.

Antique and historic.

Simpler and purer feeling than in the French section.

Aquarelles.

Aquarelles.

If in the use of oils the English are far behind the French, in *aquarelle* they at least take equal rank with them. The room dedicated to these in the English department contained master-pieces of execution as well as of sentiment. The side of one screen was dedicated to *aquarelles* by the late Mr. Frederic Walker. These are characterised by tender and delicate sentiment and by harmony of color. They all represent scenes of common life, and are each so happy in the rendering that it is difficult to say which is to be preferred. "The Old Farm Garden" is charming. It represents a scene in an old-fashioned garden inclosed in walls, over which are seen the farm building and roof. The garden is filled with bright flowers, a tree is in full blossom, and along the

Frederic Walker.

ENGLAND.

Walker.

walk is ranged a row of bee-hives. A girl, slowly sauntering through the walk, is knitting. She has dropped her ball of yarn, and a tortoise-shell cat is couching to spring at it. Here is the pure English feeling and character, all quiet and in harmony. "The Ferry" also is a beautiful picture, and as true to fact as to feeling. A boat is drawing up to the shore of the river. White swans are swimming in the water. Straight down to the ferry opens a street of red-brick houses with groups and figures scattered here and there. The atmosphere is England, the feeling is all English, and the picture is full of air and misty sunlight. "The Housewife" is a figure seated in a court-yard, shelling beans; a chair is before her, and a great butt of water on one side, and a low window is filled with flower-pots. In description this is nothing. It is the tenderness and sweetness with which it is done that make it a delightful idyl. "The Village" is a bit out of English life and scenery. There is a bridge with three arches, under which the river flows, and over the parapet of which figures are leaning lazily. An old mansion-house is seen behind, on the further side of the road which crosses the bridge, encompassed with a wall, with trees inside. Another represents "The Last Asylum," where a daughter is accompanying her old mother to the almshouse—beautiful in sentiment and delicate in execution. "The Fishmonger" also is admirable. He is leaning forward and pointing out on his broad bench covered with fishes a large turbot to a girl who is standing beside it hesitating whether to yield to his persuasion or not. This is masterly for management, color, and tone. The soft, darkened shadow of the interior is admirably given; the figures are capital in character and expression; the details are carefully studied and not obtrusive. Of a more ambitious character are "The Three Fates," who are three sour old ladies, two seated on a sofa and one standing, and delivering their oracles to a young girl who is rising from her chair. This is dramatic, entirely modern, and full of character and spirit. The other pictures are "Health to the Absent," "The Chaplain's Daughter," "The Field of Violets," all charming. Mr. Walker had also a large picture in oils, called "The Old Gate." This has much of the same excellence as the smaller water-colors in sentiment and character, but it lacks vigor of execution and is a little monotonous in tone and color. In fact it is rather like a very large *aquarelle* than a painting in oil. The figures are admirably drawn and the picture has much charm.

Frederic Walker.

Mr. A. H. Marsh sent a good showy picture of "Mussel Gatherers," representing a crowd of fisherwomen toiling along a beach, with a storm rising. Mr. J. D. Linton's "Off Guard" is also well composed, with good effect of light and dark, and painted with vigor. The parts are well subordinated to each other, and the general masses are well kept, which is a rare thing in English art.

Marsh. Linton.

Mr. G. J. Pinwell sent three pictures, "The Pied Piper," "The Great Lady," "St. James' Park," of which the best is the last named. This is a subject which suits the English mind. It represents a scene in the park, English in its character and true to common life. The figure of the man seated on a bench and looking down is particularly good. The subject does not call for a high effort of imagination, but is represented with much truth and feeling.

Pinwell.

There were several of Mr. J. F. Lewis's elaborate oriental scenes, which are painted with great minuteness and detail, and are brilliant in color; but they are of little interest as to character or incident, and are too uniformly brilliant and have too equal insistance of parts. They represent "A Street in Cairo," "The *Lilium Auratum*," "The School," "Cairo," "The Prayer of Faith." He also sent three oil pictures, all of which have the same characteristics and are scarcely to be distinguished from *aquarelles*, so thin and flat are they in treatment. "Twilight," by Joseph Knight, is powerful and interesting. There is a lowering gray sky, with a strip of light on the edge of the horizon. Shadows darken over the low deep-green moor-like swell of the ground, and in the foreground is a pool illuminated by the sky, and overgrown on its banks by low bushes. This picture, which is painted in body color, is solemn, lonely, and full of sentiment. Mr. Boyce's "Bridewell" is admirably rendered, and a capital study of the place. Mr. J. D. Watson's "Book Lore" is rich in color. The low crimson dress is well painted, the color is rich, and the composition is good in light and dark. Mr. Thomas Collier sent a masterly landscape called "Arundel Park," which is freely and vigorously rendered. Mr. E. X. Johnson's "The Anxious Mother" is delicate in sentiment and color, and painted with much care and refinement. The anxious mother is a hen, which is much disturbed because the lady in the picture has taken her chicken from her and holds it in her hand. "*Nôtre Dame de Brou-Bourg*," by Mr. S. Read, is a careful and effective study of the interior of the cathedral. "The Higher Pool," by Mr. E. H. Fahey, is admirable in color, tone, and composition. It is a study of the same place that he has taken for his oil

Lewis. Knight. Boyce. Watson. Collier. Johnson. Read. Fahey.

ENGLAND. painting "He Never Came," and is even stronger than that. The picture is effective in its light and dark, and the sky is particularly good. "The Market at Toulon," by Mr. Birket Foster, with its gay flowers, vegetables, and great yellow umbrellas, is very bright in color and clear in treatment.

Birket Foster.

Green. "Derby Day—Here they come!" by Mr. C. Green, is a very clever and characteristic representation of this scene. The eager heads and earnest action of the crowd that are pressing forward against the rope to catch sight of the coming horses are capitally rendered. Mr. H. Herkomer's "Woodcutters," which represents workmen turning the trunk of a tree they have felled, is admirable in its action and drawing, and very pleasing in its clear gray tones.

Herkomer.

Sir John Gilbert. Among other watercolors which may be noted are "The Guide," by Sir John Gilbert; several pleasing pictures by Mrs. Allingham, "When our Gudeman's Awa'" by G. G. Kilburne, and a clever head of "Saint George" by Mr. E. J. Gregory, "Sunday Evening in Chelsea Hospital Gardens" by Mr. James Macbeth, and E. J. Poynter's portrait of Mrs. Louis Courtauld.

Mrs. Allingham. Kilburne. Gregory. Macbeth. Poynter.

Crane. "The Death of the Year," by Mr. Walter Crane, is a processional picture of maidens carrying a corpse, which is pleasing and stronger in color than his oils. There is little definite character and individuality known in the figures or faces: they are all of the same type, and have a family likeness, as if they were sisters. The same observation may be made of all the pictures by Mr. E. Burne-Jones. He sent two watercolors, representing "Love among the Ruins" and "Love as Wisdom." The first represents two figures, a youth and a maiden, seated in a strange place, with strange fragments of architecture overgrown with ivy and thistles, with little regard to perspective or probability. The low gateway, for instance, has no just relation in point of size or height to the figures, and all parts are so equally emphasized that the total effect of the picture is flat. "Love as Wisdom" represents two girls in red and brown dresses standing erect and half embracing, while opposite to them stands a third in dark blue, who is apparently addressing them. A town on a hill behind forms the background. The picture is pleasing in composition, but it entirely lacks aërial perspective, and the houses of the distant town seem to adhere to the heads of the figures. Both these pictures are rich in color, and in "Love among the Ruins" there is considerable expression of languid sadness. But both are rather conceits than subjects.

Burne-Jones.

ENGLAND.

Burne-Jones.

Mr. Burne-Jones has attained so distinguished a reputation in England, that it is with much hesitation that we approached with criticism pictures which have received higher panegyric from his friends and admirers than perhaps was ever before bestowed upon the works of any living painter. One of his admirers has not hesitated publicly in his writings to say that he is the greatest artist that ever lived.*

Prof. Colvin in "Fortnightly Review."

* NOTE.—Lest I may be supposed to exaggerate the statements of Mr. Burne-Jones's admirers, I cite the following passages from an article in the "Fortnightly Review" for June, 1877, by Professor Sydney Colvin, on the Grosvenor Gallery, which may also serve as a correction to my own view. The whole article is worthy of perusal, as indicating the opinion of the new school of criticism on the new school of painting in England. Language can scarcely go farther. Professor Colvin speaks of Mr. Burne-Jones as a "master in whose inspiration there is nothing faltering or ambiguous, and in his ideals nothing harsh and unlovely. The genius of Mr. Burne-Jones will on these walls become a reality to those to whom hitherto it has been only a report." Speaking of the "Six Days of Creation," he says, "This is a favorite mediæval subject for the opening illustration of Chronicles, and occurs in some schemes of mosaic and other church decoration. But the modern work is no echo of any old; the subject has been redipped in the colors of a living spirit, and recast in the furnace of a great imagination. . . . Since painting was an art it is probable that no poetry so intense as this, no invention so rich and unerringly lovely, was ever pressed into form and color. It is better to say it without hesitation, we have among us a genius, a poet in design and color, whose like has never been seen before. To an almost incredible patience and multiplicity of workmanship, this painting joins a quite inexpressible felicity and loveliness of pictorial invention. Inch by inch, as well as division by division, it can only be studied with ever-increasing wonder and delight." Just as a born poet and inspired singer cannot put together those words that have not the sound, the spell, the soul of poetry, so this artist cannot draw a ring of hair, or a fold of drapery, or lay the tint of a flower, or a feather, or a shell, but the drawing has a charm and the color a preciousness which stirs the mind with the spell of visible poetry, an enchantment from the soul of things, an inexpressible felicity and loveliness,"—"preciousness of color," "soul of poetry," an "incredible patience," "an increasing wonder and delight," "unerring loveliness," "great imagination."—After such praise what can be added—what can be said of those whom we have hitherto held to be great masters? As for those who do not agree to this "supreme" gush ("supreme" is the word which is affected now by a certain clique of critics, and we wish to conform to this "preciousness" of diction for the moment), and who dare to criticise even the drawing, they are told that their criticisms "cannot be made with any show of reason now," and that some critics of this class "write themselves as asses and puppies before the world." Still we must honestly say that such extravagant laudation is, in our humble opinion, not calculated to be of benefit to Mr. Burne-Jones, who, whatever be his talent, has still something to learn, nor to lead with it the calm judgment even of his best friends and much less of the public.

It may also be interesting to append here two opposite criticisms of

ENGLAND.

Burne-Jones.

But, on the other hand, critics are not wanting who, admitting his great talent, protest against this excessive laudation as injurious not only to art but to the artist, by confirming him in a style, both of subject and of treatment, which in itself is not the highest, and which threatens to degenerate into mannerism, and to lead astray into vague sentimentality those who follow him. It may not, therefore, be presumptuous if we venture to choose a neutral ground, and proceed to consider his methods and his subjects.

These two pictures, as well as his "Beguiling of Merlin," which, though in oil, is partially *aquarelle* in its technical treatment and effect, have been declared to be "among his noblest inspirations," and it will be no injustice to judge him by them.

Mr. Burne-Jones is essentially a colorist, and in the two water-colors he has amply justified his high reputation. They are rich in color, and harmonious in combination of tints. The "Beguiling of Merlin by Vivian" is not, however, at all entitled to the same praise. It is monotonous and

---

"London Week."

Mr. Burne-Jones's latest work, "Pygmalion," as indicating the opposite extremes of opinion, taken from the "London Week" of May 24, 1879:

"TWO WAYS OF SEEING A PICTURE.

"Let us now see what these discordant voices have to say about Mr. Burne-Jones's 'Pygmalion' series. The following criticisms are well worth comparing carefully:

"Spectator." "Illustrated News."

"[*Spectator.*]

"'No description of which we are capable can convey in any adequate degree the intense beauty of this work. As in all supreme painting, we lose sight altogether of the artist in the vision he has created for us, and it needs a severe effort of the mind to bring itself back to the consideration of the marvellous skill which is here displayed. But when this is done we hardly know upon what to bestow our greatest admiration, whether upon the soft effulgence of light in which the picture is enveloped, the little bit of azure sky on which Venus stands, and the delicate iridescence of the doves' plumage; on the stately strength of divine beauty and power in her figure, the clinging dependence of that of Galatea, or on the expression of the living statue, which is probably the most wonderful painting of all—surprise, joy, and helplessness struggling together in one woman's face.'

"[*Illustrated News.*]

"'We are assured that in these pictures there are latent meanings as to the rise, growth, and fruition of "passion" which associates them with those productions of the minor poets of the day, which forms the "supersensuous," or rather, we should say, the ultra-sensual, school—a school which, in its worst development, is the morbid outcome of weakly, overwrought physique—which every man who respects his manhood and every woman who values her honor must regard with disgust, and would destroy everything of value in the national character. For our part, we see merely mawkish sentiment, not "passion," in these wan, haggard faces—these limp languors, this hysterical tension—together with mediæval dilettanteism, for there is nothing whatever of Greek spirit or character in the series.'

"The 'Spectator' critic, it will be seen, goes nearly into hysterics; the other gentleman is affected in a very different way. We must say that for gush, tears, and bosh generally, the 'Spectator' man throws all his fellow-laborers in the field of art far into the shade."

Burne-Jones.

ineffective in color and without perspective. Merlin is represented as reclining in a contorted and helpless attitude, with crossed legs, at the foot of some tree or thorn covered with blossoms, while Vivian, swaddled in an extraordinary dress, turns her back upon him, twisting her head round over her shoulder, and holding before her in both hands a long book, from which she is apparently reciting her spell. The figures are neither of them well drawn. Each is at least ten heads high, and Vivian, from her feet to her waist, is seven heads. The attitudes are singularly constrained and graceless, and inexpressive of the subject, and Merlin looks rather like a feeble, peevish old woman than the master magician with all the arts of sorcery at his command. Without the title to this picture it would be difficult to divine the subject.

The objection to be made to many of Mr. Burne-Jones's works, and specially to these most recent ones, is the vagueness of the theme; and it is greatly to be regretted that his remarkable talent should have taken the direction it has toward subjects either vaguely ideal or languidly effeminate, removed from the best sympathies of our age, or the highest requirements of art. One gets a little tired of the constant apotheosis of Venus and Love, of these unwarlike knights and sentimental ladies, and of this perpetual repetition of the same type of face. Here, for instance, are three pictures, in all of which, both male and female, is the same type of character, expression, and face; and a similar peculiarity may be observed in all his later works. They are all the same person, or of the same family, with the same prominent chin, the same large sickly sad eyes, hollow cheeks, and full lips. Both manly and womanly vigor is wanting to all. The men are not virile; the women are not womanly in its best sense; but a certain languidness, effeminacy, and dreamy sentimentality, as of exhausted passions, almost epicene in its character, is visible in all.

It is not because we do not recognize the ability of Mr. Burne-Jones that we venture thus to criticise him. He has great merits to counterpoise his defects; but we would gladly see his genius engaged in sturdier struggle with more vigorous subjects and themes of greater power.

Revived Mediævalism.

Mediævalism.

And this leads us to speak of the school or rather clique of art which has lately grown up in England, and in which some of the most noted names are enrolled. Admitting at once the ability of these artists, we cannot the less regret the influence they are exciting. Desiring to lift art to a more

ENGLAND.

imaginative height, out of the commonplace of life, they have carried it beyond its legitimate domain into the vague and unreal, and sought to obtain notice by eccentricity and mediævalism. In their protest against the lower school of mere *genre*, they have sought to renovate art by recurrence to earlier methods and simpler schools. Feeling, through the quaint awkwardness, *naïveté*, and rigidity of the early Italian period, a purity and sweetness of sentiment art hath since lost, they have made the mistake of supposing these to be inseparable conditions of their charm, and have wilfully assumed their technical limitations and deficiencies. The sentiment they seek is modern, but the manner is in imitation of the early Italian masters. New wine is poured into old bottles. Their pictures are animated by the spirit of the new and the memory of the old. Scorning Guido and the Caracci, and scarcely accepting even Raffaelle, they prostrate themselves before their predecessors, expecting by imitations of their defects to attain their excellences. For instance, "Love as Wisdom" is a reminiscence of early Italy in composition and character. Its inspiration is from the early Italian poets in sentiment, and of the early painters in composition. So also the "Renaissance of Venus," by Mr. Walter Crane, is plainly inspired by a picture of Botticelli's in the Uffizi, at Florence, and in "On the Banks of the Styx," by Mr. R. Spencer Stanhope, the same early, dry manner is imitated. I only refer here to some of those examples found in this Exposition, but the list might be greatly enlarged, if it were proper to cite other names and works outside the Exposition. In these works, one cannot but feel that the genius of the artist has been fettered; that his intention is willful; that his method is not spontaneous. The quaintness, rigidity, even the bad drawing, of the early Italian school is imitated, but the unaffected charm is lost. There is a touch of affectation which ruins all. So strong is the protest against beauty, through fear of prettiness, that the ugly and awkward is sought, as it would seem, with intention.

Recurrence to early Italian style.

Imitated quaintness without the unaffected charm of the early Italian school.

Another defect to be seen in some of the English work is literalness. The artist is not a co-worker with nature, but her drudge and slave. He is so afraid not to be truthful that he copies the accidents and defects of nature as well as all its unimportant details with a fatal subjection. This is specially observable in some of the landscapes, in which the parts often are over-emphasized to the destruction of the main effect. They look like timid and labored studies by a student, not free and plastic interpretations of a mas-

Literalness.

ENGLAND.

Ruskin.

ter. Mr. Ruskin has so loudly and emphatically preached the gospel of detail and imitation of nature that his followers are afraid to omit anything, and there is little distinction in the work between the common and the poetic. The opposite defect of slovenliness and meanness of execution is also frequently seen, and there is a strange oscillation between overdoing and carelessness—between doing too much and doing too little. In fact what the English school most lacks is a decided style and training, a certain hand, a command of material, and precision in drawing. Much of their work has, therefore a groping character, with no definite and absolute intention. They are happy ideas, half expressed, and a constant tendency to sentimentality.

Oscillation between overdoing and carelessness.

In the poetic and ideal school of English art the themes are at times subjects rather for poems than for pictures. They do not clearly express their meaning, but need a runing commentary of explanation. *Sermoni propriora* is their pet motto. "Love as Wisdom," for instance, might apparently make a pleasing poem in the early Italian manner, but as a picture it scarcely explains itself. So much is this felt in England, that great pains and ingenuity are expended on the titles of the pictures. These are often far more suggestive than the pictures themselves. Suppose "Love as Wisdom," or "Love Among the Ruins," had no name, could one easily divine what was the precise intention of the artist? Nay, can one, as it is?

Subjects for poems rather than pictures.

Genre.

Between these and the school of anecdote, *genre*, and familiar life, the gap is great. "Love as Wisdom" and "The Railway Station," by Mr. Frith, represent the extremes of different styles. In the familiar school of England of common life there is often a triviality and sentimentality of commonplace which is disappointing. The themes are often not worthy of the cleverness which is displayed, and the execution, so far as *technique* is concerned, is insufficient to give an interest of itself to the pictures. In these respects the superiority of execution in France is very striking. There are no oil pictures in England which are rendered with the skill which, for instance, is to be observed in Worms, Meissonier, Gérôme, Leloir, or indeed of any of the chief painters of such subjects in France. The humor is often a little exaggerated, the sentiment a little flat, and the painting weak. At times the real poetic sentiment is reached, as in the water-colors of Mr. Walker, and at times true pathos is expressed; but generally speaking there is a

Trivial themes.

ENGLAND. want of freshness and energy of conception, and firmness of drawing.

Historical.

Historical Paintings.

In the higher branches of History, the eight pictures in this Exposition, with all their cleverness and talent in general, lack power and firmness of conception as well as strength of execution. They are more scenic than real; the heart of the mystery is not plucked; they do not interest; they do not excite the spectator. They want reality. In this connection I would refer to the admirable essay of Charles Lamb "On the Want of Imagination in Modern Works of Art," as clearly showing what is needed in a great historical painting.

More scenic than real.

Reference to Charles Lamb's essay.

But to pass from general considerations to particular instances, there were many works in the English department which deserve high praise, and constitute exceptions to the general statement we have made. One observation is to be strongly emphasized, and that is that, with all its shortcomings, earnestness of purpose, purity of theme, and propriety of thought and feeling are always to be seen in English art. There are no indecencies, no doubtful innuendoes, no displays of mere nudity, no violence and brutality of subject and treatment, such as deform the French school, and but little mere *bric-à-brac* work, with no soul and nothing but the body of *technique*—all is serious or quiet, at least in its intention, and there are frequently a naturalness, sweetness, simplicity, and refinement of feeling which make up for many deficiencies. The English school in various and perhaps blind ways is feeling its way, but it is animated with high and pure purpose. It does not prostitute itself to low and unworthy aims. This it is which marked especially all the department of English art at this Exposition, and made a strong impression on artists of every country.

English art shows: Earnestness. Purity, Propriety.

Among the most charming pictures in this department was "The Reaper and the Flowers," by Mr. P. R. Morris, which is a little idyllic poem, full of sentiment and feeling, and very delicate and pure in color. The sun has set, but the light is still bright in the sky, and the trees and landscape in the middle distance rise dark against it. The old reaper with his scythe on his shoulder is going home, and five little girls, who have come out to meet him, are dancing around him, gay and flower-like. He is walking toward the sunset, and his face is illuminated with the coy light. So, too, are the faces of the children whose backs are turned to the

Morris.

ENGLAND.

Morris.

light. How their faces are illuminated, or why they cast no shadows, it is difficult to say; but no matter, the picture is charming and truly poetic. Another of Mr. Morris's pictures represents four mowers working in a field of grain. The action of the figures is well expressed, and the drawing and color good. They are earnestly at work, unconscious that we are looking at them. There is less poetic feeling, perhaps, in this than in the other picture, but the subject is well felt and rendered, and it is a serious and admirable work. Both of these pictures are under glass, and one needs to examine them closely to assure one's self that they are not *aquarelles*.

Holl.

Mr. Holl sent two pictures, both of decided merit, "The Lord gave, and the Lord taketh away," which is cleverly composed and interesting, and "Leaving Home." Here there is character, firm drawing, and truth of movement and expression. The scene is in the waiting-room of the third class, at a railway station, and represents the leave-taking of a young soldier who is leaving his home. It is simply rendered and without affectation. The group, consisting of mother, father, and sister, is seated along a bench, and the figure of the old father in especial is admirable in every way for color, drawing, and character. The sincerity and clear intention of the artist, and his ability to depict what he means, make this an exceptional picture. There is nothing mawkish in the sentiment, or slipshod in the execution, and there are strong values of darks, which is rare in an English picture. Unfortunately it is under glass, which gives it somewhat the effect of an *aquarelle*, and disturbs the eye. Why the English have this practice of covering their oil pictures with glass, it is difficult to see. The effect is injured, and there is no apparent necessity for the practice.

Aumonier.

"Toilers of the Field," by Mr. J. Aumonier, is a very pleasing picture, well composed, and agreeable in sentiment and general sunny tone. One cannot but regret that it is so *aquarelle* in treatment, that the figures are so thin and even in tone, and that the shadows are so faint. At this hour the long shadows constitute an essential feature and sentiment of the scene. A little more enforcement would have made this picture quite charming; as it is, the figures are a little too transparent, and do not come off from the ground. But, despite this, the picture is full of feeling and sentiment.

Luke Fildes.

"Applicants for Admission to a Casual Ward," by Mr. Luke Fildes, is a composition of great talent, full of dramatic character and feeling, and without affectation or grimace. It is a little gloomy and monotonous in tone and color, and

ENGLAND. wants focussing of light and dark, but it is a strong, able, and pathetic picture, done with great directness and steadiness of purpose.

Herkomer. "The Last Muster," by Mr. H. Herkomer, deserved the medal of honor which was conferred upon it. It is a remarkable picture, representing a Sunday service at the chapel of the Royal Hospital at Chelsea, with all the veterans seated on their benches and the tattered banners hanging over head. This picture, which is really a picture of portraits, is painted with great vigor, honesty, and solidity of *impasto;* but beyond this it shows a quiet dramatic sense, and a simplicity and truth of individual character such as is rarely seen. The two principal figures are particularly admirable in truth of action and expression. Besides this, Mr. Herkomer's other oil painting, "After the Toil of the Day," looks very washy and *aquarelle* in manner, and is far behind it in character and vigor, though it is a pleasing picture.

Millais. The only other medal of honor which was given to England was awarded to Mr. Millais. He was admirably represented by no less than ten of his principal pictures, of which five were portraits, two landscapes, and three subject pictures. These pictures have been repeatedly exhibited, and are already so well known that they scarcely need to be described. Of his portraits, that of "Mrs. Bischoffsheim" is one of the best, and it is spirited and well painted, though a little careless in the execution of all but the head, and has the great merit of a very strong resemblance. The portrait of the "Duke of Westminster" in his hunting dress is also an admirable portrait, simple, direct, and true to life; but still better than this is "The Gambler's Wife," which, notwithstanding its title, is plainly a portrait, and only a portrait. The head on this picture is charmingly rendered with great delicacy of color and feeling, and care in execution. Indeed, of all Mr. Millais' works in the Exposition this is the most sincere and happy, as far as the head goes. But the *fichu* on her neck is too careless—it means nothing. Mr. Millais has quite changed his whole style since those early works which first won him his high reputation, and which were characterized by fastidious and minute elaboration. Now, on the contrary, his style is free, and at times quite too free and careless, and he often contents himself with merely suggesting in the sketchiest manner what, with the pressure of his engagements, he has no time to work out. There, perhaps, might be a happy mean between these two manners, and there is at times an indication of altogether too much hurry in his work. In the portraits of his three children, for instance, the dresses are mere vague smudges of white, with no anatomy in the folds and no texture. The dresses also of the "Three Sisters" are very careless, and all the same pattern and color, while the background of flowers is a mere sketch. This reckless splashing on of incidental parts is a characteristic of English portraits. If an artist draws anything it ought, at least as far as it goes, however unfinished, to have a determinate form and meaning, and not to be, as it too often is, a mere scribble, and Mr. Millais is too clever an artist and too capable an executant to allow himself to slur over accessories in this hurried way. "The Yeoman of the Guard," clever as in some respects it is, has on the whole something a little grotesque in it. The tones of the red costume are too *voyant*. The face is dabbled and spotty in execution, and the general effect is of a huge water-color.

The two landscapes, one representing "Chill October," and the other "O'er the Hills and Far Away," which is a view of the Scottish moors, are so well known that they scarcely need to be described. In sentiment and general tone the "Chill October" is the best, and narrowly misses being a remarkable picture. But here is the same carelessness of parts, the same want of real love for the thing represented, the same hurry of execution. The background and distance are scarcely even sketched in, as if the artist had got tired of his work before completing it. The foreground is scratched in loosely; the roots of the trees are scarcely drawn at all. The only part which is really painted is the middle distance, with its dark trees bending to the stress of the wind and its chill gleamy water, and these are so admirably rendered and so good in character that they hold the whole picture together and cover the deficiencies of the rest. In the Scotch landscape, as in "Chill October," the main dark is in the middle ground, drawing the pictures into two parts, and the foregrounds are comparatively weak and unsatisfactory. Here there is much and careful study; the execution is free and the color good, but it lacks the sentiment that animates the "Chill October," and is not so happy in its expression of feeling, though it is more carefully painted. Indeed, it is to be objected that in the distance there is too much insistance of particulars which could scarcely be visible to the naked eye, and little effect of *chiaro-oscuro*.

The subject pictures by Mr. Millais are two in number, "The Northwest Passage" and "Yes or No." The latter is essentially portrait. The former, a girl seated at the feet

ENGLAND. Millais.

of her father, an old sailor, and reading from a book, to which he is attentively listening. The character and expression of the sailor, who clasps his daughter's hand, is admirable, the incident is interesting, and the story well told.

Mr. Millais' reputation is so established and his talent so decided that he can well afford to be criticised. Had his influence and position been less we should not have dwelt upon his shortcomings, which are chiefly the result of hurry and carelessness and want of real love for his work. Art is a jealous mistress, and demands devotion and earnestness. She is not satisfied with a careless nod even from so masterly a workman as Mr. Millais.

Watts.

Mr. G. F. Watts sent a number of interesting portraits of "Robert Browning," "Herr Joachim," "General Laurence," "P. H. Calderon," "The Duke of Cleveland," and "Hon. Mrs. Percy Wyndham." Of these the best is the full-length of Mrs. Wyndham, which has much dignity and breadth of style and character. Mr. Watts's genius, however, has a larger scope in his ideal subjects, of which he sends us but two specimens, in his "Pallas, Juno, and Venus," and his "Love and Death;" of these the more carefully painted is the former, which is simple and unaffected, and, though it leaves much to be desired in clearness of color and exactness of drawing from the nude, has no taint of the model, and is conceived in a true spirit. There is something large in the conception of Death, and the head of Love is expressive in action and feeling; but his figure is sadly out of drawing and strange in color. There is in these pictures, however, a lift of spirit and feeling.

Poynter.

Mr. E. J. Poynter sent three pictures, "The Catapult," "Proserpine," and "Israel in Egypt." There is much that is refined in sentiment and conception in the "Proserpine" gathering flowers, her figure showing through the half-transparent drapery in which she is robed. Both the other pictures are more ambitious in character and design, show great study and research, and are interesting and spirited. The "Israel in Egypt" represents the Israelites dragging a colossal figure through the burning noon of Egypt. The great mass of figures are well drawn and appropriate in action, the costumes are carefully studied, and nothing has been slighted. What is to be objected is that the values of all parts are too equal in color and *chiaro-oscuro*, so that the interest is too widely distributed, and not sufficiently concentrated on any main incident. In consequence the picture has a certain thinness and flatness of effect. "The

Catapult" is more concentrated and more powerful, and very clever in action and design, though a little dull in color. ENGLAND.

"Rough Weather in the Mediterranean," by Mr. Henry Moore, is a very careful study of mid-ocean. The heaving waves are full of life and movement, and the intense blue tones very true to nature. H. Moore.

Mr. Brett's two pictures of "Spires and Steeples of the Channel Islands," and "Mount's Bay, Cornwall," are immense birds-eye views of the sea and coast in broad sunlight, crowded with detail, and studied with exceeding pains and labor. Indeed, it is a painfully careful study, and despite the talent it displays and the conscientiousness of the work, one cannot but feel that the labor is in the wrong direction, and that the artist has been mastered by his subject, and rendered subservient to the facts. There is no reserve anywhere; everything glitters with excess of light; every bit is of equal value, and insists upon forcing itself on the attention. The minute is over-emphasized, as if the artist had been afraid to have anything unreported, however unnecessary, and the result is fatiguing. Brett.

Mr. Albert Moore's two little pictures of "Beads," and "The Palm Fan," which in the catalogue are called "harmonies in blue and gold," have little theme or character, but they are well drawn, delicate, unaffected, and graceful, though a little pale and chalky in color. They are of the young school of England—with which novelty is often a synonym of excellence. These two pictures were too pale and weak to produce much effect in the Exposition, but they would be charming in a little boudoir. A. Moore.

Mr. R. W. Macbeth sent two pictures, a "Lincolnshire Gang," and "Potato Harvest in the Fens." The first represents a gang of workmen and women roused to labor at daybreak. It is well composed and painted, and has a good deal of action and spirit and vigor of character. It is a little monotonous from its want of contrast in light and dark, and the faces have that peculiar lantern-like illumination which is characteristic of so many pictures in the English department, but it is an interesting picture. In light and dark, and in *technique*, the "Potato Gatherers" is much more vigorous, and, indeed, in these qualities it is one of the most striking pictures in the English department. It is firmly and forcibly painted, well composed, and solidly laid in. The sky is good, and the massed figures come up strongly against it. Macbeth.

Miss Thompson (now Mrs. Butler) sent a picture representing "The Return from Inkermann," in which we confess. Mrs. Butler, née Thompson.

ENGLAND.

Mrs. Butler. after all the great praise which has been bestowed upon this lady's work, to have been disappointed. The drawing is studied. There is character undoubtedly in some of the groups, but the figures are somewhat confusedly massed together, and there is a certain want of that virile strength and enforcement which is demanded in such a subject. The color is dull and smudgy, and of a uniform tint throughout. After the pictures of a similar class in France it has rather a tame effect. But there is undoubted talent in it, and as the work of a woman it is remarkable.

Stanhope. Mr. Spencer Stanhope is a follower of Mr. Burne-Jones, and his "On the Banks of the Styx," is an effort in the same early Italian direction, though with inferior talent. In color it is washy, thin, and ineffective, and the figures are very long, lean, and queer. The subject is poetic, and with different treatment might have been made interesting and pathetic; but as it is, it is only affected and eccentric, and willfully wrong. "*Ils sont joliment maigres*," was the comment of a French woman that reached my ears as I was looking at it.

Brewtnell. Mr. E. F. Brewtnell is of the same following, and his "Sleeping Beauty" has the same quality of queerness. The young Prince especially is very peculiar in attitude and drawing. Originality seems in this class of pictures to be confounded with oddity and awkwardness.

Sir J. Gilbert. Among the historical paintings, those of Sir John Gilbert are among the most ambitious, though, perhaps, not the best of his efforts. They represent "The Doge and Senators of Venice in Council," "Richard II resigning his Crown to Bolingbroke," "The Arrest of Hastings," and "Cardinal Wolsey at Leicester Abbey." There is in the treatment of these subjects a certain academic character of composition and action, the color is hard and *voyant*, and the drawings far from good. "Serf Emancipation," by Mr. Armitage. Armitage, represents an Anglo-Saxon noble on his death-bed, surrounded by his family and friends on one side, while opposite stand a group of serfs, some kneeling and some standing, to whom he is giving their freedom. The picture is a little academic, though well composed, but it is monotonous in color and tone, and there is little salience in character and expression. Calderon. Mr. P. H. Calderon sent seven pictures. "Constance," "Victory," "Margaret," "On her Way to the Throne," "Catharine of Lorraine," "Sighing his Soul into his Lady's Face," and "Home they brought her Warrior dead." "On the way to the Throne" is good in character and composition and is delicate in color, but it is in the pure water-color style, and it would easily pass at a little distance for an *aquarelle*. The "Catherine of Lorraine urging Jacques Clement to assassinate Henry III," is clever, but exaggerated, and the color, particularly in the background, not happy. "The Last Touch" is a very clever bit of comedy and humor, without exaggeration and splendidly rendered. "Home they brought her Warrior dead" is by far the best of his pictures here. It is strongly painted and clearly felt. The textures are well given, particularly the curtain and the yellowish white and satin coverlid. There is pathos, too, and simple unexaggerated strength of feeling, and it is altogether an interesting and effective picture. And this leads me to speak of the want of feeling and study of draperies and textures and qualities of stuffs which is ordinairly seen in the English work. The anatomies of drapery and the peculiarities of different textures are little studied. The execution is not only careless, but unintelligent. The folds and breaks are not understood and imitated, but merely blotted in with a vague, uncertain touch, and uniformly treated as if they were unimportant accessories. The picture by Mr. Calderon is known as one of the few exceptions to the general rule. Here you see what the stuff is, and you feel that the artist has represented it *con amore*. Mr. Millais sins greatly in this respect, as we have already said. His draperies and textures are the least good parts of his pictures, and he seems not to feel their value and beauty. In this respect, the English might well take a lesson from the French, whose draperies and textures are studied with great care. It is vexatious to see in the English work dresses vaguely rubbed in in color, with here and there an indeterminate and inexpressive streak of dark to break the surface. There is one kind of execution which although it does not insist on details or become niggled in execution, is broad, decisive, true, as far as it goes. This is the free manner of a master's work, and is the result of knowledge. There is another, in which the English school indulges, that is indecisive and careless, and which strives to mask its ignorance or carelessness by sloppy inexpressive touches under the pretense of freedom of style.

ENGLAND.

Calderon.

Another exception to this general characteristic is to be seen in the exquisitely felt and carefully studied draperies of Sir Frederick Leighton's "Music Lesson." This picture has great refinement of sentiment and composition, and, though a little over-labored in the execution, and with, perhaps, a touch of the *precieuse* in the almost enameled flesh, is, as a whole, charming. There is great harmony in the

Sir F. Leighton.

ENGLAND. Leighton. general tints and great tenderness of feeling. Sir Frederick's portrait of "Captain Burton" is, on the contrary, masterly in execution and strong in *impasto*, and is decidedly one of the best portraits here. We regret to say that his more ambitious attempt to represent "Elijah" ministered to by the angel, does not show the same vigor. It is not happy as a composition, and it is weak in execution. The angel is graceful, but the picture lacks that solemnity and seriousness of character that the subject demands. There are in all Mr. Leighton's works earnestness and faithfulness of study, but powerful subjects like the Elijah are less in harmony with his genius than that of a more idyllic, romantic, and poetic type.

Prinsep. Mr. V. Prinsep sent three pictures, "Reading 'Sir Charles Grandison,'" "The Linen Gatherers," and "*A Bientôt.*" "The Linen Gatherers" represents a scene on the Devonshire cliffs, with English girls coming down a slope carrying home the linen that has been bleaching in the sun. In this picture, though it represents a scene in the open air towards evening, with full light, not a single figure casts a shadow, while all the faces coming toward the spectator, and with the light of sky behind them, are self-illuminated like lanterns. There is no feeling of distance or perspective, all the figures are of equal value and distinctness in one monotonous tint, and there is no light and dark. There is the same monotony of tint and value, the same absence of shadow, and the same thinness of execution in both the other pictures, which are essentially *genre*.

This even, flat monotony and absence of shadows and self-illumination are singular peculiarities of most of the

Yeames. English pictures. For instance, Mr. W. F. Yeames's "The Last Bit of Gossip" represents a scene in the open street of Bath, with two persons meeting in Sedan chairs, the tops of which are raised while their occupants look out and chat together. The incident is amusing, there is a pretty arrangement of color, and there is character, but the whole picture is flat, as if it were printed in *cretonne*, the tones are all even, and nothing casts a shadow. There is no distance, no tone, no disengagement of one thing from another. In examining the picture bit by bit, one sees that it shows spirit and talent, but there is absolutely no light and dark. "*Pour les Pauvres*," by the same artist, has the same defects and the same

Goodall. merits. Again, in Mr. F. Goodall's picture of "The Time of Roses" the same peculiarity is seen. It represents a mother with her infant in her arms in a rose-garden, with a red-brick wall behind. It is clear sunlight, and yet nothing casts a shadow, and the faces are self-illuminating. There is much that is pretty and pleasing in parts, but it is all there as water-color, and without light and dark. The "Head of the House at Prayer," by the same artist, represents an Arab chief standing in front of his tent with his camels near by, in broad daylight, yet there is not a shadow thrown by anything. The same thing may be said also of Mr. Goodall's "Spring," which is vaporous, tender, and delicate in color, but without a shadow. Goodall.

Again, the same remark may be made in respect to all Mr. Richardson's pictures. There is something very pleasant and bright about them. In linear composition they are clever, the figures are fairly well drawn, and the incidents represented are interesting, but there is almost no composition of light and dark, all things are of equal value, there are almost no shadows, there is no principal light, and all the faces are equally illuminated. Each figure is drawn with a dark outline, and flatly filled in with color. The background and still life are painted in a thin, stringy manner, are just washed in, and have somewhat the effect of stained wood. Still there is much talent displayed in these pictures, though one cannot but regret the feebleness of the *technique*. One exception there is in his "Escaped," which represents two dogs finding a cap in the water. Here there are darks and a sense of values, but here, too, there are no shadows. Richardson.

The subject of "The Queen of the Swords" is taken from Sir Walter Scott's "Pirate," and the moment chosen is when Minna Troil moves down between two files of lifted swords, which are crossed above her head. It is drawn with spirit and animation, and is an interesting picture. "The Bill of Sale" is also clever, and has a good deal of quiet character. The "Portrait," however, is far more solid and strong in color, painted with good *impasto*, and simple, unaffected, and natural. It is one of the best portraits in the English school.

Again, the same peculiarity is seen in Mr. G. H. Boughton's pictures. None of the figures cast any shadows, and the faces are all self-illuminating. This is especially the case in the "Surrey Pastoral," where the subject is an English landscape almost in twilight, with a rising moon. In the middle ground are figures, some seated, and one crossing a brook. All is in subdued tone and pleasing in sentiment; but, though the backs of the figures are turned to the sky, their faces are all unnaturally illuminated, and seem like lanterns. The same is the case with "The Bearers of the Burden," which is also marked by a quiet monotony of tone, Boughton.

ENGLAND. Boughton. with faint yellows and browns, and almost no perspective of distance. "Snow in Spring" represents a group of young girls in a wood. Primroses are on the ground, and flakes of snow are falling. The theme is rather a quaint conceit, with little realism, but pleasing in arrangement of colors and refined in sentiment. Indeed, there is something agreeable and attractive in all Mr. Boughton's work, when one has ceased to look for solidity and truth, and is content to accept sentiment and delicate tones in their stead.

"Harmonies." "Nocturnes." "Symphonies." Here it may be observed that the phrases so constantly used in the new school of England, such as harmonies and arrangement in this and that color, nocturnes, symphonies, etc., indicate clearly a notion that a pleasing combination of tints and colors constitutes "color." It cannot, however, be too strongly insisted upon that no arrangement of tints and colors constitutes, in its proper sense, "color." What "color" means. The term "color" has a far larger and deeper significance, and embraces not so much mere arrangement of flat tints (which might equally well be made in a *cretonne* pattern) as unity and harmony of tone, depth of quality, values of colors in *chiaro-oscuro*, and solidity of representation. When it is said that Titian and Giorgone are great colorists, it is not meant only that the tints superficially laid on are agreeable in arrangement, but that the qualities of the things are rendered; that there is a just relation of parts in effect; that all is in its proper place as value; that the flesh is deep, rich, and luminous; that the gradations are subtle; that light and shade balance and give value to each other; and that there is an all-pervading presence of tone throughout every part. And this is exactly what is not seen nor apparently sought for in most modern English works. English combinations of mere tints. They rather seek for agreeable combinations of mere tints. But, besides, they are Weak in drawing. extremely weak in their drawing, which is generally without style and decision. It always seems tentative, approximative, and uncertain, and often ignorant, as if the artist had not been properly trained to draw before he began to paint. But it cannot be denied that good drawing is the very foundation of good art; and, in drawing, the English school is far behind the chief schools of the Continent. Take, for instance, the drawing in the figures of "Merlin and Vivian," by Mr. Disproportion. Burne-Jones. They are about ten heads high, while the highest ideal standard is eight, and the practical standard less. It may safely be said that no figure can be found in nature, and none in the antique, which clearly measures eight heads. But it is not only in the lengths of parts, but in the unintelligent rendering of them, that the drawing

ENGLAND.

fails. The hips are almost impossible. The neck is deformed; the proportions and balance and movement all incorrect.* Look, too, at the "Love" of Mr. Watts, where not only the color but the drawing and anatomy are exceedingly unsatisfactory. I mention these two names only because they enjoy so high a reputation, and therefore fitly should be among the best draftsmen.

Leslie.

Similar defects are to be found in the pictures of Mr. G. D. Leslie, but they need not be more insisted on. They are very flat and weak in color, are without contrast of light and dark, and have a thinness of body as if they were *aquarelles;* but a charming and refined sentiment animates them all, and they have a *naïve* grace and simplicity which is very attractive. The "School Revisited" is in especial to be noticed. The time and costumes are of the last century, and the picture represents an old schoolfellow, who sits on a bench with her former playmates, younger than herself, telling them, probably, of the outer world and its delights, and talking over old times. His pictures "Lavinia," "Fortunes," "Celia's Arbor," and "Potpourri" are all most pleasing.

Revière.

The same faults may be found also with Mr. Briton Rivière's pictures. He sent three, "Daniel in the Lions' Den," "Charity," and "The Last of the Garrison." This last, which represents a wounded dog, has a good deal of pathos. The first, "Daniel," is, however, his most important work. It is spirited in conception and original in treatment. Daniel, with his arms tied behind him, and his back turned to the spectator, confronts a group of lions. His figure is striking in its severe simplicity. The character of the lions, too, is well given. What one regrets is the monotone of color and the want of technical strength in the execution, but the picture shows much talent and originality.

Cope.

Mr. C. W. Cope's picture, "Selecting Pictures for the Royal Academy Exhibition," is very clever and well-composed. The likenesses are good, and the groups happily arranged.

Hunter.

"Trawlers waiting for Darkness," by Mr. Colin Hunter, is a strong and well-conceived work. The coming on of the dark is well expressed, and the contrasts of light and dark are good. Altogether it is a serious and striking picture.

* Professor Colvin is of a different opinion. In the article already cited from the "Fortnightly Review," after stating that in this picture "the countenances are passion incarnate, the profile of Nimiane never to be forgotten," etc., he adds that "the drawing of Nimaine's figure, hands, and feet—the numb and slackened hands of Merlin—these, for instance, are mere masterpieces."

ENGLAND.

Morgan. The "Haymakers," by Mr. F. Morgan, represents a group returning home along the road in the glow of a summer's evening. This picture is admirable in composition, color, and *chiaro-oscuro*. The sentiment is well expressed and the character of the figures well rendered. One cannot but ask, however, why the faces, though turned away from the sunset, are self-illuminating, and why, since the sky is so bright, no shadows are cast.

Landseer. Of deceased artists, Sir Edwin Landseer was represented by six of his well-known pictures—"The Indian Tent," "The Connoisseurs," "Swannery Invaded by Eagles," "Man Proposes, and God Disposes," The Ptarmigan Hill," and "The Sick Monkey." The last is the only one that merits attention, and here Sir Edwin is seen at his best. The remainder are weak and washy in execution, and very poor in color, and without strength of design or character. In fact, it must be admitted that these pictures do not at all sustain his great reputation, and have materially diminished the estimation in which he has been held.

Mason. Seven of the late Mr. George H. Mason's pictures were exhibited, all of them good in color and *impasto*, and pleasing in sentiment. Particuarly are to be mentioned the "Evensong," "Children Fishing," and "The Cast Shoe," all of them characterized by a low tone of color, a good feeling for light and dark, and a pure simplicity of treatment.

Phillip. Four of the late John Phillip's works were also here, of which the principal one was "Round the Brasero," representing a group of Spaniards gathered around the fire in the brasero. These are all a little coarse in color and character, but are clever and spirited.

Armstrong. Mr. T. Armstrong's "Music Piece" is graceful, pretty in sentiment, and pleasing in its arrangement of colors, though it is perfectly *aquarelle* in quality. Two half figures of girls in front are listening to a young priest who is playing the piano-forte in the background, or rather what is meant for the background; but in reality the picture is so totally without perspective, and all the parts are so much on the same plane, that the girls look like giantesses and the priest like a pigmy.

Croft. Mr. E. Crofts' "Morning of the Battle," with day breaking over a weary and wounded group of soldiers, some on the ground, some preparing to move at the summons of the trumpet, has much character, expression, and spirit, and shows very decided talent.

Among the portraits are to be noted Mr. Lehmann's excellent likeness of "Mr. Browning." He is also represented by his well-known and often-repeated "La Lavandaja" and "The Convent Dole," which is one of his best works." Of the late Sir Francis Grant's three portraits, "His Royal Highness the Duke of Cambridge at the Battle of the Alma" is the most ambitious, but the portrait of "Lord Gough" is far the best, and this is spirited and clever. Mr. W. B. Richmond sent a portrait of "Lady Frederick Cavendish," which is delicate in color and highly finished; Mr. Ouless sent portraits of the "Rt. Hon. Russel Gurney," "Mr. H. D. Pochin," and "Mr. William Sale," all strong and vigorous works; and Mr. J. Sant had a group of three portrait figures, called "The Early Post," all in white morning dresses, opening the letter bag, which is very fresh and English in character. Mr. Sant's "Adversity," which represents a poor girl leaning against a wall, with flowers for sale, has a good deal of expression and grace of attitude.

ENGLAND. Lehmann. Sir Francis Grant. Richmond. Ouless. Sant.

Among other pictures to be noted are "At the Prison Window" in southern Italy, by Henry Wallis, where a girl is playing a violin outside a prison grating through which a group of prisoners is looking, which is pleasing and well painted; and here it is to be observed that the girl casts a shadow; "Out in the Cold," by Mr. J. MacWhirter, representing a donkey standing in the snow outside a shanty; "Christmas Eve," by Haywood Hardy, a man with horse and dogcart in the cold, bleak, wintry evening; "Shearing Wraick in the Sound of Harris," by Mr. H. Macallum, a very clever picture with a good deal of careful study of nature; "French Savants in Egypt," by Mr. Eyre Crowe, showing considerable humor and character; and "The Lament of Ariadne," by Mr. Richmond. "What is it?," the "Apothecary," and "St. Francis and the Birds," all very carefully painted, and particularly in the still life and the birds. But perhaps the cleverest of all in humoristic perception and treatment is "Only been with a few Friends," by Mr. J. D. Watson, where the confused drunkenness of the careless home-returning drinker is admirably rendered in contrast with the rigid figure of his severe spouse.

Wallis. MacWhirter. Hardy. Macallum. Crowe. Richmond. Watson.

Humorous.

Among the humorous subjects are to be mentioned those of Mr. G. A. Storey of the "Old Soldier" asking alms and "Scandal"; also "Old Neighbors," by C. Green; and probably under this title should be ranked the extraordinary picture by Mr. E. J. Gregory called "Dawn," which is a scene in

Storey. Green. Gregory.

ENGLAND.

a ball-room, where the early light comes in and the lamps are still lighted, and a man and woman stand by a piano-forte. Whether it was meant to be humorous or not, its peculiarities are certainly amusing, both in color and drawing.

Frith.

The two large pictures by Mr. Frith of the "Derby Day" and "Charles II's last Sunday in Whitehall," and "The Salon d'Or at Hombourg," are too well known to need description, and have been already so much lauded and criticised that it is almost useless here to say anything more about them. They represent common incidents of life and character with undoubted talent, and some of the groups are strongly dramatic in character, well expressed, and well drawn. They will always appeal to a certain class of minds, to whom the poetic and ideal is comparatively a closed book, and who prefer the accurate representation of incidents of every-day life and character. Of the ability of Mr. Frith to represent these there can be but little doubt. Such incidents as the arrested felon as he is entering the railway carriage, while his wife looks out through the open door, is not only highly dramatic but rendered with great talent. So, too, in the "Derby Day": the various groups are faithfully drawn from nature, and there is something touching in the poor little tumbler who looks askance with hungry eyes at the tempting lunch, and loathsome in the half drunken faces near. Whether the representation of such subjects is the highest function of art is quite another question, which there is no need to discuss.

Sentimental.

In this connection a certain class of sentimental pictures of every-day life may be spoken of, which are often fairly well rendered, but are commonplace in ideas, and can scarcely awaken any great interest with those who crave high or ideal subjects in art and a lift above the ordinary.

"Keepsake" style.

The "Keepsake" style has little true root in art, and one was pleased to see so comparatively little of it in this Exposition. The "Mother's Darling," "The First Shoe," "The First Prayer," the "First Step," and, in general, baby pictures have been omitted.

Scenes of ordinary life.

Wynfield.

Among the scenes of ordinary life and family interiors, may be mentioned "The New Curate," by Mr. D. W. Wynfield, which is an elaborate representation of a very commonplace subject, painted with extreme clearness and precision, but with a certain quiet sense of humor and character.

ENGLAND. Alma-Tadema.

We have left to the last Mr. L. Alma-Tadema, for, although he exhibited in the English department, and his pictures almost covered one of the walls, his style, subjects, and execution are so completely foreign that he can scarcely be considered as an English artist. These pictures, ten in number, are interesting in character, clever in composition, and remarkable for their technical qualities of drawing, method, and color, as well as for the archæological study which they display. The still life, the texture and anatomy of the dresses, the imitations of stuffs, and especially of marbles, which abound in his pictures, are rendered with great fidelity and truth, and vigorously painted. Most of them are representations of so-called classic scenes of ancient Rome or Greece, as will be seen from their titles: "A Roman Emperor," "The Sculpture Gallery," "The Picture Gallery," (in ancient Rome), "An Audience at Agrippa's," "A Roman Garden" (very brilliant in color), "A Pyrrhic Dance," "After the Dance" (a naked Bacchante reposing, not among his happiest efforts), "The Vintage Festival," "*Une Fête Intime*," and "Death of the First Born". One of the most striking is "An Audience at Agrippa's," where a group of Romans are coming down marble stairs, at the foot of which is a statue. There is generally no strong theme in these paintings. They, for the most part, represent ordinary scenes of ancient life, and derive their chief interest from the ability with which the artist reproduces the costumes, furniture, manners, *bric-à-brac*, sculpture, marbles of the antique world; and in doing this no one can doubt that he shows the accomplishments of a master and a student. There are at times a little want of perspective and a little too equal values of parts, but their general excellence is indisputable, and it certainly is to be wished that his methods and skill in painting could find followers among the English artists. Though among them, he is not of them, but essentially a foreigner in his art.

Black and White.

Black and White.

Among the drawings in black and white, some were to be found which are quite equal if not superior in character and *chiaro-oscuro* to the more elaborated oil pictures in the English department. Particularly may be mentioned as admirable several by Mr. C. Green, as "The Irish Patern, or Pilgrimage," "Holiday Time Afloat," "Cripps the Carrier," and several by Mr. Gregory, whose "Among the Brigands" is capital in its effect of light and dark; "The Funeral at Sea," by Mr. J. Nash, which is simple and striking. The original drawings of correspondents, and the wood-cuts from

Green. Gregory. Nash.

ENGLAND.

them exposed by "The Graphic" Company are spirited, and executed with vigor and character. Many are without the names of the authors, but among those which are signed may be noted as very clever those by Messrs. C. Green, I. L. Fildes, L. J. Gregory, Fr. Holl, H. Herkomer, T. E. Hodgson, J. Nash, E. Hopkins, and M. D. Mauris.

Artists of London "Graphic."

SPAIN.

SPAIN.

We now come to the Spanish school, and, as it were, into a totally different world, animated by different ideas, expressing itself in a different manner, and having a different purpose and aim. This school, within the last few years, has exerted upon modern art, and particularly upon that of Italy, a strong influence, but whether, on the whole, a beneficial one is a question. The leader of the modern Spanish school, which is now so greatly in vogue, is Señ. Mariano Fortuny. To him the place of honor was given in the Spanish department. His various works covered one whole side-wall, and over these was placed his bust. He was represented by 29 works, among which were some of the most important, for size and subject, ever painted by him, as well as many smaller ones, and a number of finished studies. Fortuny's pictures early took the public by surprise, and captivated its judgment by their *éclat* of color, by a certain exactness and brilliancy of execution, and by their novelty of subject and treatment; and the place he took almost at first he maintained to the end of his not long life. Their great popularity, and the extraordinary prices which they brought, drew after him a host of imitators, and already the manner as well as the matter of this school begins to pall. The question is whether these pictures were and are entitled to the great praise that has been given to them. As they stood together on the wall, the first impression was that they had paled in color and lack the vividness which so struck us at first. Their sparkling brilliancy seemed to be going; and when it is gone, what will remain to justify their great reputation? Little, it is to be feared. They had only caprices of color, brilliancy of execution, and sparkle. All the great qualities which make works lasting and "a joy forever" are lacking. The imagination has had no play. There are no great conceptions, no poetic utterances, no inspirations of genius. They are the *apotheosis* of the palette. It is the "preciousness" of the doing, the minuteness of the execution, the touches of the brush, the multiplicity and *finesse* of details which captivate the attention; but they have no

Fortuny.

SPAIN.

soul. They never touch the heart nor stimulate the imagination. They are, in a word, the *bric-à-brac* of art, to delight collectors and what are called amateurs and connoisseurs, apparently because the former love so little and because the latter know so little. Among the principal subjects represented are "The Academy of Saint Luke," "The Court of Justice in the Alhambra," "Serpent Charmers," "Amateurs," "The Sword Sharpener," "The Poet's Garden," the "Dance of Arabs," "The Turkish Butcher's Shop," "Prisoners at the Gate of the Mosque," etc. Of these, perhaps the best in color is "Serpent Charmers." It is freer in its rendering and larger in its execution than most of the others, and as mere color is certainly a striking picture. But the subject is not expressed. It is only with the most careful examination that one can detect the meaning of the composition, and there is no interest beyond the mere *technique*. "The Poet's Garden" is equally without character or expression. Its total effect is of a mass of crude and disagreeable greens, spotted here and there with thin, ill-drawn, and characterless figures, so confused with the background as scarcely to be intelligible, and the whole producing the general effect of bright patches of color on a palette. It is not a picture at all in any true sense. There is no dramatic purpose; no story; and what character there is in the figures is forced and unnatural. In fact, they are but pegs to hang costumes on, and the costumes themselves are tin. The "Academy of Saint Luke" represents a naked woman standing on a buhl table against a richly-ornamented pink wall, on which hangs a great mirror, while a group of old men, in last-century costumes, are examining her. Everything here is confused, and without relation of parts or perspective. There are pictures and statues and painted glass, and bronzes and elaborate columns, and busts and marbles, and an infinite deal of minute *bric-à-brac*, and all the figures in costume are, as it were, veneered upon them and into them, with no relief. The idea of the picture is essentially vulgar, and what character there is in the faces and figures is offensive. There is undoubtedly great dexterity and *finesse* of touch in the details, and the nude figure is painted with great skill.

Fortuny.

"The Butcher's Shop" is so confused in color and composition as to be scarcely intelligible. It is a conundrum in blood. The picture representing Arabs leaping over a grave and firing guns into it has a similar confusion, but here, at least, there is an attempt to represent a characteristic incident of manners.

SPAIN. But without particularizing more, it may be said that here are a number of pictures without any soul to animate them, exceedingly clever in touch and *finesse* of details, brilliant, but spotty and confused in color, without sobriety and tone, and manifesting great manipulative dexterity with no imagination.

Fortuny.

Madrazo. Much of the same quality, with similar excellence and similar deficiency, may be observed in the works of his followers. Among them, of Señ. Madrazo stands prominently forward. He has much of the dexterity of Fortuny, but everything is sacrificed to brilliancy. The colors are very *voyant*, the tone of his picture very high, and the combinations of tints often clashing and inharmonious. They are all vividly painted, in fact too vividly. There is more noise than tone, more brush-work than feeling, more emphasis than truth. He sent several portraits which are broad in their manner and firm in their drawing, but they all want sobriety and quiet. One, full length, is of a lady in a dress with a violet waist, white skirt, and black round her hips, relieved against a glaring blue wall-paper, and with a yellow rose in her fichu. Another figure is a *pierrette* in a pink and blue domino, white peaked felt hat, and a black mask in her hand. It is totally pink in tone, if it can be said to have any tone, and thin and bright in tints as a picture on a prune box. There were also two portraits of children, glaring in color, all over-bright and loud. His most elaborate picture represents early morning, with the guests just leaving the house after a ball. There is very great painstaking in the drawing, considerable truth of action and character in these figures, patient exactness of detail, and minuteness of execution. The dresses specially are touched with great spirit; but the tone is not pleasant, the general effect is spotty, and, despite the *chic* with which it is executed, one cannot but be vexed to see so much talent wasted on such a subject. He also sends several small pictures, the chief distinction of which is that they are very small, and finished with extreme precision; but as to color, sentiment, or feeling, they have not much to recommend them.

Indeed, the effort of this school seems to be to startle and provoke admiration by technical *tours de force*, over-emphasized light and tints, and violent effects. They are the fashion now; how long they will please the public after their novelty is gone remains to be seen.

Rico. Señ. Rico sent a considerable number of pictures, all small, and all studied with minute attention to detail. Four of these are about 14 inches by 7, and three of them repre

SPAIN

sent buildings with figures from ½ an inch to an inch in height. One of these represents a market with about 30 figures, with horses, market-carts, and a strip of houses behind them. Another is of Rienzi's house at Rome, with some 10 little figures. Another of Venice, with houses on a canal. As wholes these pictures are hard and spotty in color, but as specimens of minute work remarkable. In quality and color they are hard. They look as if they had been painted from photographs, and have the merits and defects of photographs. Another of his pictures represents boats on the lagunes at Venice, which is hard and glittering in its quality. By far the best of all is an interior of a Moorish court. The tone of this is pleasant, the color subdued, and there is air and feeling in it.

Rico.

Señ. Ribera also sends some very clever pictures of the extreme realistic school. They are well composed and have a purpose. The drawing is good, though sharp and edgy in outline, and the figures have a little the effect of the tin Nuremberg figures, but they show a great deal of talent and strong perception of character. Specially clever is the picture representing an actor in red, standing on the stage before the curtain with the orchestra below. The heads are characteristic and the execution exceedingly careful. The street sceneis also spirited and clever.

Ribera.

Señ. T. E. Sala's "*Guillen de Vinatea devant Alfonso IV*," represents a figure in red addressing the king and courtiers ranged along a wall. There is a combination of brilliant tints of white, red, yellow, and blue, vivid in effect, but each so evenly insisted on as to create a confusion of colors. The only way to enjoy such pictures is to examine them in detail part by part. At a distance they affect one like palettes.

Sala.

Señ. R. Santa Cruz sent a picture representing a catafalque draped in black and surrounded with tall candles in a hall hung with tapestries and rich in ornament. Four servants are in service there. Two are playing cards, one lighting a paper for his pipe at one of the tall candles, and one is stretched on a red embroidered divan. The theme of this picture is striking, and it is executed with skill and care even to the minutest detail. The utter reckless heartlessness of the attendants, who are simply bored by their service and care nothing for the corpse, is well executed, and all the details are painted with delicacy, truth, and spirit. The great defect of the picture is that the parts are too evenly insisted upon and the interest dispersed, so that the total effect is a little flat.

Santa Cruz.

SPAIN.

Gonzalez. Señ. Gonzalez sent seven pictures, all of the modern Spanish school, all exhibiting talent and technical skill, and all having the defects of this school.

Casada. Señ. Casado's "*Zaida la Favorite*" represents a half nude female figure reclining on a carpet and surrounded with flowers, rich draperies, and jewels. The subject, of course, is the hackneyed one of the favorite in the harem. There is scarcely any motive which could give play to the imagination, but there is brilliancy of execution and a strong feeling for color both in the flesh tints and in the textures and draperies and still life, and the work is free in its handling. All the parts, as is usual in this school, are equally emphasized and equally brilliant, and all equally call upon the eye and insist on being noticed.

Carbonaro. Señ. Carbonaro sent a picture of the impressionist school, representing Don Quixote and Sancho Panza in the blaze of noon on a hillside. The key is so high, the light so intense, the sky so blue (*morbleu! parbleu!*), the figures so dark, and everything so forced as almost to be painful. The picture is exceedingly odd and fantastic; as it is, however, it shows talent, and if the artist's object was to startle the spectator he has certainly succeeded. But, how thoroughly in all such attempts as this the high romantic spirit of Cervantes' hero disappears, leaving only behind the grotesque and ridiculous figure for the vulgar world to sneer at! How one would like to see a true representation of that high ideal gentleman, with his perfect chivalry, and his honest faith in a world of dreams! All that we seem to understand is Sancho Panza, the shrewd and practical knave, and we look at his master with his eyes only.

Zamacois. Of all the pictures of this school, those of Señ. Zamacois are the strongest and most agreeable. They are rich and deep in color, low in tone, and full of spirit and character. After the glare and glitter of some of the other pictures we have named, those of Zamacois are grateful as twilight after a burning day. Particularly fine is the "Checkmate," in which a jester is mated by a dwarf, who is seated on the table before him, while another dwarf crouches beside him, both highly delighted at the total discomfiture of the other player. In tone, richness, depth of color, expression, and composition, this is so masterly, that it leaves little to be desired. The reds are subdued yet brilliant; the tapestry and accessories keep their place and are subordinated to the rest; the light is low and concentrated on the main figures; the story is admirably told. Altogether it is a charming picture. Beside it hangs the well-known "King's Favorite," which has the same qualities and merits. The dwarf-jester is descending the staircase of a palace, accompanied by a great dog. The courtiers are smiling and saluting him with profound respect, while he, with an air of supreme importance, passes down the stairs and scarcely deigns to notice them. Finished as this picture is *ad unguem*, there is nothing obtrusive in the details and accessories. The imitation is not forced; the humor is excellent; the color splendid. This work preceded by several years and undoubtedly suggested the "*L'Eminence Grise*," by M. Gérôme, but it is greatly superior to it in all its qualities. I particularly wish to dwell upon this picture as contrasting in general characteristics with the other Spanish pictures of this class, and showing how possible it is to be exact in drawing, minute even in detail, brilliant in color, without glare and over-emphasis of parts, or excess of light and pigments. Here there is no attempt at mere *chic* of treatment and brush-work. The work is honest and faithful, and the story clearly and admirably expressed.

SPAIN.

Zamacois.

Landscapes.

Among the landscapes may be particularized one by Señ. C. Haes, "*Les Alentours de Vreeland, aux Pays-Bas.*" A storm is coming on, the wind blowing, the sky is gray with gleams of light through broken clouds cast on the turbid troubled river, across which a heron is flying. All the reeds and trees are bending to the stress of the wind. This is a picture full of sentiment and simplicity of treatment. The artist is not consciously and pretentiously striving to exhibit his own cleverness. "*Les Bords du Wahl*," by Señ. Morera y Galicia, is also a serious landscape, with a smooth river, down which a boat is coming through the wooded banks. Another landscape merits special notice. It is by Señ. Diaque, and is simple and effective in light and dark. The ground is somber, with two trees, a pool in front reflecting the light in the sky, and vague figures moving along in the gathering dark. Night is coming on, a faint gleam of red still lingers in the west, and a yellowish dying light is in the sky. Altogether this is a reserved and able picture.

Landscapes.

Haes.

Morera y Galicia.

Diaque.

There was also a landscape by Señ. Veyredée, representing twilight on the Roman Campagna, with two great carts and oxen silhouetted against the sky, which is effective.

Veyredée.

Señ. Gonzalvo y Perez sent a "View of the Grand Canal of Venice," and several interiors of churches; all clever. Two in particular, "San Marco at Venice," are to be noticed; one with the shadows of night coming on, and

Gonzalvo y Perez.

SPAIN. the other more illuminated, but both true to nature, and with the colors kept in reserve, and admirably painted.

Historical Paintings.

Historical. Among the historical paintings were several of decided merit. "The Death of Virginia, or the Origin of the Roman Republic," by Señ. C. Plasencia, is seriously designed and shows much talent. The action and grouping are good, and there is honest intention and simplicity of treatment. The color is a little monotonous, however. The size of the canvas and space occupied by the sky detract from the concentration of the scene.

Plascensia.

Rosales. "The Death of Seneca," by Señ. Rosales, has also qualities of seriousness and distinction. The four standing figures who gaze at the body of the philosopher as it lies half out of the bath are quiet and without exaggeration. The seated figure which leans on the bath weeping is well composed. The principal light falls on the dead body. The color is somber, with a reddish-brown background. There is an attempt, not without success, to render a serious pathetic subject without clash of colors and over-emphasis.

Ferrari. Two other historical pictures, by Señ. Ferrari, are also to be noted as forcible and cleverly painted, particularly "The Burial," as well as "The Education of Prince Juan," by Señ. M. Cabells, which has much merit in parts, but is rather confused, *voyant* of color, and less reserved in treatment, but with considerable character in the heads.

Pradilla. By far the most interesting and impressive of this class of pictures in the Spanish collection was by Señ. Pradilla, entitled "Doña Juana la Loca." This represents Ieanne or Juana, the daughter of Ferdinand, and mother of Charles V., accompanying the bier of her husband, Philip the Handsome, to its final resting-place. Twilight is deepening into night, the sky is gray, the cortege has reached a desolate spot, with no house in sight save a convent, which is in the middle distance on the right, and the mad queen will not allow the corpse to be placed in a house where there are women. The coffin, covered with a black and gold pall, embroidered with armorial bearings, and surrounded with tall torches and candles, which glare and fritter in the wind, is placed upon the ground in the middle front plane. Beside it, the central figure, stands Ieanne, clad in purple and black, her hands hanging at her side, who gazes down at the bier, watching for her husband to come to life. Her attendant and court are gathered in groups, some seated and some standing, and weary of the constantly repeated scene, behind, the train of followers, bearing torches, stretches into the distance obscured by the coming gloom. Its dramatic interest, truth of character, quiet strength of color, and simplicity of treatment, render this a remarkable picture. It is everywhere thoroughly felt and rendered, without exaggeration or attitudinizing, and well deserves the medal of honor which was accorded to it. The landscape is particularly fine, in harmony with the solemn character of the scene. The sky is gleamy with gray clouds, against which, on one side, rises the convent with its belfry. A fire is burning in the front, near which is seated the main group of attendants, and the heavy smoke rises and drifts away across the picture. The figure of Ieanne is profoundly dramatic in its simplicity and touching in its expression. There is no gesticulation. Her body is quite passive. It is only the mind which is working in her, and that is astray. She has gone out of herself, forgetful of everything about her, and is communing with visionary thoughts and vague phantasies. One sees at once that she is mad, by her utterly absent, lost look. The weariness of her attendants is also very well expressed. The scene has nothing new to excite them, and they gaze listlessly at her. There is great sobriety and earnestness in the picture. It is solidly painted, well composed and drawn, animated throughout by a single purpose. It is—what so few pictures of the present day are—a creation of the imagination, where technical skill has been employed as a means to embody a noble conception, and not primarily to exhibit itself. It is out of a different world of art from the brilliant *bric-à-brac* of colors without ideas that is now in vogue, and it is a pleasure to turn from clothes and costumes and nudities and *chic*, that have no higher purpose than to show the skill of the painter, to such a serious and imaginative work. It gives us hope that art has yet a poetic office to fulfill.

SPAIN. Pradilla.

ITALY.

But to turn from Spain to Italy. The modern Italian school, as exhibited at Paris, seemed to have little independence of character or originality. It follows too much of late the leading of Fortuny, and many of the cleverest productions of its younger artists are after his manner or bred of his influence. Undoubtedly there is much talent shown by some of its painters, but there is little seriousness of purpose or imaginative force. The greater part of the pictures exhibited are of cabinet and *genre* subjects, with little that is

ITALY. Principally *genre*.

ITALY.

new, and almost nothing which is either striking in character or powerful in conception. There is scarcely an attempt to rise out of the common every-day of life and incident, and even in the treatment of these there is a lack of vigorous feeling. The general want of bone and sinew is not compensated for by spirited execution. Out of 191 oil paintings, not one is devoted to any great or powerful subject, either of character or history. The execution for the most part is weak, and though there are some striking exceptions to this statement, there are none which stand prominently forth out of the ordinary line of accomplishment, none that surprise by their excellence, none that enchant by their depth of feeling. More was to be expected than this from young Italy. Now that she has gained her freedom and consolidated herself into a nation, we thought we had a right to look for fresh germs, at least, of national feeling, and an outburst of something vigorous and free in her art. But her friends have been greatly disappointed. There is nothing new; nothing that corresponds to their hopes and her promises; nothing that shows the progress we had looked for; and, as a whole, her exhibition was, to say the best one can, only second class. She not only did not show one single great work with a strong stamp of originality or nationality in it, but some of the most striking pictures in her exhibition were inspired by foreign schools, and were the work of expatriated Italians. Undoubtedly the public demand has much to answer for in all this, but one could not but feel in looking at this exhibition by Italy that most of the pictures were made, not from any true inspiration or any lofty conception of the true functions of art, but rather, like Peter Pindar's razors, "to sell." It is sadly true that those who live to please must please to live, but to boil one's pot is not the best office of art.

No great historical subjects.

But little originality.

The most striking of all the pictures exhibited were the series of ten by Signor A. Pasini, all of which are oriental in their subjects. These are carefully drawn, and exhibit a great deal of talent. They are mainly of the school of Gérôme, though touched by the influence of Fortuny. There is not much theme in any of them, nor any high poetic intention, though they are picturesque, well composed, and carefully studied. They are a little hard and metallic in tone, but they exhibit a strong feeling for color and composition of tints. The backgrounds and architecture are not forced, but kept subordinate, and there is certainly much to praise. With all their cleverness, however, and this is indisputable, they leave us cold.

Pasini.

ITALY.

De Nittis.

Sig. de Nittis sent twelve pictures, representing actual street scenes, with figures from London and Paris. One of these, representing "The Road to Brindisi," is so totally different in character from all the rest, that it is with difficulty one can believe it to be by the same artist. It is of the school of Meissonier, and in all its qualities equal if not superior to the master's work. Hot noon on a burning road, in which is a *vettura*, could scarcely be better represented. The color is bright and transparent; the finish is extremely minute and careful, and the feeling of the time and place admirably rendered. The *technique* has not killed the spirit, as it too often does in such elaborately minute and accurate works. Altogether this is a remarkable picture. All his other pictures are of the impressionist school. The color is dull and muddy, the drawing suggestive instead of accurate, and the subjects prosaic. Of all these "Westminster" and "Cannon Street Bridge" are the best and most characteristic. The former represents a group of workmen leaning on the parapet of the bridge in the right corner, and all the rest is a vague, blotted, dull gray representation of London in the distance. The figures are well done as far as they go, and in attitude and character are true to common life. They are more or less what anybody might possibly see there any day. The whole attempt has been to represent literally a common-place scene, without any special theme; and to a considerable extent it has been successful. Whether it was worth doing is another question. "Cannon Street" represents a scene beneath the railway bridge, over which a train is passing and pouring down its clouds of smoke. There is something decidedly striking in this, and it has a poetic touch in it, despite the commonness of the fact. But Sig. de Nittis seems to have a notion that it is the function of art simply to reproduce facts, and to take whatever comes. He scarcely troubles himself even to choose, nor, when he has chosen, to do more than give a general impression. The utmost result to be hoped for from such representations of street scenes would be that given by an instantaneous photograph, with all the figures disposed by chance. If, in addition, the lens of the camera was not quite in focus, so that it blurred a good deal, one would have something not far removed from what Sig. de Nittis apparently desires.

Gioli.

"*Le Viatique*" by Sig. J. Gioli, is somewhat of the impressionist school, but is effective. It represents the Viaticum carried along at twilight, and is serious, and simple in sentiment.

ITALY.

J. Induno. Sig. J. Induno sent several pictures of considerable merit. "*Un Amateur d'Antiquités*" is well painted, and has simplicity and truth of character. It represents an old antiquary examining through a *loupe* a coin which a peasant has brought him. The figure and expression of the antiquary are particularly good. Another picture representing conscripts before a church showed decided talent. It is well composed, spirited in character, and quiet and agreeable in tone. His picture of "Emigrants" is also specially to be noticed.

D. Induno. Sig. D. Induno's "*Victor Emmanuel plaçant la première Pierre de la Galerie de Milan*" is chiefly interesting as containing the portraits of many of the chief men of modern Italy. There is not much pictorial effect to be obtained out of a crowd of black coats, but the scene is not without interest, and it is carefully painted.

Jacovacci. Among the *genre* pictures by Sig. F. Jacovacci, the "Return from the Baptism" and the "Gondola" may particularly be mentioned as well drawn and composed, and vivid in color. Favretto. "The Prescription" by Sig. J. Favretto, is also vigorous and bright in color without being excessive, and the attitudes are natural, and the story is well told. "*La Revue de l'Héritage*" by Sig. E. Pagliano, has much humor of character and incident, and is very freely and quietly painted. Pagliano. It represents girls turning over and examining articles of dress which they have inherited. It is one of the most pleasing in tone and manner of all the pictures of this class which hang on the Italian walls. Meradel. Sig. A. Meradel's "*Comment cela finira-t-il?*" is rendered with much humor and spirit, and is remarkable for the expression of the heads, though the color is a little *fade*, and perhaps the innuendo is a little broad. Bouvier. For minuteness of execution Sig. Bouvier's "*l'Occasion*" surpassed anything in the whole Exposition. It is only about nine inches long, and represents the interior of a studio, with a girl sitting for her portrait to a painter; while he is painting, the servant who accompanies her has fallen asleep, and he seizes the moment to declare his passion. The color is delicate, the textures and still life admirably rendered, the tone agreeable, and the *finesse* of execution remarkable. Signor Mion. L. Mion's "*Le Colin-Maillard*" is pleasing and carefully done. Joris. Signor P. Joris also sent a couple of pictures, "*La Voie Flaminiénne*" and "*Une Baptême dans l'Île d'Ischia*," which are pleasant and sunny, but rather too spotted with vivid Vanni. colors. Signor P. Vanni's "Mephistopheles and Marguerite" represents the scene of Marguerite in the Cathedral, with the evil spirit whispering to her. There is a good deal of talent

ITALY.

and character in this picture, and a higher attempt at seriousness of subject than usual. Signor Michitti's two pictures of "*Printemps et Amour*," and "*Le Baiser*" are exceedingly eccentric in color, and seem a little like insane Fortunys. If the intention of the artist was to startle, he has succeeded. Here is certainly, as the shopmen say, "*grande nouveauté.*" Bit by bit all is picked out with intensity of tints, but there is no relation of parts in "Spring and Love." There are naked salmon-colored children lying on bright green grass, with dazzling blue sky and sea, and straggling trees with salmon blossoms, all so vivid and violent that they strain the eye. In "*Le Baiser*," which represents a peasant trying to kiss a girl, and is not particularly happy in sentiment, there are crude masses of cabbages and greens, and red turkey combs, and trees barely sketched in, and a sky of terrible yellows and reds rumbled strangely together. The total effect of these pictures is, so to speak, noisy and impertinent, and it is a pity to see talent so pretentiously misapplied. There is no reserve, no restraint, but perpetual insistance. Sig. L. Marchetti's "*Avant le Tournoi*" has somewhat of the same defect. It is like a very confused palette of colors.

Michitti.

Marchetti.

The "Charge of Cavalry at Monzambano," by Count Rossi Scotti, is spirited in design, and with much truth of action in both figures and horses. It is drawn and painted with great care, has a great deal of "go," and is a very honest piece of work, though a little hard in color and tone.

Rossi Scotti.

The Chev. Bianchi's "*Regarde! Regarde!*" is a very pretty theme well rendered. It represents some girls looking eagerly out of a gateway at something passing outside the picture; and Sig. Volpe's "*Un Prêtre*" is quiet in tone and characteristic in expression.

Bianchi.

Volpe.

Among the landscapes were particularly to be commended two very pleasing pictures by Sig. G. Ciardi, "*Idylle; Lagune de Venise*" and "*Torcello.*" In both there is much delicacy and refinement of sentiment and simplicity of execution. "*Torcello*" is bright and sunny, and the "*Idylle*" vaporous and sunny. It represents a fisher-boy standing in a boat fishing on the broad lagunes. The atmosphere is soft and silent, the sea calm, and he stands in his boat alone, the dark center of a soft, luminous haze. Other landscapes particularly to be noted are four, by Chev. A. Vertunni, representing the lonely "Pontine Marshes," "Pæstum," "The Pyramids," and "The Sphinx," which have the well-known character and style of this artist, though they are not among his happiest achievements; a "*Coucher de Soleil*" by Chev. B. Giuliano, with girls walking along a pier; another "*Coucher de Soleil*"

Ciardi.

Vertunni.

Giuliano.

ITALY. by Sig. Poma; and "*Après l'Orage*," by Sig. S. Allason, a very effective picture, of a serious character and strong theme.

Poma. Allason. Aquarelles.

Among the *aquarelles* there were some which are very bright and clever. Particularly are to be mentioned "*Ah! combien je regrette le Temps que n'est plus*," by Sigr. A. Rotta, which is freely and carefully finished, and with good tone, color, and character. It represents a group seated outside a door in Venice at work, with children around them at play, and fruits and vegetables. The "*Baptême dans l'Île d'Ischia*," by Sig. P. Joris, previously mentioned, representing a bright landscape with a baptismal party coming down a hill, is also very pleasing, and so are the *aquarelles* of Sig. J. Gandi, "*Au Carême*" and "*Sur la Table*," which are careful and characteristic studies of peasants.

Rotta. Joris. Gandi.

AUSTRIA-HUNGARY.

AUSTRIA-HUNGARY.

We now come to the Austrian-Hungarian section, which may be taken together. Of the Hungarian pictures, the most distinguished were those by Herr Michel Munkácsy, representing "Milton dictating 'Paradise Lost,'" and "*l'Atelier de l'Artiste*." For character, composition, expression, and quality of color the former picture was certainly among the most remarkable of all the pictures in the entire Exposition, and well deserves the medal of honor which was accorded to it. It is simple and direct in character, with great truth to nature and to the highest sentiment in the attitudes and expression of all the figures, masterly in its free painting, and striking in the values of color. The tones are a little black, but everything is relatively in its place. Nothing cries out for notice, and the main interest is concentrated, as it should be, in the figures. Milton is seated in a large chair near a window, which gives the light of the whole picture. His three daughters are grouped about a table, one engaged in writing to his dictation, and eagerly reaching forward, intent to catch his words. The second is sewing. Her attention is, for the moment, attracted by what he is saying, and she listens with her hand and thread suspended. The third, who is standing, is also arrested by the poet's lines, and half turns round to listen. Milton himself, buried in thought, sits sunken in his chair, profoundly immersed in his subject, and utterly forgetful of himself. There is in all the figures a total unconsciousness of any looker-on, an absorption in one single interest, an absence of posing, and a sincerity and earnest directness of sentiment which are entitled to great praise. The story is told with wonderful truth and simplicity. The painting is extremely free, and shows a thorough

Munkácsy.

AUSTRIA HUNGARY.

understanding of values of colors, which are rich, subdued, and solemn. Nothing is improperly insisted upon, and there is no over-emphasis of parts. But above all there is the poetic and imaginative spirit. We seem to have had the privilege of looking in unobserved upon a profoundly interesting and touching scene, which is so thoroughly felt, that it subdues the spectator to its own emotion. This picture, we are happy to know, was purchased by Mr. Lennox for the Lennox Gallery in New York, where all our artists will have an opportunity to study and admire it.

Munkácsy.

The "*Atelier d'Artiste*" is also a masterly work, less interesting in its subject, but equally admirable in its treatment, in its reserve, and quiet. The artist, seated on a table, is asking the advice of his wife as to a canvas turned away from us. Both are looking at it attentively, and seriously considering it. He is not satisfied, but doubtful. She is trying to help him. Behind a screen which shuts off the left of the picture is a little model which at first we scarcely see, so perfectly is she in relation to the rest. The main interest is concentrated in the two principal figures, who are really and earnestly interested in what they are doing. There is no posing; all is simply and perfectly expressed. The color is very fine, the touch firm and solid, the values admirable.

Makart.

In eminent contrast with these two pictures is the large canvas by Herr Makart, representing the "Entrance of Charles V into Antwerp." Around this picture there was always a crowd of admirers and critics. This is essentially a decorative picture, and treated in a decorative style. The procession is marching through the picture diagonally. The Emperor himself, mounted on a charger and clad in armor, is the central figure. Accompanying him are several nude or nearly nude female figures having flowers; others are dressed richly and looking on, and there is a dense crowd of knights, soldiers, burghers, and nobles, some shouting welcome to the Emperor from windows hung with tapestries and flowers, among whom may be seen the figure of Albert Dürer. There is scarcely any attempt to render character or probability of scene. There is no definite incident or central thought; in a word, the work is purely decorative and without any concentration of interest or personality. The groups are confused and crowded almost impossibly, and there is little proportion observed in the figures, some being gigantic in height while others at their side are of life-size. Considered, therefore, from the point of view of an imaginative conception or a powerful representation of a historical

AUSTRIA-HUNGARY. incident, there is little to praise; but for dexterity of brush-work, brilliancy of color, dash of execution, noisiness and "*tintamarres*" of tints, it is remarkable. It is painted with much energy, and in every way shows cleverness, but it has no heart and soul. In color, though brilliant, it is monotonous, in tone the various planes of the picture are confused, and the total effect is rather that of a tapestry. Piece by piece it is spiritedly done, but there is no whole. Each figure seems to be posed for itself and by itself, and has little relation to the main purpose.

Matejko. Herr J. Metejko also sent a large historical piece representing the "*Union conclué à Lublin en 1569, entre la Lithuanie et la Pologne*," which has much power and character. It is a far more solid and real work than that of Herr Makart, not conceived from the merely decorative point of view, but with a true intention to represent a real scene of history. Many of the heads and figures are vigorously drawn and have great character. Particularly may be mentioned the group around the figure of the aged Pope, who is seated and holds up both hands inclosed in red gloves, and the foreground figure in blue who is rising from his chair. But all of the heads and figures are carefully studied, rendered with life and spirit, and have much individuality. There is a want of massing of parts, and of effect of light and shade, so that at first the picture, though rich in color, has a certain equality and monotony of effect; but here is serious intention, a firm hand, admirable drawing, and truth of character, and the longer one looks at it the more it pleases. Herr Metejko also sent another picture representing "*La Cloche de Segismond à Cracovie*," which is smaller, and crowded with figures of over-brilliant tints, but is clever.

L'Allemand. Herr L'Allemand's "Portrait of General Laudon" is a very vigorous work. It represents the general mounted on a dark bay horse in front of his staff. Three attendant officers are behind him on his right, a dead soldier is on the left, and behind are other mounted men. The main figure is boldly drawn, and painted in a large, free style, and takes proper prominence over all the other subordinate figures, which fitly illustrate the picture.

Kurzbauer. Among the pictures of *genre* may be specially mentioned "*La Maison mortuaire*," by Herr E. Kurzbauer, which is conceived with much sentiment. The face of the widow is full of feeling, and the central group of persons striving to console her is characteristic and well composed. This forms the central light of the picture. The second light shows some children at a table on the left, who, careless of the grief of the main group, are amusing themselves together. Herr Kurzbauer's other picture, "*Les Fugitifs*," representing a youth and a maiden who have eloped and are discovered by the family in an inn, is also good in character and expression and well painted. Herr Defregger's "*Le Jeu du Pouce dans le Tyrol*," and "*Le Joueur de Cithare*," are spirited in action, and effective in their composition of light and dark. The former represents two men at a table, each endeavoring to force over the edge the clenched fist of his adversary, while a group of peasants look on with eager interest. The latter represents a young man playing a zithern, while two maidens are standing by him. He is utterly absorbed in the music. Both these pictures show clearness of ideas and strength of character. "*Les Paysans Tyroliens*," by Chev. C. de Blaas, representing also a somewhat similar game, is rendered with talent. Herr C. Karger's "*Une Gare de Chemin de fer*" is a study somewhat after the manner of Mr. Frith, and, though prosaic in character, is naturalistic and clever. Among other pictures of this class may be specially noted Professor Schönn's "*Fête Populaire sur le Côte Génoise*"; Herr Fux's "*Sacrifice de Pigeons*," which is pleasing in color, and Herr F. Paczka's "*Un Accident*," and "*Le Tambour*," both very clever, and, especially the former, representing an old man alone looking at his violin, one string of which has snapped. Herr Aggházy's "*Tireuse des Cartes*," Herr Bruck's "*Le Déménagement*," and Herr Ebner's "*Les bons Amis*," should also be mentioned.

AUSTRIA-HUNGARY. Kurzbauer. Defregger. De Blaas. Karger. Schönn. Fux. Paczka. Aggházy. Bruck. Ebner.

The late Herr Čermak's "*Monténégrin blessé*" is a picture of much character, representing an old chieftain carried on a litter down a steep, rocky path, and accompanied by wounded companions, while a group of women stands apart or kneels, as they pass. The foreshortening of the main figure is admirable, and the expression noble. Herr Čermak's other picture, "*Retour au Pays*," is even more tragic in subject. The scene is a village which has been devasted by Turks, and a party of old men, women, and children, are just returning to it, to find their homes destroyed and the heads of their murdered husbands and fathers stuck on poles. The story is told with much pathos, and both these pictures show mastery of execution, and solidity of painting.

Čermak.

Professor Müller's "*Après la Messe sur les Place de San-Marc à Venise*" is full of vivacity of color, action, and costume, which last is of the time of Bellini.

Müller.

AUSTRIA-HUNGARY.

Landscape.

Landscape.

Jettel. Von Thoren.

This section was not very showy in landscape, but among the best may be noted those of Herr Jettel, which are Dutch scenes, cleverly rendered; several by Chev. von Thoren, of which the most striking is "*L'Orage*," which represents a thunder storm with wind and rain, which is well drawn and gives the effect of wind on trees, clouds, and figures with great spirit; "*Sur la Côte d'Istrie*," by Herr Schäffer, which is picturesque and striking, and a well-drawn street view by Herr Ribarz, representing "*Architecture Hollandaise à Dortrecht*," as well as other Dutch landscapes.

Schäffer.

Ribarz.

Portraits.

Portraits.

Makart.

Among the portraits are two by Herr Makart, which are clever and facile, but a little too pinky and decorative, and want interior character; a portait, "*Madame la Comtesse Schönborn*," by Herr Canon, which is in the style of the older masters, and is admirably painted with force and good keeping of parts and strong character; a portrait of the painter "Rudolf Alt," by Herr Griepenkerl, and 13 portraits by Herr H. de Angeli, which all show a great talent for likeness, but are generally rather literal and prosaic; one, however, of "Madame Schwabe" rises far above this, and has a good deal of distinction.

Canon

Griepenkerl.

De Angeli.

On the whole, it is clear that there is much life and excellence in the art of this section, but it is to be observed that a considerable number of the artists have studied and painted out of their own country, and sought their subjects and acquired, or at least modified, their manner in foreign schools. For instance, of those whom we have mentioned, Herren Munkácsy, Jettel, Čermak, Thoren, live in Paris, and have studied in the French school, while Defregger, Gabl, Karger, Kurzbauer are of the Munich school, and Herr Ribarz is essentially Dutch. Herr Makart, on the contrary, and Herren Metejko, L'Allemand, and Müller are of Vienna, and perhaps more exactly represent the tendencies of the national art.

Aquarelles.

Aquarelles.

Passini.

Passinger.

Among the *aquarelles* and drawings in black and white are particularly to be noticed three by Herr Passini, extremely clever, and seven by Herr de Pansinger, also showing great spirit and talent. The former has studied in Venice, and his subjects are Italian; the latter at Munich.

GERMANY.

GERMANY.

We now come to Germany. Though late in their decision to take part in this Exposition, the Germans with great energy made up for their tardiness, and in arrangement their hall was disposed with great taste, and in its general impression agreeably contrasted with those of all the other nations. In the center were tables covered with engravings and illustrated books exhibiting much talent and invention, which were open to all to turn over. The average of the work was good, and although there were no salient pictures of great force of conception or subject, there were many serious in quality and pleasing of character. Of historic and religious subjects there were few, and these are of not much importance or any striking merit. Of domestic scenes there were many, some of great merit. It is scarcely a quarter of a century ago that a revival of art took place in Germany, and some of the chief artists of that time endeavored to found a great school, devoted to the development of subjects of high historic interest, of symbolical, legendary, and religious character, and of philosophic abstractions. At the head of this were Cornelius and Overbeck. The aim was high; but, although the leaders of this school brought to it great earnestness of spirit, they were essentially weak in execution and artistic power, and they failed to carry with them the mind of the nation. They cared little for a faithful study of nature, and strove to limit art solely to a representation of ideas, without regard to truth of form and color. Overbeck, indeed, during the latter part of his career, abjured color, declaring it to be averse from the spirit of the religious subjects he exclusively treated, and devoted himself purely to outlines in charcoal or crayon. No one of this energetic band was a colorist or truly a draughtsman. The reaction from this over-legendary and romantic school on the one side, and the limited and, so to speak, monastic spirit on the other, showed itself soon among a class of artists who sought their subjects in real and common life. This school, appealing as it did to more general sympathies, soon displaced the former, and in the Paris Exposition it was this which took the lead. The difficulty of the Germans in matters of art is that their genius is more theoretical, philosophic, literary, than practical and artistic, and their art oscillates between the common and often even the ugly on the one hand, and a certain academic ideal on the other. It was pleasant, however, in the Paris Exposition, to find a freer spirit manifesting itself with better drawing and color, and a less hard and literal treatment. What is, however, still lacking is style.

Renaissance of art in Germany.

School of Cornelius and Overbeck.

Earnest aim, but weak execution.

Reaction from the romantic and monastic spirit.

Oscillation between the common and academic.

GERMANY. Every artist knows what is meant by the Düsseldorf school.
Düsseldorf school. Clever as it is in many respects, it lacks the sympathetic quality, and has a sort of mechanical hardness.

There were in this Exposition a few works of great excellence, and among these we must note an exquisite little picture by Fried. August Kaulbach of Munich, called "*Une jeune Femme avec son Fils*," which for tone, simplicity, tenderness of sentiment, and delicacy of color is remarkable. It is archaic in treatment, thinly painted on a gold ground, and is somewhat after the manner of Holbein, but it has a great charm. "*Rêverie*," by the same artist, is also a very finished and delicate picture, representing a girl in a white satin dress seated on a couch against a background of subdued tapestry, and tuning a mandoline. This is very carefully studied, rich in color, and painted with much skill, and the textures well rendered. He also sent two heads which are characterized by the same sentiment.

Kaulbach.

Knaus.

Herr L. Knaus, the well-known painter at Berlin, sent five pictures, each of them a master-piece in its way. "*Un Élève plein d'avenir*," and "*Une bonne Affaire*," have genuine humor of a rare quality. The first represents an old Jew seated on a rickety chair with a pipe in his hand, in his "ogh-clo" warehouse filled with dingy old clothes, instructing a red-haired boy, who may be his grandson, in the mysteries of bargaining. This precocious pupil thoroughly appreciates his lesson, and his teacher's face beams with approbation at his aptness. It is impossible to look at this picture without laughter, so admirably given are the character and expression of both faces. "*Une bonne Affaire*," represents the same boy putting into practice the lesson he has received. He stands alone holding in his hand a piece of money, and chuckling to himself and to you over his own dexterity. The "*Fête d'Enfants*," which represents a village festival, is full of figures well drawn and clever, but it is inferior in character and expression to the other pictures exhibited by Herr Knaus, and poorer in color. "*Un Enterrement*" represents a scene in a court-yard with the roof and ground covered with snow. A crowd is gathered there, principally women and children, chanting a hymn, and down some steps totters an old man followed by the attendants who are bringing the coffin out at the door. The figure of the old man, who half leans against the house for support, is admirable in drawing and expression. The finest of the whole series is, perhaps, the "*Paysans délibérants*," where six peasants are gathered in a little room discussing some matter of village importance. GERMANY. The oldest of them is on his feet speaking and the others are listening. There is great individuality in all the heads and figures; one sees at once the obstinate pig-headed man who means to disagree, the simple peasant who is ready to agree to anything, the fluctuating muddle-head who does not quite understand and never will, and the Knaus. open-minded man who is anxious to come to a right conclusion. The color of the picture is good. Sunlight comes in to illuminate the room from a side window, a green-tiled stove stands in the right corner, on which are hats and a blue umbrella, and there is a hen with her chickens on the floor in the foreground. The comedy is excellent; nothing is overdone.

"*Plus d'Espoir*," by Herr Fagerlin, is another picture of Fagerlin. domestic life treated with great pathos. It represents the interior of a cottage, in the background of which a man is dying or dead, while his wife accompanied by an old woman is coming forward out of the room, hopeless and inconsolable. The intensity of tragic feeling in her face and attitude, and the reflected sympathy in her old companion, who may be the mother or grandmother, are portrayed with true feeling, and altogether the picture is profoundly interesting and affecting. The painting is very careful and studied. The old brick floor, the green curtains against which the sunlight falls, the textures of the dresses are admirably given. There is perhaps a little too much the sense of painstaking, but the whole work is earnest and skillful and full of feeling.

Herr Leibl's "*Des Paysans*," though cold and gray in color, Leibl. and with no tone, is a most careful series of studies from nature of peasants' heads. The execution is hard and precise, but there is strong grasp of character and precision of detail in the heads. It represents five peasants crowded round a table and listening to one who is reading a newspaper. Outside the window is a sunny landscape. The heads are evidently careful, minutely careful, portraits, eminently characteristic and well drawn.

Herr Menzel sent two oil pictures and four *aquarelles*, Menzel. full of character and showing much ability. The largest is "*L'Usine*," which represents the interior of an iron foundry, with workmen drawing out from the furnace an iron shaft at white heat. This forms the chief light of the picture, and against it some of the figures stand in dark relief and some brilliantly touched with a lurid glow. There is vigor and character in some of the heads, and the action is well given, but

GERMANY. as a whole there is a lack of quality, and a certain hardness of execution. "*Entre deux Danses*" is a small picture representing a saloon with groups of men in diplomatic dresses, and ladies in full ball toilets which exhibits even a superior power of character drawing. The composition is good and the coloring strong. Altogether it is a very clever and characteristic painting. His *aquarelles* of "*Moines dans le Sacristie*" and the "*Repas interrompu*" are also clever, but rather cold and hard.

Pilz. "*La Leçon de Gymnastique*' by Herr O. Pilz, of Weimar, is clever and well composed and painted. The landscape and sky are particularly worthy of note. It represents a master standing before a double row of boys giving them a lesson in gymnastics. Herr Defregger's "*Bénédicité*" and Defregger. "*La Visite*" are also very clever representations of purely domestic scenes. The latter represents two peasant girls on a visit to their married sister, to whose baby they are presenting a pear; all are happy and pleased. The girls are pretty in their quaint costumes and the baby is all smiles. The "*Bénédicité*" represents a woman who is teaching the smallest of a group of children who are seated round a table to say grace. The expressions are simple and natural and the composition good, but the execution though careful is hard. Herr Werner's "*Une Conversation*" has considerable Werner. humor of expression. It represents five of Frederic's grenadiers standing on the further side of a railing and joking with two nursery maids on this side with babies; all are laughing, and the jest seems to find favor in the ears of those who hear and those who make it. The effect is bright and the execution precise. Another picture of a humorous character is Herr Meyerheim's "*Des Zoulou,—* Meyerheim. *Caffres à la Foire.*" The scene is in a booth at a country fair. On the stage are a couple of Zulus executing a war dance, while the audience are divided between terror, astonishment, and delight. There is considerable freedom in the manner of the painting, and the scene is amusing.

The "*Chasse à courre au XVIIIme Siècle,*" by the late Gierymski. Herr Gierymski, is a very clever picture by a young painter who lately died. There is capital drawing, good action, and careful study; but it is very *voyant* in color and hard of texture.

Bockelmann. "*Une Banque populaire en Faillite,*" by Herr Bockelmann, of Düsseldorf, represents a crowd in the costume of to-day outside a bank which has just failed. The painting is literal, and the color is clean, cold, and gray. There is little intensity of character and no great vividness of expression, but some of the figures are well done. GERMANY

Among the other domestic scenes of this class to be noted are the "*Baptême de l'Orphelin*," by Herr Hoff, representing a baptism, with costumes of the time of Louis XIV, which is pleasing in sentiment and arrangement; the "*Heure d'Angoisse*," by Herr Hildebrandt, where a mother and father are at the bedside of their sick child, in which there is a good deal of earnest feeling; "*La Lecture intéressante*," by Herr Scheurenberg, of Düsseldorf, which is capital in expression and well painted. Hoff. Hildebrandt. Scheurenberg.

Religious and Historical Paintings.

Religious and historical subjects were not ably represented. There were few of them, and they were not of high merit. The best pictures are those which represent homely and domestic scenes of common life. Herr von Piloty's "*Wallenstein se rendant à Éger*" is one of the largest history pieces, but it is scarcely worthy the high reputation of the artist, and is academic and conventional. Herr Becker sent two pictures, "*Albert Dürer à Venise*" and "*Ulrich von Hütten reçoit de l'Empereur Maximilien la Couronne de Poëte;*" Herr O. Knille, "*Plato avec ses Disciples;*" and Herr Baur, "*St. Paul, Prisonnier à Rome*," which is archæologically studied, but without much vitality. "*La Fille de Jaïrus*," by Herr Gabriel Max, is weak and *fade*, and on the arm of the apparently dead child he has painted with care a fly, which will indicate the spirit in which the work is conceived. Herr von Gebhardt, of Düsseldorf, sent a "Crucifixion" and a "Last Supper," the latter good in color, but without great life in character. It is treated somewhat in the early German manner, and the types of the apostles are taken from the lower classes of common life. It may be claimed that this was the fact, but the religious and poetic sense is none the less unsatisfied by such a representation. What all these pictures lack is spontaneity and poetic character. *Religious and Historical.* Von Piloty. Becker. Knille. Baur. Max. Von Gebhardt.

Portraits.

In portraiture, the heads of Herr Lenbach, of Munich, though thinly painted, are full of character and individuality. The portrait of the "Princess of Carolath-Beuthen," by Herr Richter, also should be noted, as well as those by Herr Kaulbach, which are fresh and charming, and the "*Portrait d'une Vielle Dame*," by Herr Gussow, of Berlin, *Portraits.* Lenbach. Richter. Kaulbach. Gussow.

GERMANY. the head of which is pure in color and carefully studied, but the dress and details very hard, bright, and absolute.

Gussow. Herr Gussow had also two pictures of still life and figures, one called "*L'Atelier*," and one "*Nature Morte*," which are painted with wonderful *chic* and freedom of touch. One is the interior of a studio, with an old woman washing with a piece of wash-leather a reduced cast of the Venus of Milo. The other is a study of an interior with various objects—half-finished pictures on the wall, a bust in the middle of a table, etc. These are a little hard and *voyant* in colors, but the imitation of still life is very remarkable.

Landscapes.

Landscapes. Dücker. There was a considerable number of landscapes, among the best of which are to be noted those by Herr Dücker, of Düsseldorf, "*Bords de la Mer Baltique*," with the sun setting red along a tranquil sea, and long stretch of shore, and the "*Paysage du Harz*," both of which are freer in style than the general run of this school. Baisch. Herr Baisch, of Munich, sent "*Une grande Route en Hollande*," which is a rainy scene, with a herd of cows going over the wet road, and breaks of light through a gray sky, and a windmill in the distance, a river and boat, and a woman with an umbrella. This is decidedly a clever picture. Irmer. Herr C. Irmer's "*Lac en Holstein*" is a very good specimen of the Düsseldorf school, though it has its defects of hardness. Kröner. Herr Kröner's "*Sangliers dans la Neige*" is a well-rendered winter landscape with wild boars huddling through the snow in a wood. The tones of the snow are good, and the picture interesting. Lier. Herr Adolph Lier's "*Soirée d'Automne aux Bords de l'Isar*," and "*L'Inundation*," by Herr Scherres. Scherres, are also specially to be noted as among the best in this department. Oeder. Herr Oeder's "*Paysage*" is also pleasing, Neubers. and we must also note another "*Paysage*" by Herr Neubers, of Munich, and "*Le Moulin à Vent dans la Frise*," by Herr Schœnleber. Schœnleber.

The two Herren Achenbach, whose reputation is so well established in Düsseldorf, also sent a number of landscapes. The best of all is Herr A. Achenbach's "*Vlissingue*," with a A. & O. Achenbach. stormy sea breaking over a pier, a castle wall on the right, and a steamer laboring in the distance. This is clever, but somewhat cold and conventional in character. His other pictures are more mechanically felt and rendered, though they all exhibit talent. There is cleverness, but a lack of real feeling.

On the whole, it cannot be said that the German school, despite all the cleverness it exhibited, manifested any very

GERMANY.

high tendencies, or any great achievement in the highest line of art, nothing to correspond to the lofty purpose of its great composers in what is essentially its natural art—music. In poetry, sculpture, and painting it has no names to be placed beside the great ones in that most ideal of arts. Even Goethe is tame and mechanical beside Beethoven, and for the last quarter of a century, poetry has had no great exponent in Germany. Still there is a good table-ground of excellence in painting, though there are no high peaks.

Its musical composers on a higher plane than its artists and poets.

RUSSIA.

RUSSIA.

The Russian department rather surprised us as giving evidence of a distinct nationality of character and subject, with considerable originality of treatment. It is not that there are any very high flights, but there is in many of the pictures a quality different from what is seen elsewhere, and a freedom from bondage to other schools which is noteworthy.

Originality.

Landscapes.

Landscapes.

The landscapes were particularly striking, and were mostly of natural scenes. Among these must be specially noted the works of M. Kouïndji. His "*Paysage en Finlande*" represents a sluggish river rolling out of a dark distance, with two birds flying over it. In the foreground are reeds on one side, and on the other a shelf of sloping rock, above which are three tall trees; a thunder-storm is rising and covering with its dark, threatening shadow, the middle ground and distance, while a white metallic light gleams upon the trees in the foreground, forcing them out with that strange prominence so characteristic of such moments. Here is great sentiment and truth to nature. The scene is lonely, desolate, silent, the sky heavy, lowering, and slaty—everything dreary, threatening, and wild. His "*Clair de Lune en Ukraine*" is also a most striking, original, and effective picture. Here is a group of lone houses on a high plateau in the middle distance, with a windmill and two cypresses; at its base flows a stream into the foreground; a strange, mysterious green tone pervades the picture. The moonlight gleams upon the sides of the houses, and in one window burns a candle, while the river catches a faint reflection of light as it flows down through its dark, vaguely-shadowed banks. The cypresses stand dark and solemn against the sky, which is a deep dark blue. The *chiaro-oscuro* of his picture is striking. The painting is careful, and the tones remarkable. It is a solemn, serious, silent picture, very peculiar, but very interesting and

Kouïndji.

RUSSIA.

Lindholm. original. "*Pâturage en Finlande*," by B. Lindholm, of Helsingfors, is a charming study of nature. It represents a slope of rising ground stretching into the distance, and down this at intervals are coming groups of milk-maids with pails, while along a road that climbs it on one side in the mid-distance a cart is going. The tones and gradations of light and color are given with great delicacy and truth; there is no over-insistance of anything. The foreground of broken soil and plants is faithful and perfectly rendered, and over the whole is a sentiment and refinement which is rare. The space and perspective have almost nothing to be desired. Mechtcherski. "*Forêt en Hiver*," by M. Mechtcherski, is also a charming picture, with great sentiment and truth to nature. In the middle and foreground of the picture is a dark pool, out of which blue blocks of ice have been cut; around this rise wooded banks, inclosing it as in an amphitheater, with tall, thin, serried trees tipped with snow, and rising against a dim, vague, gray sky, in which snow is gathering. The tone is pale gray and white, and there is a hush of silence over all. Altogether this is a charming picture.

No. 35—which was omitted from the catalogues, and, therefore, I cannot give the author's name—is also a very clever picture. It represents a sea scene from the shore, on which a stranded vessel lies which workmen are calking. On the right is a cliff. The sky is gloomy, and flaky, and gray, with light on the horizon—the sea dark, except where it breaks toward the shore. "*La grande Route*," by M. Dobrovolski, Dobrovolski. represents a grass-grown road with deep ruts filled with water, along either side of which, as it stretches straight off into the distance through the center of the picture, are sparsely-scattered trees, and in the mid-distance a carriage is coming down. The pools and spots of water reflect the sky, and a pink light is in the edge of the horizon and touches the clouds above. There is admirable quality Volkoff. on this picture and the scene has much character. Volkoff's "*Forêt à la Fonte des Neiges, effet du Soir*" is a winter wood-scene, with snow on the ground and a sunset effect through tall trees. The snow is particularly good in tone, cold without being painty, and the whole scene well drawn Klever. and rendered. M. Klever had also a "*Coucher du Soleil en Hiver*," which, though it has rather a scenic and sought effect, also shows talent. His "*Parc abandonné à Marienbourg, en Livonie*" is a better picture and has some character. It represents an old decaying park with groves of trees, and steps leading down into sluggish calm water, over which a scum has gathered and in which two swans are

RUSSIA.

Schichkine.

swimming. M. Schichkine's four pictures are also to be noted for their merit. One is a secluded wood-scene with a brook running through it; another the interior of a primeval forest, with tall, slender trees. In both the sentiment is admirable and the drawing and color excellent. They are serious and lonely, and no living person is there to disturb their solitude.

It will be seen that a certain silence, loneliness, and seriousness are characteristic of many of these pictures. None of these we have mentioned are pretentious or self-conscious, or noisy in character. They do not aim at showing off the skill of the artist, but have a better object, to reproduce the interior feeling and character of the place.

Aivazovski.

The same remarks cannot be made of the landscapes by M. Aivazovski, which are ambitious and vague. "*Nuit dans l'Archipel, près du Mont Athos*" represents a moonlight-scene with light misty blue sea. "*La Tempête aux Bords de la Mer Noire*" is of the same character of misty blue color. Both show talent, but they miss their aim.

Orlovski.

M. Orlovski's pictures show much ability. "*Les Faucheurs*" is painted with great care; the perspective of the immense plain is admirably rendered; the details are all studied, and the general effect bright and sunny; a little more concentration and suppression of parts would have made it far more effective, and taken from it a certain monotony of brightness. Another landscape of much merit represents a heavy sea rolling in to shore, with one great green surf-wave lifting in the foreground and on the point of breaking. The sky is gray with broken yellowish white clouds towards the horizon, and grayish white ducks are descending into the sea.

Genre.

Genre.

Kovalevski.

Among the cabinet and *genre* pictures were several of importance. "Excavations at Rome," by M. Kovalevski, is an admirably drawn and carefully studied picture, full of truth and nature, and fidelity of execution. The figured horses are capital in their action and expression, and rendered simply and without affectation. The color is subdued, without glare or spottiness, the tone harmonious, the sky grey under a clouded sirocco, the composition and character excellent. It represents a group of workmen excavating at the "*Monte de Giustizia*" at Rome, and carting away the rubbish and débris. Mr. Savitzki also sent a picture of the same class, representing "*Travaux de Terrassement sur une Ligne de Chemin de Fer*," which, though inferior to that just described, is full of animation and nature and cleverness

Savitski.

RUSSIA. of drawing. The pictures of M. W. G. Makovski are also W. G. Makovski. spirited in character and simply and genially executed. His "*Amateurs de Rossignols,*" is particularly to be noted. It represents three old men in a low room lit by a small window. They are looking at a bird in a cage which hangs above them, and endeavoring to induce it to sing. Another is "*Utile dulci,*" in which an old couple is engaged in preparing raspberries for preserving. The subject is simple, but the spirit which is put into it make it noteworthy. Jouravleff. "*Bénédiction de la Fiancée,*" by M. Jouravleff, is executed with spirit and is dramatic in feeling. The bride is on her knees covering her face. The father stands erect looking down on her coldly. There is a good deal of character in the expressions of the figures, and the still life is painted Kramskoï. with skill. M. Kramskoï's "*Les Nymphes, sujet tiré de la ballade de Gogol: une Nuit de Mai,*" is of the legendary type Mennier. and shows talent. M. Mennier also should be noted. His "Mary Mother listening to the last Words of her dying Child" is the work of a young artist and has much promise. M. C. G. Makovski. C. G. Makovski's "*Martyres Bulgares,*" and "*Procession du tapis du Prophète au Caire,*" are works of more importance of subject. They are cleverly painted, with much talent, but they are of a character which simply repels us and shocks us. Why select scenes which can only cause horror and pain?

There are also to be mentioned, as showing talent, M. Korzoukhine. Maximoff. Korzoukhine's "*Devant le Confessional*"; M. Maximoff's "*Arrivée d'un Devin à une Noce Villageoise,*" which has great Baron Klodt. vigor and naturality of character; "*Le Banc Noir,*" of Baron Dmitrieff. Klodt; "*Dix minutes d'arrêt,*" of M. Dmitrieff's, which is somewhat of the same manner as Mr. Frith, and a number of excellent portraits. Among the latter may be particular- Paroff. Kramskoï *et al.* ized some striking portraits by M. Kramskoï, by M. Paroff, M. Frenz, M. Lehman, and M. Hartamoff.

We have left to the last the largest and most ambitious picture of the whole Russian department, "*Les Torches Vivantes de Néron,*" by M. Siemiradski. This picture obtained for its author the distinction of a medal of honor, and, therefore, deserves a careful consideration. The scene Siemiradski. which it attempts to represent is the historic legend of the burning of Christian martyrs by Nero. On a high terrace are seated, in a golden palanquin which has just been placed there by negro bearers, the Emperor and his wife Poppæa. Architectural constructions cover two-thirds of the background of the picture, and the *loggie* and balconies are filled with spectators and attendants. The foreground is thronged with a crowd of figures, courtesans, guards, and senators, gaming, drinking, and lounging, and playing on musical instruments. On the right, attached to high stakes against a background of sky, are the figures of the martyrs enveloped in combustible stuffs, to which the executioners are setting fire. RUSSIA.

There is certainly something in the selection of such an incident which shows an imaginative desire at least. It was a bold conception, which demanded power and a strong dramatic capacity fully to carry out. But it is not enough to have selected a great subject; the artist must be pushed by the imaginative and executive force which he has brought to its development. As far as the hand is concerned M. Siemiradski has shown a remarkable talent. His touch is bold and free, his imitation of stuffs and objects, his painting of flesh and costumes, are masterly. His drawing is generally good. There is nothing niggled and timid in his handling, and, as mere painting, there are parts which could scarcely be too highly praised. He has all the facility and brilliancy of Herr Makart, with much more solid qualities of execution. In *technique* there is very much to praise and little fault to find. It is not here that he fails, but in the total want of imaginative grasp of the scene. The picture is full of splendid parts, but it is nothing but parts, and there is no relation between them. There is no whole, either in composition or conception, no historic truth or even probability. It is a mass of jumbled archæology and history, never quite correct, of well-drawn figures having nothing to do with the tragedy which is enacting, of groups disengaged from all the main interest, and often in violent opposition to it. The burning of the martyrs becomes a subsidiary and unimportant incident which scarcely attracts the observer, and which interests scarcely one of the figures in the picture. It is an impossible bacchanalian scene, and is without any central dominating idea. Siemiradski.

The first great and fatal fault is that the two halves of the picture are totally different in the time and hour. The main mass of the picture is in the broad light of noon, in which all the personages and details of architecture are highly sparkling. The other half is dull, and towards twilight. The burning torches of human beings which should have given the chief light, as they were the chief protagonists of the scene responding to Nero, are feeble, ineffective and secondary in light. In the incidental groups the main effect is placid; they occupy all the foreground and the principal part of the picture. Even Nero and Poppæa

RUSSIA. are insignificant beside them. They are far off and small. The others are near and large. The next fault is the want of proper perspective. It is difficult if not impossible, to understand the planes or to see how or in what manner the figures are standing. It is equally a mystery how Nero and Poppæa were carried to the positions they occupy, as there seems to be no clear way leading to it. One above the other, the heads and figures are piled up, but what supports them is doubtful at least.

Siemiraski. In the next place, historical truth and individual character are violated. Poppæa never was there. She opposed Nero in all these violences and endeavored to dissuade him from them, and in fact her opposition was the cause of her death. However, setting aside this, and the artist may claim that he was not to be bound by facts, how does this feeble, bloated, and languidly effeminate figure of Nero lounging uninterested in his litter correspond to the character of the mad emperor, whose great boast it was that he was the most powerful athlete in Rome, and who descended into the arena to try conclusions with trained gladiators, and always took pride in exhibiting himself as the prominent figure of all games and spectacles. How do this heavy and common face and figure of Poppæa correspond to her's who was the most beautiful and graceful woman of her day, who affected reserve and modesty of bearing, and avoided public meetings and crowds, and how is it that the emperor, at whose command this fearful tragedy was enacted, seems to take so total a want of interest in it? It seems rather as if he were going to sleep. And how, again, is it that no deference is shown to him by any of the crowd, who, careless both of him and of the place of the great scene, riot and revel in the imperial courts?

But deeper than all this is the want of imaginative conception of the tragedy. Conceive for a moment the scene, and say if this in any way represents it. Conceive the darkness of night coming on or already enshrouding the world, which is to be illuminated by these living torches—the excited crowd that have gathered as spectators of this brutal scene, some indignant, some sympathizing with the wretched victims, some bloodthirsty and rejoicing in this novel spectacle, some loving, some hating, all fearing the emperor, and all profoundly interested in the tragedy to be enacted. Over the darkness and half-illumination of the crowd that seethes below rises that of the athletic madman and player who has given the signal for the torches to be fired, and, standing erect and prominent before his guards that attend him, catches the full glow of the torches as they glare up against the dark abyss of the sky and flicker over the cornices and edges of the architecture and leave vast hollows of empty shadow. The lurid glare of the light shows the great protagonists in opposition to each other—the tyrant in this world in his mad and momentary triumph, the victims inspired with religious zeal and looking forward to eternal glory beyond the reach of man. What a tremendous contrast!

Siemiradski.

In the picture itself but one or two figures seem in the least degree observant or interested in the spectacle. The mass drink and play at dice and amuse themselves as if they were there for any other purpose than to see the burning of these martyrs. The emperor and the Christians who are tied to the stake are alike accessories. The palanquin is splendid, the mother-of-pearl veneering beautifully rendered, but so massive and important as to overwhelm the occupants, and in itself, archæologically considered, totally without justification of fact. Some of the spectators are in furs and rich, heavy robes, some nearly nude. There is no keeping in the feeling nor in the composition. It is a work of great decorative merit, showing much cleverness of handicraft, but as an imaginative conception it can only be considered as a complete failure.

"*La Coupe ou la Femme*," by the same painter, has similar merit as technical work. It represents an ancient voluptuary and antiquary in a room filled with *objets de vertu* and *bric-à-brac*, hesitating between the purchase of a nude slave and a rich cup. The theme is *banale* and scarcely worthy of so large a canvas. It is a colossal piece of *genre*, which would be more acceptable on a very much diminished scale of size. M. Siemiradski is a young man, we believe, and with such executive talent it is to be hoped that he will brace his mind to achieve results of deeper significance and more earnest thought than these two pictures display, and take to heart those true words of Goethe, "*In der Beschränkung zeiget sich erst der Meister.*"

Jacoby.

M. Jacoby's "*Noce dans le Palais de Glace construit sur la Néva pendant l'Hiver de* 1741," represents a chamber cut in the ice, and on a couch placed in an alcove are seated a strange, half-idiotic couple who have there passed their bridal night, while a crowd of revelers are entering the chamber and a dwarf is presenting a fan to the bride. The picture has something strangely fantastic and grotesque in its effect. The sunlight gleaming on the transparent ice, the cold,

RUSSIA. shivering glow of the icy room, the boisterous figures of the revelers, and the stupid, vacant expression of the unhappy couple make up a contrast which is singularly striking. The incident of which it is an illustration is narrated in the novel of Lagechnikoff, entitled "The Palace of Ice," and represents the marriage of the idiot Galitzin, the *protégé* of the Empress Anne, with another unfortunate of Calmuck origin. The picture displays as much talent as oddity of conception, character, costume, and color. It shows a great deal of study, and is drawn with spirit.

Jacoby.

Among other pictures which must be noted are several by M. Bogoluboff, representing a "*Combat naval, livré par Pierre le Grand, près de l'Isle d'Oesel* (a. 1719)," "*Passage des Galeres de Pierre le Grand sur la pointe de Hangä-Udd,*" "*Vue de Nijni-Novgorod,*" and "*St. Petersbourg, Nuit d'Été,*" all of which show a decided ability; M. Gerson's "*Nicolas Copernic démontrant le Système du Monde aux Hommes illustres de son Temps.*" M. Gué's "*Pierre le Grand fait subir un Interrogatorie au Tzarevitch Alexis, à Peterhof;*" and M. Edelfeldt's "*Blanche de Namur, Reine de Suède, et le Prince Haquin.*"

Bogoluboff. Gerson. Gué. Edelfeldt.

BELGIUM.

BELGIUM. We now come to Belgium, which sent no less than 300 oil-paintings, among which there were some which were striking, but on the whole there was a general lack of great vital force and individuality, though there was certainly a good level of fair work.

Historical Paintings.

Historical. Wauters. Of the historical pictures there were two by M. Wauters, which show a great deal of character and feeling. "*La Folie de Hugues Van der Goes*" represents the mad painter seated in the foreground, to whom a choir of youths are singing. His expression as he catches the familiar strain that seems to recall the past and to clear up the present is admirable. So also is that of the black-cowled monk who is guiding the singers and looking over the back of the chair to observe the effect of the music on the painter, as well as of the figures in shadow who are watching him with the same intent. The work is serious and careful, the light and dark well disposed, and the composition good. There is a common center of interest, and the story is well told without exaggeration and attitudinizing. It is a pity that he has introduced the two players in the left behind the boys in white who are chanting; they add nothing to the interest, and detract from the concentration of the group. "*Marie de Bourgogne implorant des Échevins de Gand la Grâce de ses Conseillers Hugonet et Humbercourt*" has not the same force and individuality, but is interesting, well composed, and expressive, without affectation. These two pictures obtained for M. Wauters the medal of honor for Belgium, and they justly deserved it. BELGIUM.

There is also a good deal of character in M. Cluysenaar's "*Canossa, l'an 1077*," which represents Henry IV humbling himself before Gregory VII. It is boldly painted and well drawn and composed, but a little tame in general effect. The figure of Henry is a little too cringing to be true to his character. He submitted at last, but reluctantly and angrily. Gregory is better, but hardly up to the mark of that imperious and overbearing Pontifex, and there is a lack of intensity in the queen and the attendants. But the picture is serious in purpose, and executed with ability. M. Cluysenaar has also a portrait of a little boy lounging in a great gray fauteuil, which is admirable in character, expression, and color, and full of nature. "*Charles V à Yuste*," by M. A. de Vriendt, represents the emperor seated and looking at a picture held up by two monks. It is well painted, but a little academic in treatment. All the pictures of this artist deserve to be commended, as well as those of M. J. de Vriendt, and particularly "*La Justice de Baudouin à la Hache*," by the latter. Cluysenaar. A. de Vriendt. J. de Vriendt.

M. Verlat's "*Nous voulons Barabbas!*" is a striking and also a disagreeable picture. There is a good deal of force, both of character and *impasto*, in many of the heads, but they are all vulgar and repulsive. This, of course, he intends they should be, but he has carried this to an extreme, and there is nothing in the picture to counterbalance this vulgarity. The composition is not fortunate, and the color is *criarde*. His other pictures of animal subjects are coarse but clever, and certainly do not lack vigor and individuality. Verlat.

Among the other historical pictures should be also noted "*Messaline sortant de Rome et insueltée par la Populace*," by M. Hennebicq; "*La Mort de Didon*" and "*Le dernier Combat du Gladiateur*," by M. Stallaert; "*Baudoin V appelant le Peuple aux Armes pour le Défense de la Ville*," by M. Carlier. Hennebicq. Stallaert. Carlier.

Genre.

Of the cabinet and *genre* pictures, there were some which deserve special commendation. "*Un Concours de Chant (le Jury)*," by M. D. Col, is very clever, well disposed in light and dark, and carefully painted, and exhibits much hu- *Genre.* Col.

BELGIUM.

mor. Hundreds of cages with canaries line the walls. The judges sit on a platform attentively examining them placed on a table below them. "*La Sortie du Restaurant*," by M. [Hermann.] Hermann, is, for size and character, one of the most important. It represents two men overcome by drink, and coming out of a restaurant after an orgie, accompanied by two *cocottes*. There is certainly considerable cleverness and expression in this picture, but the subject is unworthy the talent and labor bestowed upon it. "*Secours au temps*," by [Verlat.] M. Verlat, represents a child attacked and overthrown by a wolf, which in turn is seized by a dog. The color is hard, but the attitude and expression of the child are very good, [J. Verhas.] and the story is well told. The "*Inondation*," by M. J. Verhas, [F. Verhas.] and "*La Fête de Papa*," by M. F. Verhas, are agreeable in color and composition. Among other pictures which [Verhaert.] should be mentioned were four small canvases by M. Verhaert, "*L'Esprit Vaincu*," "*La Soubrette Intriguée*," "*La Convalescente*," and "*La Bibliothèque*," which are well painted and good in color; some clever and original little pic- [Impens.] tures by M. Impens; several by M. Lagye, after the manner [Lagye.] of Leys, particularly "*Les Bohémiens*" and "*Statuaire*"; [Robie.] some flowers and fruits by M. Robie; several clever pictures [Madou.] by the late M. Madou; "*Chien regardant une Mouche*," by M. [J. Stevens.] J. Stevens, which is natural and amusing; "*Rhétoriciens* [Markelbach.] *d'Anvers*," by M. Markelbach; and a characteristic figure of [De Braekeleer.] "The Geographer" by M. de Braekeleer, which represents a man in his shirt-sleeves studying an atlas.

[Willems.] M. Willems sent ten pictures, all of the same class and character, which is clearly indicated by the titles, "*La Visite*," "*Le Baise-main*," "*La Toilette*," "*L'Offre de la Bague*," "*La Présentation du Futur*," etc. The still life, furniture, vases, stuffs, and dresses are all executed with great elaboration and skill. The personages are mere models or lay figures to show off their costumes and laces and silks and satins and velvets. They have little to interest us in character.

[A. Stevens.] M. Alfred Stevens sent no less than sixteen pictures, and to his admirers these form one of the attractions of the Belgian department. One regrets to find them, for the most part, inferior to his former work; and though they have a certain distinction of sobriety in color, they have little to say which interests or affects us. Among the *criarde*, hard, and noisy pictures which abound, it is grateful at least to find in these a subdued quality of gray tones which soothes us almost like silence. But they err even in this direction, and, seen together, have a monotony of effaced color which is not satisfactory. There is a good deal of trickery, too, of

BELGIUM.

half-lights and reflected lights, and they lack substance and quality. The subjects are not striking. They represent generally a lady in her boudoir alone or with a friend, with dim candle-light or shrouded day, and it is nearly always the same lady. There is little emotion or character, no force, and scarcely any incident. The most striking of all M. Stevens's pictures here was a portrait of a boy in a gray velvet dress, and a greyhound at his side. This is admirable in quality and character and delicate in tone, and altogether a masterly work that justifies his high reputation. The velvet dress is charmingly painted.

A. Stevens.

Landscapes.

Landscapes. Coosemans.

Some of the landscapes were clever, but there were none of any very high rank. Among the best may be mentioned three by M. Coosemans, and particularly one of a dark, marshy ground filled with pools and high grasses, with dark, pollarded trees with ravens perched on them and fluttering about them, and a dull, slaty sky, with a gleam on the horizon. This is strongly painted, and is gloomy, solitary, and effective. M. Van Luppen's "*La Flandre*" and "*Avant l'Orage*" are also effective. M. Tscharner's "*Après l'Hiver*," several by Mlle. Marie Collart, M. F. Lamorinière, M. de Knyff, and M. Boulenger, among others, must be noted. M. Clays sent seven landscapes, all representing seaports and ships with brown and white sails and blue and white skies with mixed clouds. These are clever, but mannered. When we have seen one we have seen all. They are repetitions of the same subject with the same treatment.

Van Luppen. Tscharner. Mlle. Collart. Lamorinière. De Knyff. Boulenger. Clays.

Portraits. Winne.

Among the portraits was one by M. Winne which is very lifelike in the expression of the eyes, that seem to follow one about. His other portraits also are clever.

SWITZERLAND.

Genre.

SWITZERLAND. *Genre.* Robert.

In the Swiss department there was little to detain us of distinguished merit. One of the largest was "*Les Zéphyrs du Soir*," by M. L. P. Robert, which is legendary in theme and represents a number of nude and wild female figures floating over a green slope covered with low trees. This picture received a medal from the Salon in 1877. Though well drawn, it is feeble in tone and character. M. B. Vautier's "*Le Dîner de Circonstance*" represents a company of *bourgeois* and functionaries gathered around a dinner-table.

Vautier.

SWITZERLAND. The color is rather dry and monotonous, but it shows much careful study of character, and conscientious work. The heads are expressive, and are evidently portraits, and the action and scene are true to life. Durand. M. Durand's "*Le Mariage à la Mairie*," "*Un bout de Conduite*," and "*Le Marché*," are all spirited. The first represents a scene at the *Mairie*, where a bridal party has been waiting with impatience for the arrival of the bridegroom. The "*Bout de Conduite*" is a file of Bohemians and bear-leaders walking through the snow escorted by gendarmes. These are brightly painted and the comic element is well expressed. Stückelberg. M. Stückelberg's "*Diseuse de Bonne Aventure*" has much merit, and is out of the common. It represents two girls with a donkey, and an old woman on a wall looking at them to tell their fortune. Ravel. M. Ravel's "*Il pleut*," which is spirited, represents a party of tourists detained in a mountain inn by a storm of rain. Burnand. M. Burnand's "*Fournée au Village*" is also clever, and realistic in the heads of the peasants.

Landscapes.

Landscapes. Of the landscapes, there were few which were national, and these are not of the best. The landscape painters seem rather to have caught their inspiration in other countries. Of those who have been faithful to their own may be noted Koller. Jeanneret. Rudisuhli. M. Koller's "*Orage sur les hautes Alpes*," M. Jeanneret's "*Gorge de L'Areuse*," and M. Rudisuhli's "*La Source*" and "*La Solitude*." Of those who have devoted their talent to Botter. foreign scenes, M. A. Botter's views from Camargue are specially to be noted. Of these the "*Etangs de Vacares (Camargue)*" was the strongest and most original in this department. It represents jutting points of dark land pushing out into flat water. Heavy clouds lower over the scene, and Girardet. the sense of loneliness and desolation is well felt. M. Girardet's "*Plage de Tanger*" is a bright and sunny sea, with figures and donkeys moving along the shallow shore, and Pata. the waves breaking in along its curve. M. Pata sent some Castan. marine views on the coast of Normandy; and M. Castan "*L'Intérieur de Bois dans le Berri*" and "*Les Bords de la Creuse à Gargilesse*." Fifteen drawings of birds, by M. Robert. Robert, are executed with great delicacy and elaboration, and should also be noticed.

NETHERLANDS.

NETHERLANDS. The Netherlands did not sustain the great reputation of their olden days when their art was illustrated by great names, and in the light of these great works the modern products of their school strike one with disappointment. Clever as some of their artists show themselves to be, they do not strongly impress one, overshadowed as they are by our memories of Rembrandt, Van Dyck, Cuyp, Hobbema, Ostade, Metzu, Wouvermans, Paul Potter, Berghem, Ruysdael, and Van der Velde. The passion for light and dark, the hurry, spirit, the *finesse*, the sharp originality which characterized the early school are wanting in the present day, and the Netherlands, like Italy, suffers by comparison with its great ancestry in art. NETHERLANDS.

In place of this vivacity and pungent sense of reality we have a school of Impressionists. Unable to reproduce the vivid character of the early school, they have sought to create an effect by loose and vague, though often vigorous, brush-work. There is as much affectation in over-sketchiness as in over-elaboration, but the modern over-done and over-elaborated schools of *genre* have provoked a reaction in quite the other direction. The Impressionist school is a protest against our finish of parts, and though there is justice in its aim, it is at times carried so far as to be equally false on the other side. If this tendency is to be observed in the schools of other nations it is specially to be seen here. Impressional school. Over-sketchiness *versus* Over-elaboration.

Undoubtedly what is needed in art more than stuffs, however cleverly imitated, is stuff of the mind and imagination, and the overstudy of *technique* has tended to degrade the higher spirit of art. We have fine words and phrases, not poems. We have too much of Euphues and the Arcadia, too little Hamlet and Lear. Of this school of Impressionists there are some eminent masters in landscape, such as Messrs. Jovels, Mesdag, Maris, Verveer, Artz, and Bakhuyzen. All of these have, despite their individual differences, a similarity of treatment. Their pictures are loosely painted, suggested rather than finished, and seek for scarcely anything beyond general effect. There are, however, great vigor and character in some of their works, and often boldness of execution, and sentiment.

Landscapes.

Two of the most remarkable and poetic landscapes were by M. Mesdag, "*Bateau de Sauvetage de Scheveningue sortant pour porter Assistance à l'Équipage du Bâtiment Anglais le Hopewell* 11 *Novembre*, 1869," and "*Retour de ce Bateau.*" These are coarse and carelessly free in execution, painted with a heavy brush, and merely dashed in upon the canvas without detail or finish; but they are eminently dramatic, spirited, and affecting. The soul of the incident is seized, *Landscapes.* Mesdag.

NETHERLANDS. and the work has been done in the fervor of feeling. The first represents the launching of the life-boat. The horses and carriage, which have brought it, stand there with a flagstaff and a flag blown out by the gale. It is a wild day, toward sundown. Gray whitening clouds cover the sky, the boat is laboring in the mid-distance on the turbulent waves that break heavily in turbid and confused masses of billows, and a crowd is on the shore massed together darkly and watching its progress. One or two dark birds hover in the wild sky. The vessel that is to be succored lies far off in the horizon. The second picture represents the return of the same boat. There is the same gray, turbulent, rolling sea. The sky is broken and wild, and a red gleam breaks out along the horizon, against which the wreck is seen. The dark crowd is still there on the shore bringing in the crew that has been rescued. Altogether both of these pictures are gloomy, wild, and impressive in their character. The grouping of the figures is well managed, and all that one regrets is that they are such mere sketches which can only be seen at a distance and to a certain extent with the eye of faith. Nothing is really completed. It is as if they had been dashed hurriedly in on the spot under the influence of a powerful emotion, and then left. "*La Levée de l'Ancre*," by the same artist, is in the same style. The sky is blue, the water wild, the wind blowing.

Mesdag.

Bakhuyzen. M. Bakhuyzen's "*Paysage près de Leide*" is also of the Impressionist school, but very clever, vigorous in its drawing, and full of life and color. The town with red-tiled roofs, and a windmill beyond the river, rises against a blue sky with great gray clouds. The river is gray, with bluish reflections. The composition is good; there is a great deal of air and light in the picture, and the painting is free and strong. It is made out solely in masses and values, with no details, and must be seen at a distance.

Bilders. Again, in "*Paysage en Gueldre*," by M. Bilders, there is the same treatment, and much vigor. It represents a meadow of broken sandy soil with large trees, under which cows are feeding.

Maris. M. Maris's "*Sur la Plage*" and "*Paysage Hollandais*" have similar characteristics. The first represents a cold, gray sea, which is merely scratched in, and a sloop riding on it, darkly against the sea and sky.

Israëls. M. Israëls sent four pictures, "*Seul au Monde*," "*Les Pauvres du Village*," "*Le Diner des Savetiers*," and "*L'Anniversaire*." All of these are of a gray, effaced, and somber tone.

with no vivacity of color, as if the artist had desired to accentuate the seriousness of the subject by the dreariness of his color. They are all scenes of humble life, and all have an accent of sincerity in feeling and intention. In texture, they are wooly, in execution they are intentionally sketchy and impressionist. But the values are well kept, there is no exaggeration, and they interest from their depth of feeling and simplicity. The mind has been at work. If he does not perfectly achieve, he has ideas and sentiment, and does not pin his faith on to the mere *technique* and mechanics of his art. NETHERLANDS.

M. Poggenbeck's "*Paysage Hollandais*" represents a landscape with a smooth river running diagonally through the picture through deep green banks on which willows are growing, while cows are standing in the still water. The sky is gray, the effect clear and sunny, and there is a good deal of life and feeling for nature. In execution it is far more finished than those which have been mentioned. Poggenbeck.

M. Mauve's "*Paysage avec des Moutons*" represents sheep in a snowy, wide, flat landscape, with a man in the center, who is the only dark spot in the picture. This is rough, but clever. Mauve.

M. Artz sent two pictures, "*Sur les Dunes*," and "*Contre Vent*." The latter represents three peasants, a mother and two children, returning home through a gray, dull country, and with an overcast sky. It is a little in the manner of Millet, and not without sentiment. Artz.

M. Roelofs's three landscapes are all worthy of special note, "*Paysage près Vreeland*," "*Forêt en Automne*," "*Vue près Abcoude*." One of these represents a pool of water with scum on the surface, reedy grass on both sides, and trees beyond, reflecting darkly in the water. It is bold, effective, and full of light. Roelofs.

M. Burger's "*Pendant la Guerre*" is clever and vigorous. All the able-bodied men of the place have gone to the war, and two young girls and a boy have taken upon themselves the duties of plowing. It is a broad field with a gray sky, through which dark birds are flying zigzag. Among the other landscapes which should be noticed, are "*Paysage près d'une Ville de Hollande*" and "*En plaine*," by M. Apol; "*Forêt*" and "*Paysage sur les bords de l'Yssel*," by M. Borselen; "*La Matinée dans les Polders de la Hollande*" and "*Un temps de Bourrasque*," by M. Gabriel, rich in color; "*Dans le bois*," of M. Bock; and "*Le Coin de Ferme*," by M. Kuyper. Burger. Apol. Borselen. Gabriel. Bock. Kuyper.

NETHERLANDS. It will be seen that the painters in the Netherlands have drawn their subjects chiefly from their own country and national life, and not from foreign lands. There was, in consequence, a certain character of nationality in their work which was attractive, and in their landscapes especially they showed vigor and originality.

Genre.

Genre. Among the cabinet and *genre* pictures there were some which were striking. Particularly are to be noticed the extremely clever pictures by M. Haanen, "*Ouvrières en Perles à Venise*" and "*Meneghina, type Vénitien.*" The first is a very spirited picture, representing a number of girls and women in a factory-room stringing and sorting the pearls of Venice. They are chiefly young girls, who are seated and ranged along a wall, with an old woman in the center, who is superintending their labors and working herself. The girls are extremely pretty, and their heads and action are very easy, characteristic, and natural. The painting is good, the spirit lively, the color gay without being excessive, the composition and attitudes excellent. One would like to hear what they are talking about, they are so simple and bright and pleasant to look at. There is a remarkable sense of grace and *couleur locale* in all the figures.

Haanen.

There is great humor of character and incident in the "*Corpus Delicti,*" of M. Boks. The "*corpus delicti*" is a soldier's cap which has been discovered, and the maid has been called on to account for it to the family. The old gentleman, who is seated, points impressively to the cap, and the maid, who stands before him, shrugs her shoulders and pretends to know nothing about it. Three other servants are in the room who have been summoned for explanation, and the wife is just about to ring the bell. There is a great deal of spirit in the rendering of this scene. The characters are well portrayed and the touches are humorous without caricature.

Boks.

Dame Konner. "*L'École de Peinture,*" by Dame H. Konner, is also spirited and cleverly rendered. It represents an old cat with her four kittens, which are rummaging about in a painter's studio. The old mother quietly reposes on the top of the frame of a picture, while her kittens are in all sorts of mischief, one staining her paws with the paint on the palette, one peeping over a canvas. The character of the animals is very well given. They are painted with great truth to nature, and the humor is quiet and amusing.

"*Hiver en Frise*," by M. Bisschop, has a good deal that is interesting in subject and is well painted. It represents the interior of a hut of fishermen, where a young lady is having her skates sharpened by another girl. The costumes are pleasing, and the details all carefully rendered, and with taste. NETHERLANDS. Bisschop.

M. Melis's "*Sois Sage!*" which is of the same school as M. Israël's, is worthy of special notice, as are also the two pleasing compositions by M. Ten Kate, "*Les Maraudeurs*" and "*La Boule inattendue*," and M. Verveer's two pictures, "*Deux Mères, (poissardes de Schéveningue*") and "*La Veuve et sa Consolation*." All of these are of the same school, and all subjects of humble life in the Netherlands. Melis. Ten Kate. Verveer.

DENMARK.

Passing from the Netherlands into Denmark, we find little that is very striking or original. The style is generally that of smooth, flat elaboration. The landscapes are thin and without much character, but a few have a pleasant distribution of parts and of lights. Among the best may be noted the "*Rerage de l'Île Moen*," by M. C. A. Koelle, which represents a yellow sand bank with weeds and shrubs sloping diagonally down the picture, and a fresh blue sea rolling in on a pebbly beach, which is pleasing. "*Paysage des Landes*," by M. V. Groth, is in some respects an effective picture. It represents the Landes in mid-day in summer. The marsh, flecked with spots of light, is well rendered, the water is transparent, and the distance good. The sky, which is poor and map-like, detracts from the value of the picture. M. Kyhn's "*Au Coucher du Soleil*" is a winter sunset in Denmark. The sky is lowering and slaty, with a lurid red break on the horizon seen across a stretch of overshadowed snow. There is considerable feeling in this. M. Aagaard's "*Ruisseau dans un Bois de Hêtres*" is an exceedingly elaborate river running through green banks in a forest of trees. It is rather weak, but is pleasant in its distribution of light, and the water is transparent. DENMARK. Koelle. Groth. Kyhn. Aagaard.

The historic and religious pictures were tame, and had no special qualities to call for extended examination.

Cabinet Pictures.

Of cabinet pictures, the most effective was the "*Intérieur d'un Forge*," by M. Kröeyer, which shows strength and talent. It represents figures beating a hot bar of iron, the reflected light all coming from the forge. M. Rosenstand's *Cabinet.* Kröeyer. Rosenstand.

DENMARK.

Bache. "*Italiens jouant à la Morra*" is spirited in action and design. M. O. Bache sent four pictures, "*Après la Chasse au Sanglier,*" *Sur Knippelsbro,*" "*Élans Tués,*" "*Dans la Cour d'un Moulin à Eau.*" "*Sur Knippelsbro*" represents a dray with two horses coming breast forward into the foot plane of the picture. "*Dans la Cour d'un Moulin*" is also a picture of horses and figures, and in both these pictures these are well drawn and good in action.

Jerndorf. The portrait of "M. Matthison-Hansen," playing on the organ, by M. Jerndorf, though hard and clean in texture, is drawn and painted with great fidelity, and is evidently a good likeness; "*La jeune Fille qui écrit une Lettre,*" by M. Dalsgaard. Dalsgaard, has also a good deal of sentiment and gentle character.

NORWAY.

NORWAY.

The Norwegian department was, with some exceptions, exclusively composed of landscapes, and these show remarkable originality, *verve*, and strength. They are peculiarly national, not only in their subjects, but in their character and sentiment, and their manner is quite different from that which is elsewhere seen. One of the most remarkable landscapes in the whole Exposition was to be found here. Gude. It is the "*Paysage Écossais*" of M. Gude. It is painted with a masterly freedom and truth. The water gushes, and dazzles, and dances, in the broad sunlit path of light that flashes across it, and in the light fresh breeze the little sailboat seems almost to move along the waves. A transparent shadow envelops a dark ridge of land that thrusts forward in the mid-distance, rich with verdure. The manner in which the water is painted is quite peculiar. Seen very near, it seems composed of accidental spots and dabs of singular color, but at its proper point of sight it is full of motion and life; and here it may be observed that, throughout all this section great skill is shown in the rendering of water, as, for instance, in the "*Plage de Lister,*" by M. Thulow. Thulow, the "*Crépuscule,*" by M. Nielsen, and the "*Fjord* Normann. *Norwégien,*" by M. Normann, which is a dead-still oily sea, with no reflections, that just feels the swell, and is glassed over with a misty smoothness. M. Normann's "*Minuit à Lofoten*" is also a striking, poetic, and peculiar picture, representing the midnight sun in Norway. A tall cliff stands out into the sea, catching the full glow of the light, which is repeated on a sail in the mid-distance. The low purple-blue sea rolls in upon the beach, where lies the wreck of an old Nielsen. hulk. M. Nielsen's "*Crépuscule, Vue de Côte*" is very tran-

NORWAY.

quil and pleasing in color and composition. In the gray embayed sea that washes along the curved coast is a large dark sloop rising against the sky, and along the shore stands a cottage, with nets hung out to dry. Men are rowing along a dark boat with furled sails; a ship lies motionless in the offing; above is a misty gray sky with breaks of thunderous light. Schanche. M. Schanche's "*Sur le Côte ouest de la Norwége; clair le Lune*" is also a very clever landscape, as are also the two "*Paysages*," by M. Jacobson, Jacobson. one of which represents a path through woods with tall, dark trunks, with gleams of sunshine seen behind them. "*Le Soir d'Automne (intérieur d'un Village)*," by M. Grimeland, Grimeland. has also much merit. It represents a road leading off from the foreground straight through the picture and passing under a mid-distance arch flanked by houses, over which a cool, transparent shadow is cast. Sinding. M. Sinding's "*Perdu!*" represents a heavy sea breaking in at the base of a tall, black, iron-rusted cliff, where the dead body of a sailor is lying. There is a great deal of truth in the movement of the greenish water that wallows in, and altogether the picture shows power. Smith-Hald. M. Smith-Hald's "*De la Côte méridionale de la Norwége*" is remarkable for its truth and realism. It represents a pier, on which is a house with snow-covered roof, and at the farther end a steamer is pouring forth a column of dark smoke, while a crowd of passengers is landing and coming down the snow-covered road, already trampled in places into mud. Along one side of the pier is ice and snow, adhering to the beams and posts, and encumbering the water. Bennetter. M. Bennetter's "*Vikings en Mer*," though a little hard, has a good poetic sentiment. There is also something striking in Baade. M. Baade's "*Nuit orageuse sur la Côte de Norwége*," and "*L'Île de Hestmand (Soleil de Minuit.*") Munthe. M. Munthe's "*Paysage d'Hiver*" represents a snow-covered fishing village on the borders of the sea. Nothing could be sadder than the leaden, sombre sky, the wretched huts huddled together, the unpitying snow, the bleak despair of everything in this striking and pathetic landscape.

Dahl. But to turn to a totally different scene, M. Dahl in his "*Trop tard*," which is a landscape and figures, gives us a bright sunny day and flashing green water, all gay and brilliant. A couple of peasants are in a boat, which has just put off from shore, and are laughing at their companion, who has arrived just too late. There is a good deal of *bris* in this picture, and, though it is crude and *voyant* in color, it is amusing. The green reflections of the sunny water under the boat, though a little showy, are well given.

NORWAY.

Askevold. M. Askevold's "*En route pour le Chalet*" represents a great barge laden with cattle, which is pushing off from shore, with another barge farther away. This is well drawn, and spirited in movement and composition, and the cattle are excellent. The sky and distance are scarcely up to the mark of the rest. It is of the Düsseldorf school, and, though a little over-accentuated, shows much talent. "*L'Asgaardried*

Arbo. (*Légende Norwégienne*)" by M. Arbo, illustrates a Norwegian legend that the Asgaardried (a troop of Norsemen on their way to the dwelling of Ases, in the Walhalla) is composed of the dead who have not done sufficient good on earth to deserve heaven, nor sufficient evil to merit hell, and their punishment is to gallop continually through the air to the end of the world. As long as order reigns they are quiet, but whenever there is war, their laughter and the dashing of their arms is heard overhead. M. Arbo in his picture represents a crowd of these wild and visionary horsemen with flashing eyes, that rush through the sky, and he has made a

Lerche. powerful and effective picture. M. Lerche's "*La Réfectoire*" and "*Chronique Scandaleuse*" must also be noted for their cleverness.

Portraits.

Portraits.

Rusten. Patterson. Among the portraits may be mentioned that by M. Rusten, which is clever and photographic, and one, by M. Patterson, of a woman with folded arms seated at a table covered with a red cloth, on which there are flowers. This has considerable originality of treatment and tranquility of character.

Heyerdahl. There is something very peculiar in M. Heyerdahl's "*Adam et Ève chassés du Paradis.*" He has not sought for beauty or charm. The figures are on the contrary ugly and graceless, and the types of form and face low, but he has managed to put a certain savage character into their expression and attitudes as of aborigines, and there is something striking and uncommon in the motive which he has sought to work out. They are not our original parents in the perfection of humanity, but rather naked gypsies passionately rebelling against their decree of expulsion. The idea is certainly novel, but it is not without force. There is another "Adam and Eve"—not in the catalogue, in the Scandanavian section, and therefore I cannot give the name of the painter—which is wholly from another point of view. M. Heyerdahl's is gloomy and rebellious; this is sunny and indolent—a fruit-loving Southern couple in a bower.

SWEDEN.

There was not much very characteristic in the Swedish section, or of any high achievement. An exception must be made, however, to this statement in favor of the striking historical picture by Baron Cederström, representing "*Le Corps de Charles XII porté par ses Officiers à travers la Frontière Norwegiénne* (1718)." This is a serious work, exhibiting a good deal of character and originality. It is winter; the ground is covered with snow; the sad procession winds solemnly down a steep declivity around a projecting turn in the cliff that hangs over the way. The soldiers in blue and drab march sternly on in serried ranks, bearing on a litter the exposed body of the dead king. The group forms the right side of the picture, the left is open country, and a peasant, dragging at his side a dead eagle, stands uncovered and watches the procession as it files along. The character of the heads is earnest and strong, and the whole effective. There is nothing common about it in treatment, composition, or feeling. Baron Cederström.

"*Les Saltimbanques; avant la loi Tallon,*" by M. N. Forsberg, is a distressing episode of human life and heartlessness. It represents a master saltimbanque privately exhibiting his pupils and their dexterity to a debauched looking man, apparently an *impresario*, who is seated and languidly looking on at the exhibition with a cigar in his mouth. Two or three thin children clothed in the tumbler's dress are standing by, waiting their turn, while one is thrown backwards on his hands and feet with his poor little body strained into a curve. There is a great deal of character and truth in this scene. The figures are well drawn and expressive, and altogether, distressing as it is, it shows power. Forsberg.

M. Hagborg's "*L'Attente*" represents a woman with uncovered head, a child in her arms, who is standing on a pier which juts out into the sea. It is fresh in color, well drawn, and has a good deal of nature, sentiment, and unconsciousness. The cool breeze blows her hair and garments, and she stands looking out on the sea in expectation. Hagborg.

M. Hellqvist's "*Marguerite*" is a large picture representing the interior of a Swedish house in which Gretchen is seated with her spinning-wheel. Her figure is rather cold and thin in character, but the still life is well given. The canvas is, however, too large for the subject, which has little dramatic interest, and could better be represented in a far smaller size. Hellqvist.

SWEDEN.

Mlle. Börjesson. Borg et al.

Among the other noteworthy pictures of *genre* were "*Moines jouant à la Boccia*" by Mlle. A. Börjesson, "*L'État d'Innocence*" by M. Borg, and "*Souvenir de la Picardie*" by M. Salmson, "*Genre*" by M. Fagerlin, and the pictures by M. Jernberg.

Wahlberg.

M. Wahlberg sent a number of landscapes, two of which are night scenes. Of these the best are "*Mare sous Bois à Smoland*" and "*Mois de Mai*," which show a deal of talent. They are bright in effect and picturesque. In the moonlight scenes the skies have an extraordinary effect as of colored marbles. There should also be noted, as worthy of praise, the interesting landscapes by M. de Gegerfelt, and M. Skänberg.

Gegerfelt. Skänberg.

PORTUGAL.

PORTUGAL.

Portugal need not detain us a moment. She sent but seventeen pictures and these were of no peculiar importance.

GREECE.

GREECE.

Rallis. Gyzis. Nikiforos. Pantazis. Altamura. Mlle. Génodios.

Greece sent forty-four pictures in oil, among which are to be noted specially the three by M. Rallis, of "*Soubrette, sous Louis XIV, arrosant des Fleurs*," "*Après l'Enterrement—souvenir de Mégare*," and "*Esclave jouant de la Guitare*," and three by M. Gyzis "*Fiançailles en Grèce*," "*Fête d'Arabe*," "*L'Art jouant*." The first of these by M. Gyzis, in particular, has much that is characteristic and pleasing and national. Nikiforos' "*Canaris*" is also to be noted, as are some of the works of M. Périclés Pantazis, and two canvases by M. Altamura, "*L'Incendie de la première Frégate Ottomane à Erissos*" and "*Un Combat naval*," and some portraits by Mlle. Génodios, in aquarelle. Unfortunately neither Xeuxis, Apelles, nor Polygnotos, have contributed anything.

UNITED STATES.

UNITED STATES.

We have no nationality of style. Our artists follow foreign methods.

We have thus far given precedence to the foreign schools of painting, for such is naturally the rule of politeness to strangers, and we now come to the consideration of our own paintings. We regret to say that, with all the talent here exhibited, there is no nationality of style, purpose, or sentiment. We have no American school, distinguished in its characteristics from those of foreign nations. Our artists, with but rare exceptions, have followed in the train of foreign masters, adopted their methods, studied in their studios, and thought after them. We have some from Munich, some from Düsseldorf, some from Paris, some from Rome; and one's first impression on entering our department was that we were in a cosmopolitan society, where many manners and peoples are represented, and where we look in vain for America. Here and there on examination we found a national subject, inspired by the life of our country; but they were few and far between. When I speak of nationality of subject and style, I do not mean that the perpetual Indian—the Monsieur Tonson of our art, the Marquis de Carabas of popular ideas—should reappear. We have already been sufficiently bored by him and all connected with him. But there is nothing in our art which answers to the new life and thought, the freshness and vigor, the refined speculation, the hearty self-reliance, independence, and originality that is seen and felt in our country. No matter what the subject is, a nation should be able to stamp on its work the impress of its own originality, to distinguish itself by national characteristics. It is not, for instance, because the subjects of Emerson's, Longfellow's, and Lowell's poems are drawn from American life that we feel they are truly American poets, or because the works of Alston are illustrations of our own history, that we recognize him as the greatest painter our country ever produced. It is because, whatever be the subject, there is som thing peculiar in the style, character, and thought that we recognize as born and bred out of that which is eminently American. The refinement, the grace, the subtlety, the incisive penetration are different from what is seen in the literature of other nations. Is Hawthorne less Hawthorne because he writes "The Romance of Monte Boni," and wanders through the gardens and amid the ruins of Italy? Can he not throw over Rome the same enchantment of mystery and subtlety that envelops the scenes of early Puritan life in New England? Does it matter whether Longfellow writes of the "Belfry of Bruges" or the "Village Blacksmith" at Cambridge? Is he not equally Longfellow? Are not Mr. James and Mr. Howells as much Americans in Paris and Venice as in Boston? Is not Mr. Mark Twain the same humorist abroad that he is at home? In our literature we have already reached nationality. The peculiar flavor of our life and thought is there exhibited. But in art we are what we were three-quarters of a century ago—essentially imitative; and this is not because we have not originality, talent, even genius, if you will; but we are like pupils that follow the beck of their masters, and dare not trust our own inspirations.

Our artistic sense not up to our originality in other regards.

Alston an exception.

Literature.

Poetry.

Humor.

Undoubtedly what we want is training of the strictest kind. Every youth that can daub a canvas or scratch to-

Need of training.

UNITED STATES. gether a bust is lauded to the skies and told he is a genius. Common people love the common. Uneducated people love the literal and uneducated, and the mass of our people are uneducated in art. To be able to discriminate truly requires knowledge as well as natural feeling. We have the last. We have not the first. The artist is seduced and flattered at first to his injury, and then he is dropped and neglected.

Need of governmental recognition. But how should there be any great national development in art when the nation does nothing to foster it; when we are wanting in national schools, academies, and galleries; when there are no prizes for high achievement, no honors to bestow, no fit recognition of excellence, no proper means of study; when the artist is, to a certain extent, considered a trifler, outside the great current of serious life, the main course of which sets strongly along the great bed of politics and business, while art is but a side pool of dead water for holiday loungers? Out of such elements as this where did art ever flourish? In the best days of Greece the artist was in the front of its civilization. In the *Renaissance* he was a glory and a power, recognized by the nation, honored by the world, and courted by the great. Embassies were confided to him. Honors were poured upon him. When Rubens was selected out of all the world to be sent to England on his embassy, one of the foreign ambassadors, entering his room, found him engaged at his easel. "Ah!" he exclaimed, "your excellence, I see, amuses yourself with painting." "No," answered Rubens, "I amuse myself with diplomacy."

The artist overlooked in the din of politics.

In ancient Greece the artist was in front. And in the *Renaissance*.

Rubens, the ambassador.

Our artists expatriated. In consequence of the present state of things in America the artist, as I have already said—but it will bear repeating—is forced to expatriate himself in order to find the means of study and the development of his powers. We have no great national galleries for study. And when he returns to his country he must rely on private patronage in order to live, and on private collections of pictures for study. And what is that patronage? Is it calculated to foster in him a strong national feeling? Unfortunately, our *connoisseurs* go to Paris for their pictures, as our ladies go there for their dresses. They pay enormous prices for *genre* pictures of mere temporary fashion by distinguished names, while their own countrymen in the next street are treated with neglect and indifference. True, there are exceptions to this rule, but there are always exceptions to all rules. As for the nation, when it has commissions to give, can it be pretended that they are given as they should be; that the ablest of our artists ordinarily obtain them; that a high and educated

No national galleries for study.

Our patronage of foreign art.

To what kind of artists are government commissions awarded?

judgment, founded on knowledge, is exercised in their distribution, and that fair play is given to the artist? UNITED STATES.

I glance at these considerations as accounting for the undoubted want of national character seen at our exhibition in Paris. I think I am safe in saying that this absence of nationality was universally felt by all persons who visited our department, and was commented upon largely. Our painters, for the most part, paint—as they speak,—the languages of the countries where they study, some badly, some well, some even very well, but always with a foreign accent. It is unpleasant to say this, but the truth must be told.

Foreign tone of American pictures.

Landscapes.

In landscape, where one would naturally expect to find many characteristic reports of our country, there were scarcely a dozen American scenes; and there were but few attempts at anything historical, religious, powerful, or of the highest class of subject. The great proportion of the pictures were of *genre* subjects, with a considerable number of landscapes of foreign countries, and a few portraits.

Limited range of subjects.

Dana.

Mr. Dana, to whom a third-class medal was awarded, exhibited three pictures "*La Plage de Dinard*," "Solitude," and "A Gale of Wind." All these pictures are strong and emphatic, and executed with vigor and freedom. The gale of wind on the shore with a group of men, horses, and carts, hurrying before a rising storm, is spiritedly rendered and good in color. The "Shore at Dinard," with men gathering sea-weed, is also clever. But the most important of his pictures is "Solitude," which is a view of mid-ocean at night, with heavy warring blue billows, and a broken stormy sky through which the struggling moon casts its flash upon the dark and turbulent waters; not a sail or boat or vestige of humanity is there. It is the lonely, desolate, hungry solitude of ocean. There is a great deal of simple strong feeling in this dreary scene, and it is rendered with masterly and poetic sensibility.

Bridgman.

On the opposite wall hung a striking picture, by Mr. Bridgman, representing the "Funeral of a Mummy." The center of the composition is occupied by a barge on which is carried a catafalque bearing a mummy case, at the side of which are figures of mourners. In the prow of the barge is an altar with priests and musicians, and at the stern a group of women lamenting. The barge is towed by a boat with rowers, and another barge beyond heads the procession. These are seen dark against a clear sunset sky and rocky hills on which the red reflection of the light is

UNITED STATES. cast, glowing. This was one of the most serious and important pictures in the American section, and obtained for its author a medal of the second class. It is carefully painted with much study in all its details. The composition is good and the sentiment well felt. Particularly are to be commended the clear translucent sky, the sun-tinged hills, and the pure reflections of the water. It is entirely of the school of M. Gérôme. Interesting and full of merit as it is one cannot but help wishing that it had more of Mr. Bridgman's own individuality and less of M. Gérôme's. When Mr. Bridgman shall have emancipated himself completely from the over-influence of his master, there is evidence in this picture that he has ability to achieve even more admirable results. The only fault that we find in it is that, spirited and clever as it is, it has not yet broken free from the trammels of its school.

Bridgman.

Shirlaw. Mr. W. Shirlaw's "Sheep Shearing in Bavaria" is a clever picture of the Munich school representing the interior of a barn with men and women shearing sheep. The execution is entirely of the character of the school in which he has studied and has its merits and its deficiencies. The faces are well studied, and there is considerable vigor of touch and brush work, but the composition is confused, and there is a little too much attempt at *bravura* of style, without the previous study to justify it.

Lafarge. Mr. Lafarge's "Valley of Paradise at Newport" is somewhat in the style of some of the English landscapes. It represents a long stretch of simple unaccentuated plain reaching out to the distant and dimly seen sea. The gradations are very delicately rendered, and the work is simple, almost *naïve*, and without trickery or pretence of execution. With a lower horizon it would be more effective, for there is scarcely interest enough to sustain the long perspective of grassy plain, but the picture is pleasing and honestly rendered, and has much that is attractive.

Hamilton. Mr. Hamilton's "*Cerise*" as mere *technique* is eminently clever—one of the cleverest in all this section. It is of the French school of execution, and of the worst French school in sentiment. It is irredeemably vulgar. It represents a *cocotte* lolling back in her chair, with her legs exposed, laughing with a dreadful leer, showing her teeth and playing with a green parrot. On the floor at her feet lies a copy of the "*Journal pour rire*," admirably imitated with a half-colored caricature, and champagne bottles. There was nothing in the whole Exhibition so daringly low and vulgar as this, and which ventured so far in innuendo. It is to be hoped that the talent displayed in this picture will be for the future devoted to better purpose.

Vedder.

Mr. Vedder sent three pictures. "The Ancient Madonna" representing a lady looking at an early Italian panel, which is carefully finished, rich in color, and pleasing. "Young Marsyas" is represented seated on the ground, which is covered with snow, and playing his pipes, while a group of rabbits is gathered round him and listening.* This picture is idyllic in sentiment and agreeably composed, but as yet it is only finished in parts and deserves to be carefully worked out. His third picture, of the "Cumæan Sibyl," is original in conception and striking in character. The Sibyl, a brown wild figure of a gypsy character, with her hair and garments blown by the wind is seen striding across the campagna clasping her book to her breast. A fire burns behind her, the smoke of which streams across the picture, and hills with snow peaks stretch off in the distance, flecked with spits of sunshine and rising into the sky, that is strewn with massive clouds.

Bacon.

Mr. Bacon's "Land! Land!" represents a scene on board a steamer when land is descried, and the passengers, among whom is a pretty girl, are starting up to catch a glimpse of it. The incidents are well given, and the scene is natural. It is somewhat of the character of subject and execution of the English pictures of the same class.

Winslow Homer.

Among the few pictures representing American life and character, were those of Mr. Winslow Homer, which from this very circumstance had an attraction. They were "The Country School House," "The Visit of the Old Mistress," "Snapping the Whip," and "Sunday Morning in Virginia." The last represents a group of little negroes reading the bible. "Snapping the Whip" is a game of school boys on the green. The other titles explain themselves. These are all small, and though there is a certain amount of character, they have much to be desired in execution.

Church.

Mr. Church's two pictures, "The Parthenon" and "Morning in the Tropics," are not good specimens of his talent, and one cannot but regret that he should not have been better represented. Those who remember his striking representations of "Niagara" and of the "Northern Seas" will be disappointed. His "Morning in the Tropics" is luxuriant but feeble in its idealism, and the "Parthenon" some-

*An admirable wood engraving of this picture may be found in "Scribner's Magazine" for June, 1879, which gives the true quality and feeling of this picture, and is in itself an ample answer to the criticism on it in "*L'Art.*"

UNITED STATES. what dry and thin. Neither has the vigor that we should expect from Mr. Church's brush.

Richards. Mr. W. T. Richards's landscapes were "In the Woods," "The Forest," and "Spring." The first shows talent and is carefully studied, with almost painful care in all its details. It has a good deal of merit, but the feeling as well as the execution is a little dry and mechanical.

Johnson. Mr. Johnson's "Corn-Shucking" has something spirited and is fresh in treatment. It is an American scene and represents long lines of laborers seated in a field and husking corn.

Graham. Mr. Graham's "View in a Cemetery in California" has a good deal of merit. It is unpretending in character and has good work in it.

Weir. Mr. Weir's "Forging the Shaft" has a good deal of force and character and is cleverly rendered.

The "Scene on the Hudson" is a very clever study after the French school. Gray shelving rocks topped with large trees, with a blue sky and white clouds, rise over a pool of water at their feet. The composition is good, and there is spirit in the execution. Mr. Jones's "Return of the Cows" is also a careful study from nature of a landscape in Bretagne with considerable vigor and truth. Mr. C. C. Colman's "Ancient and Modern Venice," representing a black steamer on the lagunes against a dim misty view of Venice, is pleasing in sentiment and tone, and his "Panel Decorated with Flowers" very graceful in composition and decorative in color. The "Entrance to Venice," by Mr. Bunce, is in imitation of the manner of Turner, the color thickly laid on and smoothed over as with a palette knife. It represents fishing boats with colored sails on a still sea against a misty sky, and though a little vague and undecided in touch is sunny and pleasant in tone. Mr. W. Eaton's "Harvesters in Repose" is a reminiscence in style and intention of Jules Breton, and agreeable in composition and sentiment. The field is half reaped, a man and woman are under a haystack, and the mother is nursing her child. Mr. F. D. Williams's "*La Marne*" is a French landscape by a clever student in the manner of his master. Mr. E. M. Ward's "Venetian Water Carriers" is carefully studied and shows talent. It is a little too much, however, on the same plane and in the same tone, and the absence of shadows weakens its effect. His "*Sabotier*" also has merit. Mr. Yewell also sent some careful and picturesque characteristic Oriental scenes, representing the "Mosque of Kait-Bey" and the "Carpet Bazaar at Cairo," very faithfully executed. Mr. Quartley's

Jones. Colman. Bunce. Eaton. Williams. Ward. Yewell. Quartley.

"Morning Effect in the Port of New York" is a vigorous rendering of the actual scene. Mr. Tiffany's "Duane Street in New York" represents a group of old houses, shops, and booths of the previous century, and is a very clever study, executed with vigor and feeling. UNITED STATES. Tiffany.

Mr. Wylie's "*Mort d'un Chef Vendéen*" is of a higher grade of subject, and has strong character and expression, the promise of which unfortunately has been cut off by the recent death of the artist. Wylie.

Mr. Loomis's "*Un Délit de Chasse en 1500*" is also clever, but has more happy reminiscences than originality. Mr. Hovenden's "Interior in Brittany in 1793" is spirited, well drawn, and carefully painted. It represents an old workman seated on a table, surrounded by his family, and examining a sword and glancing down along the edge of the blade to see if it is sharp and even. There is a good deal of character in his head and action. Mr. Kensett's "White Mountains" is not a good specimen of his work, and looked poor and thin on these walls. Mr. Howland's "*Le Gué dans la Vallée*" is vague and obliterated, and somewhat of a reminiscence of Corot's manner. Mr. McEntee's "Autumn Idyll" and "The Fall of the Leaves" are slight and sketchy, but pleasing, and give the sentiment of this season. "A Cat," by Mr. G. B. Butler, is remarkably well painted and true to nature. Mr. Beckwith's "Falconer" is bright and good in color, and recalls a similar subject by Couture. "Hasheesh Smokers," by Mr. E. Benson, is an Eastern room with great arches and pillars, misty with blue smoke, through which a shaft of light piercing the roof is cast upon the floor, while the hasheesh smokers in picturesque costume are lying about or seated cross-legged in groups. The dim smoky atmosphere and the Oriental costume and dreamy luxury of the scene are well given. Mr. S. Colman's "Train of Emigrants crossing a Torrent" is a bit of Western life and scenery which is interesting in subject and characteristic, but a little monotonous in color and hard in execution. Mr. Vinton's "*Fête d'un Paysan Breton*" is fresh in color, and though sketchy, is spirited; and Mr. Wilmath's "Ingratitude" is clever. Among other pictures must also be specially noted Mr. S. R. Gifford's "San Giorgio at Venice;" "My Daily Visitor" and "A Page," by Mr. Shade, which are clever and careful; "*Aux Courses*," by Mr. E. L. Henry, representing a drag before an old gable-roofed country house in England; Mr. R. S. Gifford's "New England Cedars"; Mr. Inness's "St. Peter's in Rome," in which the sky is particularly good; and "The Passing Show," by Mr. J. B. Brown. Loomis. Hovenden. Kensett. Howland. McEntee. Butler. Beckwith. Benson. Colman. Vinton. Wilmath. S. R. Gifford. Shade. Henry. R. S. Gifford. Inness. Brown.

UNITED STATES. This last has a good deal of humor and expression. It represents a row of boys looking out of the picture at something passing which excites their curiosity and merriment. The action and expression of the different faces is good, but they all seem studies from the same boy, which is to be regretted. We must not omit also to mention a clever and conscientious landscape of "The Beach at Villiers," by Mr. Boit.

Brown.

Boit.

Portraits.

Portraits.

Healy. Porter. May. Vinton. Le Clear. Schonborn. Sargent.

There were a dozen portraits, among which are to be noted Mr. Healy's "Lord Lyons," which may rank among his best works, a striking portrait of a lady, by Mr. Porter, and Mr. May's clever head of "General Tevis," and a vigorous head by Mr. Vinton, a portrait of "Mr. Parke Godwin," by Mr. T. LeClear, a portrait by Mr. Shonborn, and a portrait by Mr. Sargent, showing much promise.

Aquarelles.

Aquarelles.

Abbey. Robbins. Tiffany. Greenough. Richards.

Among the water colors and drawings in black and white may be mentioned a very clever *aquarelle* by Mr. Abbey, of a "*Bureau des Diligences*," which is gray and subdued in tone, and has a good deal of quaintness and character. The figure of the woman in black, with a large straw bonnet and brown shawl, is admirable. The "Farm-house in New England," by Mr. H. W. Robbins, is a capital rendering of a homely country house. Mr. Tiffany's two aquarelles are strong and clever, particularly that of the "Steps of the Cathedral of St. Melaire on Market-day at Morlaix." The crayon portrait, by Mr. Greenough, is also to be noted as drawn with care and feeling. The "Shore at Connecticut," by Mr. Richards, in *aquarelle*, is also a clever work.

SCULPTURE.

FRANCE.

SCULPTURE. FRANCE.

Having concluded all that I have to say about the paintings, the remaining countries having sent nothing which demands any special consideration, I therefore pass to the consideration of sculpture; and in this department of the fine arts, the palm is to be given to France. Faint as the reflex is of the great schools of ancient sculpture, there is still a striving here after some at least of their qualities. Their essays are more serious, on the whole, than those of other countries; their subjects less corrupted by the sentiment of *genre;*

there is often careful modeling from nature, and although there are no works which are great, there are many respectable—some, indeed, which are excellent. It must be confessed, however, that there is a want of dignity and high purpose almost everywhere visible, as well in France as in Italy and other countries. Attitudinizing, affectation, and excess of action are but too commonly confounded with grace and power, and there is a general absence of that repose which is the great quality of all the best work of the ancients. On the other hand, there is careful study of the model, and often a good deal of *finesse* of execution. The *technique* is good, as a rule. It is the higher excellences which are lacking.

Careful modeling, but want of high purpose.

Excess of action, want of repose.

Good *technique*.

Sculpture in the highest sense is a serious art, and demands simplicity, concentration, and style. It is also a limited art, and abides in strict domains. It disdains the merely picturesque; it is degraded by the contact of *genre*. The charms of color, the illusions of life are denied to it. Its province is restricted to form, and its dealings should be with the ideal. No imitations of the common and the actual, however well done, will satisfy its requisitions; no mere copying of the model will suffice; no mere excellences of execution will compensate for the want of ideas. It cannot pass beyond its limits without a loss of character. It must accept its restrictions, and by its dignity, its grace, its simplicity, its power, justify its right to exist. The least touch of affectation or conscious posing, the least corruption of sentiment, debases it. With its feet planted on the real, it must lift its head above the common into the ideal. Far more restricted than painting in its means, in its demands it is higher, and what is often charming on the canvas would be intolerable in the marble. Its aspect is calm and serious; it is forbidden it to laugh, and almost even to smile. Its spirit is tragical and not comical. It has to do with character, not anecdote. It must bear itself with dignity, or it becomes contemptible. Its sentiment must be pure, its feeling deep, and its boundaries are power on the one side, grace and beauty on the other. This, at least, is sculpture in its highest sense. In our own day it has been forced to other service, and often to a humble sphere, but always with a loss of character. It really has nothing to do with the trivial things of common life, and when it enters the field of *genre* it abdicates its highest office, and must necessarily certainly fall below painting.

Domain of sculpture.

More restricted than painting.

Triviality and *genre* inadmissible.

In the highest class of sculpture there was scarcely an attempt in the Paris Exposition. There was not one single

Absence of high class sculpture.

FRANCE.

work of a great purpose, or a great subject, not one salient statue embodying a grand idea, and showing the high water mark of its powers. But again there were, especially in the French department, several which are sincere, earnest, clever, and pleasing.

Attitudinizing.

Excess of action.

The most serious fault to be found with French sculpture is its almost invariable attitudinizing, consciousness, and excess of action. It wants repose, quiet. It is contrived and not spontaneous. It attempts to impress by forced gesticulation and contortion, and endeavors to compensate for intensity by exaggeration, for grace by affectation. There is almost always a little too much. It cannot be calm and serious, and self-contained. It seeks to surprise, demands admiration, insists too strongly, poses, and constantly oversteps the modesty of nature. In moments of passion it tears its passion to rags. It will not be quiet and simple but fatigues us by overstatement. Its very grace is tormented, its attitudes sought and strained.

Repetition of the model.

In the next place, it lacks what is an essential requisite of a great work of sculpture—style. It repeats too faithfully the model and cannot free itself from the individual. In its imitations the modeling is often admirable, but one feels that it is the model which has ruled the artist. It is common to suppose that, given a good model and a good imitation of it, the result will be necessarily nature; but this is a great mistake. Nature is wider and embraces more than all the models that live. Nature is not "Lisette" nor "Antoine," however handsome and graceful they may be, but the Protean secret that is hidden unembodied anywhere in perfection and glances through all the possible forms of all possible Lisettes and Antoines, and it is this that the artist is to seek and to find, taking what is in harmony with his dominant idea, what comes fitly in to aid him in his expression, what rhymes and coalesces and unifies with his thought. In this way he arrives at style, as the great sculptors of Greece did. Their work was no copy of any particular model, but a re-creation out of the knowledge derived from numberless models and from a constant study of life in all its forms. In the "Venus" of Milo, in the "Theseus," there is style, there is no imitation of any particular person. The truth is that the model to the sculptor should be his dictionary or grammar at most. It will help him in his ignorance and keep him correct in his uses of form, but it will, if he be not careful, strangle his imagination, and seduce him out of the ideal and true, into the particular and accidental. It will not do to copy

Greek sculpture, not copies but re-creations.

FRANCE.

any *portefaix*, however strong, and call him "Hercules" or any gentleman and call him "Apollo," or any *gamin* from the street and label him "David," nor will any amount of merely careful study of any individual result in an embodyment of an idea or in a noble style. There is in modern sculpture altogether too much of this. What strikes one in the antique work is a certain scientific standard of form and temperament and established rule of proportions, a definite and decided general character independent of individual peculiarities and accidents of the model; and this is precisely what we lack in modern sculpture—a clear and educated style, in place of mannerism. Style is of course a difficult thing to define but not difficult to feel when it is reached. For instance, in M. Jules Breton's "*Glaneuse*," though it is a painting, one feels a certain sentiment of nobility and breadth of character that reproduces a feeling akin to that of Greek sculpture, and removed from all sense of mere *genre*, while in the statue of "*La Rosée*," by M. Captier, which, for delicate workmanship and careful imitation of the model, is one of the most admirable of all the French works here exhibited, there is a total want of style. It is the model and an exceedingly good one, but it is nothing more than a capital study.

Scientific standard in the antique work.

Style.

There is still another particular in which the French school is very careless and deficient, and that is in its draperies. Not only are they not well composed, but they are often quite without organization and study—mere masses without distinction of form and anatomy, which might pass in a picture, but which are quite unsatisfactory in marble. It is to the study of the nude that they have given their best efforts. Not that one would desire the kind of imitative work in stuffs and textures which forms the characteristic feature of the Milanese school, but there is a happy mean which neither holds.

Careless draperies.

Let us now leave these general considerations and proceed to particulars.

In the three halls devoted to French sculpture, there were no less that 389 works, executed by 189 sculptors. It will, therefore, plainly be impossible to do more than glance at a few of the principal ones, for the limits of this paper are necessarily too restricted to do more. This large number of works and of sculptors plainly indicates, however, the warm interest there is in France in this branch of art, and the large patronage that is given. Italy had only 180 works of 116 sculptors. One of the most important works in the

French halls of sculpture.

FRANCE.

Dubois.

French section was by M. Paul Dubois, who enjoys in France a high reputation, both as a painter and a sculptor. It was the monument to "General de Lamoricière," destined for the cathedral of Nantes. This represents the dead hero lying extended on a catafalque under a canopy, at the four corners of which are seated figures representing "Military Courage," "Charity," "Faith," and "Meditation"—a queer combination, reminding us a little of the figures in "The Groves of Blarney."* The architectural parts are designed by M. L. F. P. Boitte. The figures are by M. P. Dubois. This is a serious work, showing talent and deserving of much praise, but it cannot be said to be particularly original in conception or careful in treatment. The statues are boldly modeled but quite unfinished, and, indeed, generally very sketchy, and they lack any high motive and style. "Charity," a half-draped figure holding two nude infants in her arms, is well composed and tender in sentiment, and is the happiest of the four in conception. But it is not Charity. It has nothing ideal in its character. It is a Breton peasant with her two children, and the coarse drapery which envelops her lower limbs is rustic, and altogether too careless and unfinished. It would, indeed, seem as if the artist had aimed at carelessness of treatment and surface, for the figure is really only a large and clever sketch. "Military Courage," which is a figure in helmet and armor, is too plainly a reminiscence of the "Lorenzo de Medici" by Michel Angelo called "*Il Penseroso.*" "Meditation" is represented by an old man, nude to the waste, leaning on a book. This, again, has nothing ideal in its character. It is cleverly composed, has a good deal of expression, and is well modeled, but it is an academic study of the model, and is not spontaneous in pose. It is any old man. The least good of all is "Faith." These figures are none of them in the pure school of sculpture. Their inspiration and their execution is rather pictorial than sculptural.

Chapu.

M. Chapu's "*Jeanne d'Arc à Domremy*" represents her in her laced corsage and peasant dress, kneeling, with her hands stretched down and clasped at her knees. There is great feeling in this figure. The expression of the head and the modeling of the arms are admirable. There is seriousness, there is character, there is sentiment. The draperies and the lower part of the figure leave much to be desired, but the earnestness and unaffectedness of the work are

*"All heathen gods
And nymphs so fair;
Bold Neptune, Cæsar,
And Nebuchadnezzar,
All standing naked
In the open air!"

greatly to be praised. M. Chapu's statue of "De Berryer" is by no means so happy, either in conception or in execution. The gesture is theatric, the robes not well disposed. He has one hand on his heart, and the other thrown out in declamation. The allegorical figures of "Eloquence" and "Fidelity," which accompany it, are not worthy of his talent. They are common in their pose, coarse in their execution, and strangely incorrect in their anatomy. The figures for the monument to Schneider are better conceived and executed; the female figure, seated on the plinth of the monument, is pointing the attention of a boy beside her to the statue above. Both are in the costume of to-day, as worn by the operatives and women of the place and the foundry. The boy is nude to his waist, and his feet are in *sabots*. The woman is in a simple peasant's dress. Here there is concentration and simplicity, and the work is eminently deserving of praise. Chapu.

M. Mercié's "David" is a clever statue, which had a great success when first exhibited and justifies his reputation. It was his first and perhaps is his best work. It is a bronze figure of a nude youth, with his head swathed in a handkerchief, who is in the act of sheathing his sword after killing Goliath. The head of the giant is on the base, and one foot is placed on it. The pose has something a little theatric (which we must always expect in French sculpture), but there is spirit and originality in the design and careful study in the workmanship. It was decidedly one of the best figures in the section. We must, however, confess that the *gamin* idea of David, which seems to prevail everywhere in France, is not only far from satisfactory in itself or true to history, but has been utterly worn-out by repetition. How many Davids were in this Exposition, and not one who was not a *gamin!* "*Gloria Victis*," which is a later and far more ambitious work, is full of flutter, display, and excess of action, and is deficient in sobriety, simplicity, and that self-restraint which are essential to a great work in sculpture. There is talent, undoubtedly, but not happily directed. Mercié.

M. Falguière sent two works, "*Tarcisius, Martyr Chrétien*," and "*Un Vainqueur aux Combats de Coqs*." Both these statues are very clever. Tarcisius is a youthful figure, full of sentiment and feeling in face and attitude. The "*Vainqueur aux Combats de Coqs*" is a naked youth, running along with cocks on his bent right arm, and with his left arm extended, snapping his fingers. It is light in figure and spirited in action, but it has nothing in common with the Greek spirit. Falguière

FRANCE.

Vauthier. M. Moreau Vauthier sent eight works. His "*Petit Buveur*" is simple, natural, and without affectation. It represents a boy kneeling and filling his cap at a fountain to drink. The theme is not new, but it is agreeably rendered.

Ding. There was another, "*Enfant à la Source*," in bronze, by M. Ding, which was one of the simplest and best composed statues in the whole Exhibition. The modeling is good, the action natural and without affectation, and the composition admirable. It has a good deal of the antique spirit in it.

De Vasselot. Another figure, which is attractive for its simplicity and unconsciousness, is the "Chloe," by M. Marquet de Vasselot. It is a young girl, quite nude, seated and looking down sideways, while she clasps one knee, which is raised. It is quite pure in sentiment and removed from the feeling of the model, and the action is graceful. It is not (as so many statues here are) consciously nude, nor does it know we are looking at her, and in the present state of art this is a rare and exceptional quality.

Delaplanche. M. E. Delaplanche sent six works. His "*Sainte Agnès*" is charming in sentiment and tender in feeling. The girl saint holds a lamb in her crossed arms pressed against a palm branch to her breast. The composition is pleasing, and there is great sweetness of character, refinement, and simplicity. The least good part of the statue is the drapery, which is a little clumsy. "*Éducation Maternelle*," by this sculptor, is also simple and good in action, save that the head of the mother seems to turn the wrong way. He also sent "*La Musique*," *statue, bronze argenté*, representing a woman playing on a violin. The upper part of this statue is expressive, but the execution is very incomplete, and the draperies rude. His "*Le Message d'Amour*" is well modeled, but the sentiment is *fade* and insipid, and the attitude conscious. It represents a woman quite nude (a model) holding a dove with both hands up to her ear.

Baujault. M. Baujault's "*Le Premier Miroir*," in marble, is a thin girl, at the half-finished stage of puberty, looking down in the water and making her toilet. The age is not a specially pleasing one, and all the characteristics of it are strongly dwelt upon. In pose it is rather stiff and over-smooth in surface, and what can be more empty and worn-out than such a theme. Still it had a success when first exhibited at the *Salon*. Of late the unperfected forms of adolescence have been very much repeated in French statuary, and particularly by the Taenger school, who have affected somewhat the dry, lean manner of Donatello and the early Tuscan school, as the English painters have the forms of Carpaccio and Botticelli. But we have had quite enough of this.

M. Aizelin's "*Orphée descendant aux Enfers*," though it is not Orpheus, is a quiet statue, well modeled and without exaggeration, and has something almost antique in its intention. M. Albert-Lefeuvre's "*Jeanne d'Arc, Enfant, entend 'ses Voix'*" has much sentiment and speciality of thought. Jeanne is listening, intently listening, to the airy voices in the void, forgetful of all else, and this expression and character is well rendered. M. Allar's "*Enfant des Abruzzes*," a figure of a boy lifting a jar, is also clever. M. Hiolle's "*Arion*" is well composed, and though it is a little frigid in sentiment, has much merit, and is in a good school. M. Hoursolle's "*Cette Âge est sans Pitié*" is modeled with great care, and is an admirable study from nature. It is a nude boy lying on his back, and holding up in his right hand a bird and with the other he has an instrument to torture him. Mr. Becquet's "*Ismael*" is also a nude boy on his back, with his mouth open and his eyes closed and arms thrown back, while beside him is his empty flask. This is well modeled, but contorted in pose. M. Lafrance's "*St. Jean*" is a queer lean boy, with a drum-like belly, holding up both his hands, intentionally awkward, and apparently screaming. This shows a determination at all cost to be original, but one would be sorry to have such an idea of St. John. M. Montagne's "*Mercure s'apprête à trancher la Tête d'Argus*" has considerable merit in its composition, but is plainly a reminiscence of Thorwaldsen's treatment of the same subject. M. Guglielmo's "*Un Suivant de Bacchus*," which represents a Faun dancing, is a clever and spirited bronze, with much animation of movement—perhaps a little too much. "*La Jeunesse d'Aristote*," by M. Degeorge, is clever in composition, simple in its attitude, and well treated. It represents a young Greek leaning back in a chair, cross-legged, with his head propped against his hand, and holding in his lap a scroll. Among other statues to be noted are "Mercury," by M. Delorme; "*Jeune Faune jouant avec un Chevreau*," by M. Barthélemy; "*Méléagre*," by M. Beylard; "*Rêverie d'Enfant*," by M. Chabrié; and "*Le Bohémien à la Source*," by M. A. Ross, which has a good deal of cleverness; "*L'Amour Piqué*," by M. Idrac, which, though excessive in action and not very happy in theme, indicates talent.

FRANCE. Aizelin. Albert-Lefeuvre. Allar. Hiolle. Hoursolle. Becquet. Lafrance. Montagne. Guglielmo. Degeorge. Delorme. Barthélemy. Beylard *et al.*

M. Schœnewerk sent four statues: "*La Jeune Tarentine*," "*Jeune Fille à la Fontaine*," "*Hésitation*," and "*Mime Dompteur*." The first illustrates these lines of Chénier:

Schœnewerk.

> "Elle a vécu, myrto, la jeune Tarentine!
> Son beau corps a roulé sous la vague marine"—

FRANCE. and is simply a nude woman, lying in an extremely contorted attitude, her hips forming the highest point of the statue, while the head on one side and the legs on the other are thrown down in a steep slope. The attitude is painful, if possible, and the sentiment cold, and the idea, if there be any idea beyond that of a naked body, quite unexpressed. "*La Jeune Fille à la Fontaine*" is far more pleasing in every way. It is a nude figure, with both legs stiffly together, who is bending forward to fill a cup at a stone fountain. It is well modeled and has a certain grace, but it is the movement of a woman who has not been used to be without her clothes, and feels her nakedness. "*Hésitation*" is the old theme of a nude female figure dipping her foot into a Schœnewerk. stream. Whatever merits these works of M. Schœnewerk may have—and they certainly have merits of technical execution—they cannot be considered as very original in subject. Of some higher character and quality is the "*Mime Dompteur*," which represents a mime taming a leopard, and is very clever and spirited, and alone deserves the medal he received.

This overdoing of every action, which is so prevalent in France, finds its exponent in a remarkable degree in the Captier. "Timon of Athens" and "Mucius Scævola" of M. Captier. There is no common sense in them. No pretense to represent the possible thing. Every muscle is strained, the brows are knitted, the toes clenched, and in a word the whole action is extravagantly contorted and over-emphasized and Cambos. exaggerated. "*La Femme Adultère*," by M. Cambos, sins also by this excess of action, though by no means to the same extent; the statue is, however, clever, and specially to be commended for its draperies. The same may be said Chatrousse. of "*Les Crimes de la Guerre*," by M. Chatrousse, which is essentially pictorial and not sculptural either in subject or in treatment, and as well as of *Ève après le Péché*," by M. Delaplanche. Amy. Delaplanche, and "*Le Remords*," by M. Amy, in which the action is strained and the passion external. It is impossible to produce the effect of power and intensity by this means. No matter even whether a pose is natural, it must also seem natural, nay to a certain extent even necessary, but never sought. Over-expression and over-statement always foil their own purpose.

Cabet. "1871," by M. Cabet, is a draped seated figure, half veiled, bent over, and leaning on her hand. Here much more care than is common in French sculpture is paid to the disposition and development of the draperies; and the intention of the figure, which is mourning over the sorrows of that year, is serious and good. It does not quite reach the high mark aimed at, but the aim is good and the work good. FRANCE.

Two painters by profession, M. Gustave Doré and M. Gérôme, exposed—the first an elaborate vase and the other a colored figure of a gladiator. These are both essentially pictorial, and not sculpturesque. M. Doré's vase, or rather gigantic flask, is encrusted over with nude figures in every variety of attitude, male and female cupids, nymphs, and Venuses, all in very high relief, indeed almost and often quite relieved from the ground. There is a great deal of device-work on this, and it shows great facility of invention; but it is purely decorative in character and has a confused effect as a whole. Mr. Gérôme's "Gladiators" is a group of clumsy figures, so overcharged with armor, helmets, leggings, and accouterments of the arena, that little else than these is to be seen. The action is theatric and the proportions and composition unsatisfactory. They might stand very well for a group in a picture of a Roman arena, with all the embellishment of color and material, but as sculpture it is a failure. Why is the principal figure cased in chain-mail? Doré. Gérôme.

M. Guillaume's three works, "*St. Louis*" in terra cotta and his two terminal figures of "Anacreon" with Cupid in his arms, and "Sappho," are anything but happy illustrations of his talent. Neither the conception nor the modeling either of figure or draperies can be commended. His "*Mariage Romain*" is a work of higher character. Two figures, entirely draped, are seated holding each other's hands and waiting for the priestly benediction. There is gravity and dignity here, and though the modeling is not what one would wish, yet the subject is serious and the conception simple and impressive. His "Orpheus" shows a lack of high ideal power, and has a touch of sentimentalism in expression and of the model in execution. Guillaume.

"*Trossulus, Petit Maître de la Décadence Romaine*," by M. Eude, with a little dog under his arm, is spirited and has humor of character, and so has "*Un Secret d'en Haut*," by M. H. Moulin, which represents Hermes with his caduceus whispering into the ear of Priapus (a terminal figure) some scandalous jest or anecdote. This is indeed carrying sculpture out of its proper province. Both of these works are essentially French, and Trossulus and Hermes both Frenchmen of the Directory period. They have the affected and fantastic manner that then was in vogue, and Mercury handles his caduceus as if he understood "the fine conduct of a dandled cane." But worse than this is the low Eude. Moulin.

FRANCE.

innuendo of this group, which is thoroughly unfit for the dignity of marble.

Mad Bertaux.

Madame Bertaux sent a "*Jeune Fille au Bain.*" As for the most part nobody is naked now unless one goes to the bath, we have a constant run upon this subject, and whenever an artist wishes to represent the nude, and has no special inspiration we are sure to have either "Venus with a Cupid," an "Eve," or "a woman at the bath," coming out, going in, dipping her foot or her hand into the water, preparing for it, afraid of it, or looking at herself reflected in it—all these studies may be classed together as studies of the nude, and commonplace in conception, and with little that is original or interesting. There are, of course, a number here; there always are everywhere. Madame Bertaux, however, has struck a theme which is a little out of the common. Her "*Jeune Fille*" is half lying down with her legs gathered up under her and straining her head over her shoulder to see some queer animal that is crawling on her back, and to this is appended in illustration these lines of Victor Hugo:

"Elle est là, sous la feuillée,
Éveillée
Au moindre bruit de malheur,
Et rouge, pour une mouche
Qui la touche,
Comme une grenade en fleur." ("*Les Orientales.*")

Nothing can be more French than these lines, but they seem rather to point to a *genre* picture with color, than to a treatment in marble.

Noël.

The large group of "Romeo and Juliet," by M. T. P Noël represents Romeo stretched out stiff and dead, and Juliet kneeling with her head down to his, and naked to the waist. This subject is not very happily treated, and even if it were, such dimensions are altogether disproportionate to it. What might be striking in a small picture becomes empty in a large group in marble. The composition seen from some points of view, and particularly from behind Juliet, is unfortunate. M. Croisy has also given us in life size the incident of "*Paul Malatesta et Françoise de Rimini,*" in respect of which the same remarks might be made. It is not a subject for sculpture, save, perhaps, in small dimensions, and it is more fitted for painting.

Croisy.

Among other works which must be noted for their merit are the "*Poëte,*" by M. Lanson, and the "Dead Christ," by M. de Vasselot.

Lanson.
Vasselot.

Two colossal works also demand attention: "The Republic," by M. Clésinger, which is placed in the open air and

Clésinger.

was inaugurated after the opening of the exhibition with august ceremonies, is a figure seated on a square block, clad in breastplate and helmet, with flowing draperies falling from the shoulders and covering the legs, and resting the left hand upon a tablet, on which is inscribed "*République Francaise—Constitution, 25 Ferrier,* 1875," while the right hand, extended to the knee, holds straight up a sword. Clésinger. There is nothing either new or striking in this figure. Its proportions are unfortunate. The head is too large, the figure short and stumpy, and there is a want of dignity and spirit as well as height of stature. The composition and arrangement of draperies is not happy, and the total effect is unsatisfactory.

Another colossal work is the head of "Liberty," by M. Bartholdi. Bartholdi, which was exhibited in the gardens. This is the head of the figure which it is proposed to place, when completed, in the harbor of New York, as a pharos, symbolizing Liberty enlightening the world. Of course a head of such colossal proportions is seen to disadvantage without its proper height, but seen as it is now placed, it seemed rather empty of character and of modeling. It had the stereotyped frown of the academy. The hair, too, was scarcely expressed at all, except as one rounded mass, and, in a word, it left much to be desired. In another part of the exhibition the entire figure is shown in fairly large proportions, so that one can judge of it in the whole as a composition. The straightly thrust up arm is not agreeable, and the action of the figure is strained and theatrical. In so colossal a statue one must not seek for charms of detail. It is the total mass only which will impress, and therefore it is of greatest necessity that the silhouette on all sides should be harmonious and well composed. If this fails, all fails, and here it is precisely that the figure does not answer what one could wish. Whether this figure, made as it is intended, will be solid enough to resist the force of a violent gale when finally placed is a question upon which I do not enter, but it is one which demands most serious consideration.

Among the figures and groups of animals and men, there Cain are some which are striking, and especially are to be commended those of M. Cain, representing a lion and lioness disputing for a wild boar, and a combat of tigers, which show great vigor and mastery. M. Mène also sent a number, Mène. which exhibit his well-known cleverness in the treatment of animals, and there are colossal figures in the gardens. The

FRANCE. Rouillard. Fremiet. Jacquemait.

"Ox," by M. Cain, the "Horse," by M. Rouillard, the "Elephant," by M. Fremiet, and the "Rhinoceros," by M. Jacquemait.

Portrait-statues.

There was also a considerable number of portraits, statues, and busts, many of which are clever. The only question with many of them is whether they do not show too strong a determination on the part of the artist to be clever at all hazards, and to insist on your notice. The busts are generally free in their execution and spirited; so free that they are often intentionally and pretentiously careless of detail and careful study, and seek only to produce an effect—so spirited at times that they run into excess of action and expression. Among those which are specially to be noted are, a bust in terra cotta by M. Doublemard of "*M. Coquelin, Cadet de la Comédie Française, dans le Rôle de Thomas Diafoirus dans 'Le Malade Imaginaire',*" which is spirited and natural; "*Le Baron Zangiacomi,*" by M. Houssin, which is lifelike and clever; some by M. Gautherin, and especially a charming bust in terra cotta of "*Mlle. M. M.*"; those by M. Moreau-Vauthier of "M. Gosselin," "M. Laurens," and "M. Langlois"; the portrait of "*Général de Wimpffen,*" by M. F. Richard, and "Cardinal Guibert" among others by M. Oliva; "Georges Sand," by M. Millet; several by M. Paul Dubois, and M. G. Crauk, and M. E.-L. Barrias, and among those by the last artist, one in especial of "*Madame Olivier,*" with both hands holding gloves; some by M. Guillaume, and specially the "Archbishop of Paris;" "*M. Prugneaux,*" by M. Crauk; "*Madame Doche,*" by M. Delaplanche; and "*Mlle. Leblanc,*" by M. Noel; several by M. Vasselot; and "*M. Lefort des Ylouses,*" by M. Granet.

Doublemard. Houssin. Gautherin. Moreau-Vauthier *et al.*

Bas-reliefs. Medals.

There were scarcely any examples of bas-reliefs, and those which existed were of no special merit. The medals and coins were generally excellent in workmanship, but it would be impossible to particularize them here. America has much to learn by a close examination of them. Our own coins are a disgrace to our nation.

We now leave the French sculpture and proceed to that of Italy, which is certainly entitled to the next place.

ITALY.

ITALY.

If Italy disappointed her friends and well-wishers (and that is the world, for who wishes ill to her?) in her paintings, she has still more grievously disappointed them in her sculpture. In this exhibition she showed every kind of talent, except a serious one. The subjects to which she seems almost exclusively to have devoted herself during these late years are of a trivial and often a low order of *genre*. Her sculpture is for the most part wanting in dignity of purpose and seriousness of style and subject. Her old traditions seem to have died away, and the ruling school of to-day is occupied with mere mechanical and literal efforts at imitation, and more belonging to the workman than the artist. Here indeed is shown great mechanical dexterity of mere workmanship. The marble is freely handled and forced to minute imitation. Laces and flowers, silks, satins, and velvets are admirably rendered; common forms are carefully copied from casts or studied from nature; but this is all. Great conceptions, purity of style, dignity of design, are not even aimed at, and the great proportion of the works exhibited seem to be the outcome of a merely commercial spirit, intent on business, devoted to profit and anxious for money. The great problem seems to be how to make something that will sell, how to catch the vulgar eye, how to work for the market. The consequence is, that the most silly, tawdry, trivial, and worn-out themes are taken and wrought out with exceeding attention to all the minutiæ of the accessories in the hope to make them attractive. Statues of little children abound, with a dog, with a cat, with a bird, with a butterfly, with a rabbit, with a rose, with a cock, blowing their porridge, learning to read, saying their prayers, playing blindman's buff, looking into a mirror, coquetting, peeping from behind their hands, some nearly nude with a little chemise, some covered with flowers, some in elaborate frocks with frills and laces and curls and sashes, some running, some laughing, some crying, some sleeping, some pouting, some smothered in flowers, some with open parasols. These are the mothers' darlings, and their dresses are wrought with the greatest attention, the little hem of the chemise carefully copied, the lace-work and frills wrought *a giorno*, the meshes of the stockings laboriously imitated, the roses, the little shoes with their bows, the buttons, the curls elaborated to the utmost. Then there are the ugly boys, the *gamins*, shivering after their bath and putting on a damp shirt, squabbling, crying out newspapers, having their faces washed. Then there are the pretty boys, the young geniuses with pencil and book. After this you have the maternal element—the mother in combination with the child, teaching him to walk or to read or to pray, combing his hair, putting on his shoes, anything you like. Flowers

Want of dignity in style and subjects.

Mechanical dexterity.

The commercial view.

Trivial themes

ITALY.

Costume and demi-costume.

are thrust in everywhere to show the dexterity of the workmen. It is the apotheosis of dresses. After these come the costume figures, with mask and domino and hat and feather, indecently dressed with tight-strained drawers, and nuder than if they had nothing on, and leering at you sideways or smoking a cigarette. Then we have the everlasting girl at the bath, nude or with close-fitting *maglio*, about to dive or dipping her foot in the water, and the *espiègle* girl half-hiding and shrinking from sight. Flowers and plants play a great *rôle*. One has children and flowers, girls selling flowers and surrounded by them; "Cupid and Psyche" emerging from masses of flowers; women with wreaths and grape leaves, and all worked out in the most elaborate way. All this strikes one as very sad. If sculpture has no higher function than this, it seems scarcely to have a right to exist at all. However well executed, whatever mastery such works show over the material—and it must be admitted that the mere workmanship is often very skillful and the imitation admirable—one only can feel that they degrade art and pander to low and common tastes.

Flowers.

Genre.

If we turn to subjects of a higher class, the range of ideas is scarcely higher. There is everywhere a want of imaginative conception, of true feeling, of serious purpose. *Genre* has tainted everything; "the trail of the serpent is over it all." The accessories are of more importance than the main figures; imitation has usurped the place of creation. It is not that there is a lack of talent. There is talent enough, but there is a lack of faith and of feeling; a lack of high aim, a lack of elevated thought, of poetic sensibility. When the work comes out of the common it falls into the extravagant, it strives for the picturesque, it avoids the sensible and dignified, it affects the literal.

But, leaving these general statements, let us examine some of the most prominent works. There were two extremely clever statues of life size, but purely *genre* in their treatment: one representing the "Death of Mozart," by Sig. Carnielo, of Florence, and one, the "Suicide of Jacques Ortiz," by Sig. Ferrari, of Rome. Painful as both of these are, so painful indeed that one cannot but wonder at such a selection of subjects, they both show great talent, and have nothing ordinary about them. The accessories and draperies are copied literally from nature, with little selection, but the attitudes are striking, the expression true, and the execution good. The feet and thin cadaverous hands of Mozart look like casts from nature. Dressed in a ruffled shirt, with a blanket over his legs, he is lying back in a great *fauteuil*,

Carnielo.

Ferrari.

propped by cushions, in which his head is thrown back sideways, and in his lap is an open score of music. ITALY.

Three very spirited and clever *genre* groups were exhibited by Sig. Focardi. "I'm First, Sir!" represents two ragged newspaper boys; one with a penny between his teeth is planted on both feet spread wide apart and pressing back his companion, and each is stretching out a newspaper and crying out to a customer "*I'm first, sir!*" "You Dirty Boy!" is an old woman in a cap, with bare arms and tucked-up sleeves, who is holding a boy by the head and washing him with soap and a sponge. He has all the upper part of his body naked, with a large towel tied around his waist and falling nearly to his feet. Both hands are stretched forward over a tub, and he is squeezing his mouth and eyes tight together to exclude the smother of the lather. The expression of both figures is admirable for its truth, and the humor is contagious; one cannot but laugh, it is so well done. The third represents a man dancing and grinning, to lull a screaming baby to sleep, which he dandles in his arms. These works had a great success in the Exposition, and in their way they deserved it. One could only have wished to see anything as well done in a higher sphere of art. Focardi.

"*La Chanson d' Amour*," by Sig. Barbella, of Chieti, is very much of the same character, and is modeled with much spirit and truth to common life. It represents a peasant trying to kiss a peasant girl. The action is good and natural. It is in terra-cotta. Barbella.

"Canaris at Scio," by Sig. Civiletti, of Palermo, was one of the most serious works in this section, and is modeled with skill and truth. It represents two nude figures, only girt about the loins, in the prow of a boat. One is seated with an anchor in his right hand, the other kneeling, with his left hand on his companion's shoulder, and pointing out something in the distance at which both are looking earnestly forward. The expression and character of the heads is good, the grouping clever, and there is unity of action and feeling. It well deserved the medal of the first class which was conferred by the jury. Civiletti.

Sig. Monteverde exhibited four works: "Jenner Vaccinating his Son," an allegorical figure of "Architecture," model of the "Monument to Count Massari," and "Boy with a Cock," all in marble except the model of the monument, which is in plaster. The "Jenner Vaccinating his Son," which is life size, was the largest and most remarkable piece of *genre* sculpture in the whole Exposition. Careful study of details and precision of workmanship can scarcely be carried fur- Monteverde.

ther. It represents Jenner seated and dressed in the costume of his day, with queue, shorts, and high-collared coat and buckled shoes, his legs cramped under him, his feet raised on their toes, and holding on his knees his son, who is quite naked and stretching out in fright his arms and legs. Jenner clasps him, however, firmly, and holds his head compressed under his chin, while he bends forward crouching over him in an attitude of extreme tension, imprinting the grasping fingers of one hand in the boy's arm, and pinching tightly in the other the instrument of vaccination, while his attention is fixed with intensity upon the exact point which he is to puncture. Whether so simple an operation required such intensity and concentration of purpose is altogether another question. One would naturally have expected the father to soothe the child and perform the vaccination tranquilly, as it is scarcely to be considered an operation of difficulty; but had he been couching him for cataract, or performing the most delicate operation involving life and death, he could not have been more concentrated and strained in attention or fixed his child more strongly as in a vise. However, Sig. Monteverde has taken another view. He supposes the moment to be a supreme one of anxiety and difficulty, and though to our minds the anxiety and questioning were all antecedent necessarily to the operation, he thinks differently, and he has striven to give his idea. In this he has succeeded. There is intensity of attention. One also asks why, when the father is dressed to the least minutiæ of his costume, the child should be stripped naked; whether it would not have been easier to vaccinate the child by tranquilizing him instead of frightening him. The imaginative sense does not seem to have been strongly at work in the conception of this group, and as a composition it is singularly contorted. Seen from behind, the father's head is not visible. There is only a tall collar visible, and he seems decapitated, while seen from the side the group is very confused and straggling. But setting apart all considerations as to the fitness of such a subject for sculpture, and as to the conception and composition of it, and confining ourselves to the workmanship, careful study of details, and mere modeling, this work deserves great praise. The body of the child is admirably modeled. It is fleshy and delicate in its contours. The hands of the father are as full of nature as if they had been copied from a cast. The minute wrinkles and folds and texture of the skin are all given with great fidelity. Then, too, there is patient labor in all the details of the dress, in the shoes, in the stockings—every thread of which is expressed—in the coat—in a word, in everything. This it is which attracts the common mind; and a hundred persons are struck by the stockings to one who considers the meaning of the whole group. It is a work which impresses by its parts and its details. Here is its merit; here is its defect as a work of art.

Monteverde. The "Statue of Architecture" is in a higher vein, but even here one sees no ideal life; neither the head, the arms, nor the hands are those of a muse, and there is a certain strictness, coldness, and academic character which are scarcely compensated by care in the execution.

The model of the "Monument to Count Massari" represents his corpse swaddled closely about, so as to cover the arms, and lying stretched stiffly on a sort of couch, over which a winged angel bends from behind the head, propped by both hands against the top of the couch. This is only sketched in execution, and in this respect, therefore, lacks the interest which attaches to all his other works here exhibited. It will probably be carefully finished, however, in the marble. As it is, it leaves much to be desired. The angel has not an angelic presence. The arms are of a low type, the head wants refinement and nobility, and the draperies are not happily treated; nor is it very clear what the conception of the artist is, or with what intention the angel is standing there.

The "Boy with the Cock" is a piece of pure *genre*, excellent in treatment of the marble, and possessing scarcely any interest beyond this.

The realistic school. All of these works are of the realistic school, so called, which being interpreted means generally the prosaic and literal school, which studiously avoids all effort for ideal qualities, insists that the common is the best in nature, and at all events is good enough for art, and endeavors to impress us by literal imitation of even the accidental, rather than to make a purged selection of the best. Sig. Monteverde is a leader in this young school in Italy, and exercises, young as he is, a very considerable influence over a certain clique, and it is for this reason that I have felt compelled, while acknowledging his talent, to point out in some measure his shortcomings, but leaving him personally apart, and speaking generally. The doctrines and faith of this school are not those upon which the greatest artists of the past have worked; they are not the principles upon which the noblest works, either of antiquity or of the *Renaissance*, were wrought. They are equally opposed to those that animated

ITALY.

Phidias and Apelles, or Raffaelle and Titian, and they do not lead to the highest eminences of art. In this school the poetic nature, afraid to spread its wings, limps encumbered along the earth, and the heroic spirit is dwarfed to common-places of every day. If, however, the function of art is to lift the soul, to enchant the heart, to embody the beautiful, to gather the perfect flower of thought and feeling—and there are still some who have this faith—it is sadly forgetful of its true office when it descends in search of mere novelty to the common, low, and accidental; mates itself with mechanical imitation in order to delight the ignorant and vulgar, and laughs to scorn the inspiration of the muses. It is pitiable when one sees an art that used to lord it in the higher spheres, abjuring its birthright by lurking in the pot house of mere *genre* to hob-a-nob with mean companions. I am well aware that these are not palatable words, but I am quite sure that they simply express the almost universal verdict of the most enlightened class of those who have an earnest love and a true knowledge of art. There is surely something better for sculpture to do than to represent an ugly, shivering gamin buttoning his shirt-sleeves after his bath, or striving to pull his wet shirt over his head; better than the silliness of beruffled and becurled children walking out under a parasol, or playing with a dog, or a cat, however well executed. What we want is ideas, poetic inspirations, heroic thought and character, creations of power and beauty, not mere handicraft.

The heroic dwarfed to commonplace.

But, to continue with our review of the statues. Sig. Ximenes, of Florence, exposed a figure of a youth in circus dress, balancing himself on a globe (*L'Équilibre*). This is cleverly represented; the adjustment of difficult equilibrium admirably done. Was it worth doing? He also had a group of "*La Rixe*," which represents two boys quarreling. To this the same praise cannot be accorded; it is full of exaggeration and grimace. Sig. Gomito had a figure of a fisher-boy squatting down, with his cap between his feet, and just seizing a fish off his hook. It is hideously ugly and vulgar in type, but exceedingly clever in expression. He intended him to be ugly and vulgar. His object was to represent something literal and repulsive, and he has succeeded. But why should a creature who is ugly and repulsive in fact become interesting in art? Why should an attitude which, however natural, is disagreeable, awkward, and ungainly, be selected for the permanence of sculpture? Sig. Butti, of Milan, sent a statue which he calls "*La Grimace*," representing a *gamin* in a torn straw hat, with

Ximenes.

Gomito.

Butti.

his waistcoat buttoned over his loins back side before, who is sticking out his tongue and looking at himself in a mirror. Sig. Barzaghi, of Milan, sent a "Blindman's Buff," "*Petite Coquette*," "*Sylvie se mirant dans la Glace*," and "*Moïse sauvé des Eaux*," all of which are in the literal and decorative-dress school of Milan. But there were scores of similar subjects in this section on which I will not waste time, but cite a few of the titles, which are all that are needed to show how art is going: "*Un petit Masque; que connais tu?*" "*Joie enfantine*," "*La Rose des Amours*," "*L'Amour non aveugle*," "*Le premier Bain*," "*Le Gamin*," "*La Prisonnière d'Amour*," "*La Prière forcée*," "Hush a bye Baby," "*À Maman*," "*Enfants dansants*," "*L'Innocence*," "*La Promenade*," "*La Rose candide*," etc. In most, if not all of these, the dresses, the textures, and the flowers are worked out with great elaboration. The hair is deeply drilled and chiseled, and the mechanical labor is never shirked. Sig. Tabacchi sent three statues, a "*Baigneuse*," a "*Péri*," and "*Hypatie*." "*La Baigneuse*" is a girl in a close-fitting *maillot* shirt which exposes all her figure as if it had been glued to it, standing with both feet close together, and both hands joined over her head, bending forward and preparing to dive. This greatly attracted a certain class and had a success. The *maillot* is carefully wrought out and the workmanship and modeling excellent; what of the subject? what of the pose? In the "*Péri*" and the "*Hypatie*" there is a more serious attempt at a higher class of expression, but they are exaggerated in attitude and character, and want repose and dignity of design. The "Hypatia" is far the better of the two, save that her hands are in excess of crispation as well as her feet, but it shows a good deal of talent and good workmanship. Sig. P. Calvi sends an "Ariadne" in the Milanese school of treatment, and Sig. Malfatti a "*Liens d'Amour*," representing a floating, female figure, with a great deal of hair, and a Cupid at her feet, pulling about her a branch of leaves—also in the same school of decoration. There are two "*Bérénices*," one by Sig. Borghi and one by Sig. Peduzzi, with outstretched hands, both of the same school, with abundance of elaborately worked hair, and very careful execution of textures; and also two "*Cléopâtras*," one by Sig. E. Braga, of Milan, representing her walking forward, nude, except that around the loins some drapery is tied, with the vulture head-dress, armlets, and necklace, and a slave kneeling at her feet, on whose shoulder her hand rests; and another, by Sig. Papini, representing her "*Vêtue en Vénus ou en Isis, va à la rencontre d'Antoine*,

Barzaghi. Trivial titles. Tabacchi. Calvi. Malfatti. Borghi. Peduzzi. Braga. Papini.

ITALY.

pour se justifier auprès de lui et le captiver par ses Charmes." This statue out-Herods Herod. Cleopatra is lying extended almost nude on a great couch, on which are full draperies, and leering over the pillow with an expression that can scarcely be characterized. This is not the Queen of Egypt, but a vulgar, shameless courtesan. God help us! Is this the wondrous creature of whom Antony said: "Age cannot wither her nor custom stale her infinite variety."

Papini.

Bottinelli. "*La Modestie*," by Sig. Bottinelli, of Rome, is a figure of a very different character. She is a young girl, completely enfolded in delicate and well-composed draperies, looking down, with her hands crossed before her and holding a few flowers. There is a great deal of sweetness, simplicity, and refinement in this statue. It is quite without affectation or posing, and is carefully executed.

Majoli. Sig. Majoli exhibited a serious statue of "Michel Angelo," which also has the merit of simplicity of treatment and composition. It represents the great artist seated on a square block, holding in one hand the chisel and in the other the mallet, and looking up at his work.

Pozzi. Borghi. Villa. Salvini. Tortone. Rota. Sig. Pozzi, of Milan, sent a statue of "Michel Angelo" as a youth; Sig. Borghi, of Milan, a statue of "*Cola da Rienzo*," as a youth; Sig. Villa, of Milan, a statue of "*Pic de la Mirandole*," as a youth; Sig. Salvini, of Bologna, a statue of "Giotto" as a youth; Sig. Tortone, of Turin, a figure of "Napoleon" as a youth; Sig. Rota, of Genoa, a figure of "Salvator Rosa" as a youth. All of these show a decided cleverness in the treatment of such subjects, and all of them are well and carefully executed in all the details of costume; but, of course, they are essentially costume figures. That of "Giotto" is particularly good and simple, and so is that of "*Pic de la Mirandole*."

Signa. Maraini. Luchetti. Dini. Among other statues of a higher class of subject to be mentioned are the "Sappho" before her fatal leap, by Signora Maraini; the "Spartacus," by Sig. Lucchetti, and the "Death of Epaminondas," by Sig. C. Dini, of Turin. But subjects of this class are exceedingly exceptional in this section, the greater proportion of statues being purely *genre* in their character, and these almost stand alone.

Riggi. Borghi. Among the portrait statues was one by Sig. Riggi, of "Savonarola," seated in a chair with open staves, clad in his monkish robes, with a cowl on his head, crossed legs, and a book in his hand; and one of "Oliver Cromwell," by Sig. Borghi, of Milan, in plaster, also seated, and somewhat grotesque and exaggerated. There were also a few busts, among which may be specially mentioned one of "Mazzini,"

Gangeri. Maccagnani. Calvi. Benvenuti. Cencetti. Giani. Belliazzi. Borghi.

by Sig. Gangeri; two busts in *terre-cuite* extremely well modeled and full of character and study, by Sig. Maccagnani, particularly the head of an "African," and one of "Othello," in bronze, with marble draperies, by Sig. Calvi, and one of the "*Innominato*" in "*Gli Promessi Sposi*," by Sig. Benvenuti, and two "*Incroyables*," by Sig. Cencetti, of Rome, busts in marble, extremely clever in character and expression and full of humor. Sig. Giani, of Como, sent a statue of "*Balilla que je la jette!*" a youth in the act of throwing a stone, which has considerable spirit; and Sig. Belliazzi, of Naples, a statue of a "Peasant Boy," in the *ciocciáre* costume, asleep, which is admirable for its nature and simplicity. There is nothing affected, nothing overstated, and the sentiment is very pleasing. It was one of the very best *genre* statues in all this section, if not the best. The very worst, certainly as far as taste and sentiment go, was "*Le Masque*," by Sig. Borghi, of Milan. It represents a creature with skin tights on her legs, closely strained drawers, ruffled jacket and boots, who stands with one hand on her hip, holding a cigarette in the other, her head turning at you sideways, and with an immense bouquet and broken champagne bottle at her feet. Bad taste can scarcely go farther. There was also another figure, in a somewhat similar dress, holding a mask in one hand, which is not quite so bad in taste.

Amendola.

We must not leave the Italian sculpture without referring to a most extraordinary group of Cain and his wife, by Sig. Amendola, of Naples, in which the intention of the artist has been to represent two degraded aborigines and wild creatures, ill-organized, low in type, and brutal in expression. Their hands and feet are furnished with overgrown pointed nails several inches long; and Cain, standing with his hands down at his side, digs his nails into his flesh. This is certainly an original conception of the subject, and certainly Sig. Amendola has succeeded in representing Cain and his wife as exceedingly repulsive creatures, though they are our ancestors. Upon the whole one doubts, in looking at these, whether one would not at once prefer the ancestry insisted on by Dr. Darwin.

I may, perhaps, have given too much time to the consideration of the sculpture of Italy, but it seemed necessary to particularize many works for the purpose of giving a clear idea of the tendency of the late schools, and to justify my general remarks.

ITALY.

Italian and French schools compared.

Comparing the Italian and French schools, the defects of the first are triviality and poverty of ideas, and an over-elaboration of emphasis on what is merely accessory—on dresses, flowers, hair, textures, everything which can show off mechanical workmanship. The defects of the French school

French overemphasis of gesture, and loose sketchy method.

are overemphasis of gesture, tormented attitudes, and a certain posing and uneasy consciousness. The tendency to be observed and lamented in much of the French work, and particularly in the portrait busts, is a loose and pretentiously sketchy manner. This is carried at times so far as to become impertinent. There is often really no modeling, in the just sense of that term. Mere effects are sought. There is no proper surface or refinement of planes, but little clay pellets are dabbed on almost recklessly without being leveled, so that they produce the effect of an unhealthy and diseased skin, or of a surface defaced and rotted by time and exposure. This is particularly observable in the terra-

Models for bronze.

cotta and bronze busts and figures. Ordinarily it is thought that a figure to be cast in bronze should be specially elaborated in the model. The opposite opinion and practice obtains in France; as for translating some of these works into

French careless work, affecting ease.

marble in their present condition, it would be quite impossible without totally remodeling the surface. All this is mere affectation of careless and masterly ease, caught from the sister pictorial art. It is pure improvisation, spirited at times, but wholly incomplete. In the draperies the same fault is seen. The character and anatomies of the folds are not given. They are often mere unformed lumps and masses of clay which stand for draperies. In these respects the

Italian over-elaborateness.

French are far behind the Italians, who err, perhaps, in the opposite extreme of over-preciseness and elaborateness of imitation of textures and individualities. There was nothing, for instance, in all the French section, which for mere accuracy of modeling can compare to the work of M. Monteverde in his group of "Jenner and his Son." Nothing to compare with the extreme finesse of execution, for instance, of the naturalistic hands of the father, or the nude flesh of the child.

ENGLAND.

ENGLAND.

Sculpture.

We now come to the English section. The art of sculpture cannot be said to flourish in England. It has never produced a great sculptor. The only exception that possi-

Flaxman.

bly could be made would be Flaxman, but he, with all his genius, inventive power, and almost Greek feeling, was essentially great as a designer and not as a sculptor in the broadest sense of that word. His outlines from the Greek poets and dramatists are graceful, beautiful, refined, and, at times, even powerful in conception, but in modeling or marble his execution, either in bas relief or in the round, was inefficient, and failed to embody what his mind conceived. Chantrey was essentially a portrait sculptor, and in the higher branches of the art he scarcely attempted anything. The busts of Nollekens are sometimes striking for character, but in his ideal figures he was weak. Gibson, with all his talent, can scarcely be considered a great man, nor can such a title be accorded to Bacon, Roubillac, or, indeed, any of the chief names of the past in English sculpture.

Chantrey

Nollekens

Gibson.

Bacon.
Roubillac.

There is something, possibly, in climatic influences which renders the English mind more sensitive to color than to form, but whatever be the reason the fact can scarcely be controverted that its greatest artists have been painters; that it can boast many an eminent name in painting, and almost none in sculpture. Even in its painting its weak side has been form and drawing, its strong side color and sentiment; its weak side the heroic and ideal in art, its strong side domestic scenes, landscape, and portrait.

England excels rather in painting than in sculpture.

The works of sculpture exhibited by England were few. Against 474 paintings in oil and water color, it had only 46 pieces of sculpture; nor can it be honestly said that these are of a very high order of merit, or exhibit any salient strokes of imagination, or any specially admirable qualities of execution. Of these, nearly half are portrait busts and statues, and but a very small proportion of the remainder are ideal subjects.

Perhaps the most important work, and one that aims at the highest style, is the "Athlete Wrestling with a Python," by Sir Frederic Leighton, the accomplished president of the Royal Academy. In its workmanship and study it does high credit to Mr. Leighton's talent. The execution of it is faithful and careful. Nothing is neglected and slurred over. On the contrary, if it errs, it errs rather in the over-expression of the muscles in their insertions, and the over-insistance on particulars which nature strives to conceal. The great fault to be found with it is in the pose, which is scarcely one that any man would take in struggling for his life with so formidable an enemy. He is so planted that he has no leverage with which to counteract the Python. He could not exercise any power in his present action. His left arm and leg are perfectly helpless, as far as any force is required. To bring his power into play the action of the legs should

Sir F. Leighton.

ENGLAND. be reversed—the right planted forward as the lever of his right arm, the left planted behind. This criticism proceeds, of course, on the supposition that Sir Frederic did not intend to represent the athlete as entirely in the power of the Python. If he did it falls to the ground. It would, however, seem by the right arm that the struggle at least was meant to be an equal one. Nor is the action of the athlete's head what one would expect at such a moment. Instead of being bent forward and on one side, which gives it rather a sentimental than a determined look, it would seem rather that it should have been erect and drawn back in opposition to the head of the Python. Undoubtedly Sir Frederic Leighton has his justification for this reversed action of the lower and upper parts of the body in the Borghese "Gladiator" and in the "Apollo," but in both these figures the action is momentary and even at that a little academical. No man can strike out strongly over a leg bent and placed behind the other, as in the "Gladiator," nor can he stand in the attitude of the "Apollo" for more than a moment without falling. In fact, if any one from recollection will strive to assume the pose of either of these figures, he will find that the leg he naturally puts in advance is in these statues the leg that is behind. The artist has sought for variety at the expense of truth. Sir Frederic may excuse us, however, a criticism which places him in such company, and may prefer to be wrong with such celebrated statues rather than right with nature. Undoubtedly, after all criticism, the statue is an honest and earnest work, worthy of such an artist.

Sir F. Leighton.

Boehm. Mr. J. E. Boehm sent three statues, one of "a Clydesdale Stallion rearing," and held by a groom at his side; one a portrait statue of "Thomas Carlyle." The first, which is quite life size, is very spirited and shows a good deal of force, though in action and composition it recalls the horses of Marly. The horse, which is a powerful animal, is well modeled, his action is good, and well deserved the second-class medal accorded to the artist. The portrait statue of "Thomas Carlyle" is of the naturalistic school. He is represented as seated sideways in an arm-chair with his legs crossed, and clothed in a dressing-gown. The head is characteristic and clever, and the statue has a good deal of nature. The dress is more sketchily executed.

Foley. There are six large portrait statues by the late Mr. Foley, of "Edmund Burke," "Oliver Goldsmith," a "Parsee Merchant," "Thomas Grattan," "Lord Clyde," and "Professor Faraday," all of which have the qualities of this well-known artist, who excelled in statues of this kind. They are well posed and fairly modeled, but they have no very special character and individuality. They are more to be praised for the absence of great defects than for the presence of distinguished merits; but what can be done with a modern portrait statue?

Fuller. Mr. Fuller's "Castaway" and "Peri" were also exhibited. They are fair specimens of that lamented artist's work, and exhibit his usual care of execution. Among other statues must be mentioned Mr. Joy's "Forsaken," a woman on her knees, with her body and head thrown back and clasped behind by her hands, with her dead infant lying head down in her lap. The action is excessive and the hair strange, but there is character. Mr. McLean's "Ione" is pleasing in composition, has a pretty turn of head, and the draperies are well disposed. She is seated and holding a tablet on her knees. Miss Grant's "St. Margaret and the Dragon" must also be noticed as one of the most important among the ideal works, as well as an interesting and pleasing *genre* figure, by Lord Ronald Gower, of "Marie Antoinette," which does him great credit. Among others must also be mentioned a "Cupid taming a Panther," by Mr. Simonds, and Mr. W. Calder Marshall's "Tali Players" and "Nausicaa."

Joy. McLean. Miss Grant. Lord R. Gower. Simonds Marshall.

Watts. Mr. Watts, the distinguished painter, also tries his hand at sculpture, and sent an ideal bust of "Clytie," which is treated purely from a painter's point of view; great insistance being made upon surface treatment of the flesh. This, despite the painter's hand, which is everywhere visible, is an effort at the grandiose school of Michael Angelo, in form, but though the aim and intention are high, this cannot be said to be successful. The anatomies are very defective; the shoulders are entirely different from those of a woman, and are evidently those of a man, while the bosom, not only in its modeling and form, but in its rough texture and curves, is rather that of an old woman, than of a young maiden, like Clytie, in the fresh bloom of youth and enthusiasm. The head is turned back over the right shoulder straining after Apollo, but this action is carried far beyond the possibility of nature; no head can be turned so far back without breaking the spinal column, and the consequence is that the mastoid and the trapezium muscles are not and cannot be properly rendered. The back, too, is quite incomprehensible in its outline and anatomy. These defects are extremely to be regretted, for there is a large spirit in the intention, there is a feeling for the heroic, and the work is anything but common and petty. It is not by sudden excursions out of painting that the successes of sculpture are to be achieved. Each

ENGLAND.

art has its own peculiar difficulties, and continuous, patient study and practice can alone give excellence in either. The sculptor's painting always has the quality of his peculiar art, and the painter's sculpture has always the character of painting. The modes of thought, the ideas of composition, are different in the two arts, and although it is undoubtedly a great benefit to an artist in either branch to make attempts in the other, and thus enlarge his experience and knowledge, the painter very rarely produces a good work of sculpture, the sculptor very rarely a good work in painting.

The sculptor-painter or painter-sculptor.

Portrait-statues. D'Epinay.

Mr. D'Epinay sent three portrait busts, "Her Royal Highness, the Princess of Wales," "Miss Florence Hamilton," and "Madame D'Epinay," which are of the French school, and one knew not why they appeared in this section, except on account of the persons represented. The portrait of "the Princess of Wales" is rather a half-length than a bust, adorned with heavy draperies which shroud the pedestal, and is carefully and elaborately finished. Most of "Madame D'Epinay" is colored, both dress and head, in imitation of life, and is treated from a picturesque point of view, as is also the portrait of "Miss Florence Hamilton," who is represented in a broad-brimmed hat and ostrich feather. Mr. Brodie sent two busts of "Her Majesty Queen Victoria" and 'the Right Hon. Baroness Burdett Coutts;" Count Gleichen, a portrait of "Garibaldi," and "King Alfred the Great," which is ideal; Mr. Adams-Acton, a bust of "Zenobia," and "Lady Victoria Campbell"; Miss Grant two busts of "Sir Francis Grant" and "Lady Augusta Stanley"; Mr. A. Bruce Joy a bust of "Mr. Max Müller."

Brodie. Count Gleichen. Adams-Acton. Miss Grant. Joy.

RUSSIA.

RUSSIA. Antokolski.

We now come to the Russian sculpture. There were fifty-one works including medals, and of these those of the highest aim and importance are by M. Antokolski. He sent seven works. "*Ivan le Terrible*," "*Le Christ devant le Peuple*," "*Pierre le Grand*" (marble bust), "*La Mort de Socrate*," "*Le dernier Soupir*," "*Portrait de W. Stassoff*," and "*L'Enfant mort*" (*bas-relief en marbre*). "Christ before the People," to which the post of honor was given, represents Him draped in a strait dress with few folds, standing erect with both feet together and both hands straight down at His side and tied closely there by a cord round His body. There is no attempt at action. The pose is almost *raide* in its formality. The divine element is scarcely sought to be rendered, nor is there even loftiness of character and expression. It represents simply a suffering man with his hands tied to his side.

It is of the naturalistic school, and this is evidently all the artist desired. Of course, in such a subject, the eye sees through the mind, and the very title of the work is a half victory. But to own the truth, though the work is good and careful, it lacks the higher qualities of the imagination. It does not embody our idea of Christ at such a moment, or indeed at any moment, whatever He was in fact—whether the divine Saviour of the world, or only a lofty and spiritual man, it is impossible to accept this as an inspired representation of Him.

RUSSIA.

Antokolski.

The "Death of Socrates," by the same artist, fails in the same way. The philosopher is stretched half out on a great round-backed chair, his legs thrust out before him, his hands hanging down. Were it not for the well-known features, it would scarcely be possible to believe that this was Socrates. There is neither grandeur, nor dignity, nor power in the figure. It might be any half-naked beggar asleep. No matter what the fact was, this does not answer to our idea of Socrates, and our ideas are as much facts and often more real than the actual facts out of which they sprang. In such a work as this is, the artist who fails to answer the sympathetic expectation of cultivated minds upon the subject, may be said to fail utterly, no matter how good his work is, as work.

But though these works leave us quite cold, there is another work of M. Antokolski, which has profoundly touched us, and that is the *bas-relief* of "*L'Enfant mort.*" This is exquisite in feeling and modeled with rare delicacy and refinement. It has a touch of nature and sentiment which goes to the heart, and it could only have come out of a deep and sad experience.

Tchijoff.

M. Tchijoff sent five works: a bust of "M. Gromoff," "*Colin-Maillard*," "*La Petite Folâtre*," and "*La Leçon de Lectur*," "*Le Paysan en Détresse*." The "*Colin-Maillard*" and "*La Petite Folâtre*," are subjects scarcely fit for sculpture however well done. The other two groups are far superior in character and intention, and especially "*Le Paysan en Détresse*," which has great simplicity and pathos, and is very well executed. It represents a peasant seated with his head bent down and leaning on his hand, while his little son stands between his legs leaning against him with his hand to his mouth in an attitude of mute and sorrowing sympathy. The expression of both figures is earnest and sincere. There is no affectation, there is much nature.

Runeberg.

Among other works to be noted are three groups of "Psyche," by M. Runeberg, gracefully cold, and character-

RUSSIA.

Lanceray.

Alexeieff, Steinmann, Bock, et al.

less; some small and clever groups of animals by M. Lanceray; a series of eight medals by M. Alexeieff, three by M. Steinmann, and one by M. Koutschkine; and a remarkably well executed mosaic of "*La Mise au Tombeau, d'après le tableau de C. Dusi*" from the Imperial Academy of the Fine Arts at Saint Petersburg. M. Bock sent a "Head of a Faun" in marble, and a "Minerva surrounded by Children," M. Koukharevski a "Martyr in Prayer;" M. Laveretski a "Head of a Jew;" M. Pruszinski a "St. Sebastian;" M. Rigner two busts of "Juliette" and "Washington," a *bas relief;* M. Stigel an "*Amour;*" and M. Takkanen a "Venus and Cupid;" and these were all.

Casts from nature.

Dr. Levitoux.

There were also in a small room, placed apart by themselves, two very remarkable casts from life of two nude female figures, one lying on her back, the other on her belly. Nothing could excel the perfection of these casts for exactness and absolute representation of the model. Not a wrinkle is lost. The texture of the skin is there exactly as in life. The very goose-flesh of the shivering girl is given. In fact, this is literal perfection as far as simple reproduction of nature goes. No modeling could aspire to equal it in mere exactness, no eye could report, no hand could finish with the absoluteness that is here seen. Every pains has been taken with colored windows and curtains to give the semblance of reality to these forms. There one can see the result of absolute naturalism without ideas, and what is the result? It is curious; it is interesting from a certain point of view; it is valuable as a report of nature, but it is not art. It has nothing to do with mind, with soul, with emotions and feelings and thoughts, and it is not art. The rudest sketch of a master, the rapidest outline with feeling in it, the most blotted scribble of an idea has an interest of a totally different kind and far beyond this. It is empty; it is dead; it is soulless. Compared with a true work of art, these casts are like a dictionary as compared with a poem. The materials, the words, are all there. It is only the ideas which are wanting to combine and give soul to them. I think no lesson could be given to those whose faith it is that absolute copying of nature will necessarily result in art, more staggering than is given by these two casts. Here, as you look at them, you cannot help feeling that the perfectest possible imitation, the most exact and minute reproduction of the model, the perfection of mere material workmanship alone and of itself only rouses curiosity and awakens surprise, but does not enter even into the outer-

Perfection of exactness.

The despair of a literalist.

Naturalism without ideas.

Lesson for copyists of nature.

Implicit reproduction.

most confines of art. There, in that region only, ideas, thoughts, feelings live, abide, and embody themselves in never-dying forms. RUSSIA.

GERMANY.

Germany exhibited 24 works of sculpture, of which 8 were busts, 7 groups in marble and bronze, 5 single figures, and 4 statuettes. Herr Charles Begas sent two works, "Satyr and Bacchus," a group in marble, and a bust of "M. de Marées." Herr Reinhold Begas had 5 works. "*L'Enlèvement des Sabines*" and "Mercury and Psyche," both groups in marble; busts of "Madame Hopfen" and the "Artist Menzel," and "Venus and Cupid," a group in bronze. The "Satyr and Bacchus" is of the old school and is well treated, though there is nothing special in its conception. The "Mercury and Psyche" is heavy in its forms and somewhat academic in its treatment, though it has good qualities. The "Psyche" is rather a stout Deutsches Mädchen than the airy embodiment of the soul. The "Rape of the Sabines" shows more vigor and spirit, but it is over-violent in action, angular in composition, and French in its energy. His bust, or rather half-length, of "Herr Menzel," is his best work here. It is bold and characteristic and well worked out, and has much individuality in the head and the hands. GERMANY. C. Begas. R. Begas.

Herr Wagmüller's "*Monument Funèbre*" is an interesting work, well composed, well modeled, and with tender sentiment and expression. It represents a female figure seated in a sarcophagus, at the four corners of which are sphinxes. She leans forward sideways, resting her left arm on a tablet, and holding a palm branch in the other, and half caressing and watching over a nude child that is seated on the sarcophagus under her protecting presence. His other works are three busts and a group in marble of a "*Jeune Fille et Enfant.*" Wagmüller.

Herr Hildebrand sent "Adam," a statue in marble, a "*Berger dormant*," and an "*Enfant buvant.*" The best of these is the "*Berger dormant*," which is gentle and pure of feeling, and, though not imitated from Thorwaldsen, somewhat recalls his treatment of similar subjects. Hildebrand.

Herr Sussmann-Hellborn's "*La Poésie Lyrique et la Chanson Populaire*" has a good deal of merit, and, though allegorical, is not hackneyed. It is inspired by a thorough German spirit, both in form and in conception. Sussmann-Hellborn.

Among the other statues must be noted "*L'Amour impertinent*," by Herr J. Kopf, "*Le Satyre et Amour*," by Herr Kopf.

GERMANY.

Hartzer.

Hartzer, though the themes are not new and the treatment not very original.

On the whole, there cannot be said to be any great strength of purpose or peculiar originality in the German sculpture, though they have this merit, that they do not descend to the trival in *genre*, and their works are wrought in a serious spirit. But, on the other hand, they rather fall into what is called in France *le poncif*, by which they mean the repetition of well-known forms of composition, motives, and treatment, and the use of common-places, which lack distinction and individuality.

AUSTRIA-HUNGARY.

AUSTRIA-HUNGARY.

The Austrian-Hungarian sculpture was chiefly devoted to portraits, busts, and statues, and large decorative allegorical figures. There were no less than three different figures of Victory, two by Herr C. Kundmann and one by Herr Lax, his pupil, a "*Pallas Athênê*" and a "*Helios*," by Herr Benk, as well as a large allegorical figure of "*Industrie artistique*," by Herr Kundmann, and designs for statues of "Leibnitz," of "Pitton de Tournefort," "Linnaeus," and "Buffet," by Herr Costenoble, and of "Gessner," by Herr David, eleven figures, all intended for the Royal Museum of Vienna. Besides these, there were colossal statues of "Albrecht Dürer," by Herr Schmidgruber, and "Michael Angelo," by Herr Wagner, for the Palace of the Association of Artists at Vienna, and a colossal statue of "Beethoven" and a group of bronze of "Prometheus," for the monument to Beethoven at Vienna. Certainly it must be admitted that here is evidence of a large public spirit, of interest in the development and patronage of art, of a warm recognition by the nation of her great men, and of a generous outlay of money to which the attention of the American Government may be distinctively called, as indicating the true policy of a great nation. Some of these works show much talent and all are of a serious character. Among the best are the statues of "Albrecht Dürer," "Michael Angelo," and the "Art Industry," of Mr. Kundmann. The statue of Beethoven is a good work, but a little heavy and not very well finished. This character of heaviness was perhaps, the general defect of all the colossal works in this section. But they were there seen too low and at a disadvantage, and when placed at a proper height and distance will probably have a lighter effect. The same defect cannot be attributed to the statue of the "Emperor of Austria," by Herr Tilgner, which goes to the other extreme of

Kundmann. Lax. Benk. Costenoble. David. Schmidgruber. Wagner. Tilgner.

heaviness and long legs, and produces anything but a graceful or agreeable effect. But what can an artist do with such a costume? On the other hand, Herr Tilgner exhibited some very clever and characteristic busts, among which specially may be noted those of the artist "Herr Führich" and of Herr "Lobmeyr." The "Combat of the Centaurs and Lapithæ," on a silver shield, by Herr Tantenhayn, though a little violent in action, is exceedingly spirited. So, also, are some of the busts of Herr Beer, and particularly one by Herr A. K. F. in terra-cotta, though it is rather ostentatiously careless in execution.

AUSTRIA-HUNGARY. Tilgner. Tantenhayn. Beer.

BELGIUM.

BELGIUM. Brunin. De Groot. De Vigne *et al.*

Belgium exhibited 59 works, of which 25 were busts and medallions, by M.M. Brunin, De Groot, De Vigne, Elias, Fraikin, Martens, Pecher, which are chiefly in the same school as the French, and some of which are clever. The remainder of the works were chiefly *genre* in their character, and among these the most noteworthy were a "Woman and Child of the Roman Campagna," by L. Samain, a "*Souvenir de Jeunesse*," by M. Desenfans, which is a plaster model of a boy leaning against the trunk of a tree, with a bird tied by a string in his hand. This is a careful study from the life and well modeled. The action is good and the parts well felt. "*Le Lézard*," by M. Bouré, which is a statue in marble of a boy lying on his belly and playing with a lizard, is also simple and well modeled, and "*L'Exercice*," by M. Laumans. Among the few works of a higher aim of subject are the "Calista hesitating between Christianity and Paganism," a statue in bronze, by M. Van der Linden; "*Daphnis*," a group in marble, by M. Catteer, and several statues by M. de Vigne, of "*Dominica*," "*Volumnia*," "*Psyché*," and "*Narcisse*." It cannot be said, however, that in the Belgian sculpture there was anything eminently characteristic and original to distinguish it from other similar work of the same class, and therefore it need not detain us longer.

Samain. Desenfans. Bouré. Laumans. Van der Linden. Catteer. De Vigne.

No noteworthy sculpture from other nations.

Nor need we delay longer with the sculpture of other nations. The works sent by them were few in number and of no special excellence or character. The exhibits of Spain, Norway, Sweden, Portugal, Switzerland, and the Netherlands require no comment; and Greece is perhaps of all the lowest. The sacred fire has utterly died upon her altars, nor even in her ashes leaves a spark from the glory of the ancient days.

UNITED STATES.

UNITED STATES.

No sculpture.

It remains to speak of American sculpture, and this is easily done. There was none. It was, as I have already said, excluded from the Exposition by the necessities of the case, by the slow action of the government, by the inadequacy of means, and by the impossibility within the limited time to obtain either a place or the statues to fill it. All that appeared in the American section was comprised in two exceedingly clever and spirited small statuettes in plaster, by Mr. Montague Handley, representing "A Rough Day on the Campagna," and "A Cattle Driver on the Campagna," which were there merely by accident, and by two or three of Mr. Rogers's well-known groups, which were huddled away on the tops of the cases in the Educational Department—almost out of sight. I have already protested against this omission of all works of sculpture, and here I again protest. It was unfair to the nation, it was unfair to the sculptors. It was equivalent to advertising to all the world that in sculpture we have achieved nothing of sufficient importance to be exhibited. This is totally false, and those of the world who knew that it is false turned with surprise to ask the reason for this omission. Could any of us give a satisfactory answer?

Statuettes by Handley.

Rogers.

MUSEUM OF THE TROCADERO.

FRANCE.

Trocadero.

But, turning from all the displays of modern sculpture, if we entered the palace of the Trocadero, we seemed as it were to pass into another world. Adequately to describe what was there to be seen would be to write the history of art from the early ages of Egypt to the last week of the past century. What a wonderful exhibition was here, for the artist, for the scholar, for the connoisseur and amateur, for the weaver, the goldsmith, the worker in metals, and porcelain, and embroideries—in a word, for every class, from the high to the low! What opportunities were here given for study, for improvement, for comparison, for delight! Here were the remains of the primitive ages of bronze and stone, of the after-products of Egypt, Greece, Assyria, Etruria, and Gaul, and the whole barbarian world, where one might study their arts, their customs, their manufactures, their development from the rudest to the most refined epochs. Here were the exquisite *terra-cottas* of Tanagra, the opaline glass, pictured vases, the varied bronzes, the marble *bas-reliefs* and statues, of Greece, Rome, Etruria; the medals of all nations; the relics of decaying art in the Christian and mediæval

Marvelous archæological collection for the scholar and the workman.

Remains of the bronze and stone ages. Of Egypt, Greece, Assyria, Etruria, Gaul.

Ancient art

world; the treasures of the *Renaissance*, with their enamels and plaques, coffers and caskets, dishes and crosses, and reliquaries; their majolica, ceramics, and *niello* work; their tapestries and altar pieces, and illuminated books and missals; their carven ivories, diptychs, and lustrous plates; their armor and implements of war; their helmets, daggers, shields, and breast-plates, the *torques* and *fibulæ* of the Gauls and Huns, with the medals of their kings—in a word, the artistic remains of a score of centuries. As I lingered here, day after day, I could not but sigh, to think how utterly America is wanting in all these ancient spoils of time and art. How slight is the national interest in all such treasures. How, amid the continual contests of party for place and power and money, these finer fields of action are left to lie uncultivated and unconsidered, with none, or few, to give them reverence.

FRANCE. *Trocadero.* Ceramics. Tapestries. Missals. Arms and armor.

The mere catalogue of this museum occupies a large volume, and here I can only pass them by with one hurried glance. The first room of the Trocadero was devoted to the relics of the earliest period, and of Gaul previous to the Roman occupation. The collection of stone implements and weapons here was very complete, and among them were a number of Lacustrine objects found in the Lake of Brienne, and lent by Dr. Gross. Then came the bronze and iron objects, with the stone moulds in which some of them were run, with helmets, armor, and weapons. There, too, were the skeleton and relics of an ancient soldier found in a tomb at Gorge Meillet (Marne), with his weapons and helmet, and his horses' bits, and a wheel of his chariot, and a gold armlet, fresh as when it was first beaten out, clasping the bone of the humerus. Then there were Polish antiquities, with a series of *votos* found at Vichy, and Gaulish *fibulæ*, and golden belt, and bracelets, &c.

Ancient Gallic period. Lacustrine objects. Polish antiquities.

Here, however, the interest was more archæological than artistic. The second and third rooms were devoted to art, and here were gathered together a series of relics of the ancient as well as of the mediæval world, and of the *Renaissance*, which might well detain us for many a day. But I only stop to note here the small *terra-cotta* figures found at Tanagra, of which the collection is not only very large, but the most important and interesting which has ever been seen together. These are but trifles in one sense. They are the free *genre* work of the Greeks, not aiming at finish or completeness, but slight and sketchy figures, adorned with color, evidently cheap, carelessly executed, and often mere squeezes from a mould, made for the people, and rep-

Artistic collection. Mediæval. *Renaissance.* Free Greek work in *terra cotta.*

FRANCE.

resenting the life, costume, character, history, and religion of the Greeks. But what life, what feeling, what dignity, what grace and refinement, are here to be seen; what intelligence and delicacy in the composition of the draperies; what simplicity and *naïveté* of design; what refinement of color! Here one sees what it is to be a naturally artistic people. There is no effort, no affectation, no grimacing, no attitudinizing, no over-insistance, no over-elaboration. The work is fresh, free, and spontaneous, the movement natural, the draperies beautiful. Of course there are great differences of mere execution between the different figures, but the same spirit runs through all. It is as if modeling came to them, as reading and writing to Dogberry, by nature. Here is a school in which modern sculptors may well take a lesson, and catch an inspiration for grace and beauty. Not that these works are accurate in particulars, or finished in execution, for they are not. It is not this that gives them their charm; it is the overruling and ever-present something which is imponderable and above calculation that has spontaneously expressed itself in them, and takes you with a sweet and natural surprise. They were "born so," as Topsy says. They are the natural growth of a large and graceful artistic nature.

Tanagra terra cottas.

ARCHITECTURE.

Architecture.

We now come to the architecture, which I shall treat in a very cursory manner. Without illustrative drawings it is scarcely possible, by mere description, to convey to the reader an intelligent impression or to justify special criticism. But if this be difficult in regard to painting and sculpture, it is almost impossible in architecture; and thus far I have labored under great disadvantages in not being able to illustrate by engravings at least the chief works which have been noticed. Besides, the field is too large to be occupied in this report, and it must be left to other and abler hands.

Exposition Buildings.

Exposition Buildings.

Main building.

The main buildings of the Exposition were constructed under the direction of M. Kranz by M. Hardy, architect of the *palais*, assisted by M. Duval and M. Dion. The criticisms to which they have been exposed have been various; and this was to be expected, all the more that they conformed to no established school and to no recognized style or epoch, but aimed at combining many mixed styles, sometimes successfully and sometimes unfortunately, and adapting them essentially to construction in iron. These iron constructions are modern, and here is a field for novelty, of which the architects endeavored to avail themselves. As the buildings were only temporary, and not intended to be permanent, a free opportunity was offered to daring innovation and bold tentatives of effect such as rarely occurs, and on all sides we saw trials which sometimes succeeded and sometimes failed. The restriction of time must be taken also into consideration in judging of the result. They were necessarily planned and built rapidly, and little opportunity was afforded for reconsideration and study. As far as the interior plan is concerned, it was excellent—simple, clear, and admirably adapted to its purpose, and this, after all, was the matter of prime importance.

Main Building.

Independent of the main building, and differing from it in design and construction, the municipality of Paris erected for itself a special pavilion. This was intrusted to M. Bouvard as architect. Iron in this building was largely employed, but subordinated to the uses of construction, so that it did not make a leading feature of the architectural effect. On the whole the result was good and in many points original. There were six large doors, surrounded by frames of iron which were ornamented with enameled tiles, and on either side were deep panels decorated with large designs in the same material. A great deal of color was used, and the objection was that it was not harmonious in combination and was too crude in tints. But though this polychrome treatment cannot, in this instance, be considered as quite satisfactory, it clearly shows, with happy combinations, what admirable effects might be produced. The interior disposition was very simple and good. This building is to remain, and to be transformed into a municipal gymnasium.

Municipality of Paris Building.

The palace of the Trocadero is also to be permanent. This was designed by MM. Davioud and Bourdais, and is intended for a permanent exhibition of retrospective art. It is a mixture of many styles—Greek, Roman, Byzantine, Arabian, and *Renaissance*—and yet it has a character as a whole differing from all, and is essentially modern, and the effort of the architects has been to construct a building adapted to the purposes for which it is intended, and not merely an exterior elevation which, though admirable in itself, has no proper relation to the interior or to its use as a building. In this they have struck the right note. It is use that is the corner-stone of architecture, and ornament should be subordinated to and superposed on lines of construction. One of the great faults of modern architecture is that to ornament an independent significance is too often given, con-

Trocadero.

FRANCE.

tradictory to construction, and the exterior bears no proper relation to the special purpose of the building. When one sees a Greek temple constructed for a bank, or a dimly-lighted Gothic structure for a hotel or modern house, one may be sure that somebody has blundered. MM. Daviond and Bourdais have not fallen at least into such an error. The interior has not been sacrificed to mere architectural effect from without. The difficulties of their programme were great, but on the whole they may be said to have been fairly surmounted.

Trocadero.

Music Hall of the Trocadero.

In the center is a vast hall, 50 meters in diameter, and intended for music, capable of holding 6,000 persons, surrounded by two stories of piered porticos and windows, the outer curves of which are developed on the *façade*. This is flanked on either side by two pavilions with gilded cupolas and two long curved lateral galleries spreading out like arms and adorned with porticos with columns, under which the visitor can walk and overlook the panorama of Paris. On either side the central rotunda is a lofty tower, rising over 260 feet in height, and the central hall is crowned with a lantern, on the top of which is a gilt figure of "Fame," by M. Mercié. The chief defects which have been found with this building is that the façade is uncertain, the cage of the concert hall nude, the hall itself defective in acoustic qualities, and the two great towers both too high for the main part of the building, and too narrow, and the lantern by which the rotunda is crowned is poor and ineffective. It must also be confessed that these constant curves diminish the dignity and grandeur of the structure.

La Rue des Nations.

Street of Nations.

A great feature of the Exposition was to be found in the so-called *Rue des Nations*, where, on one of the main avenues traversing the zones allotted to the products of various nations, each nation erected a characteristic building and *façade* illustrative of its architecture. The first in importance, and decidedly the best of all, was that of Belgium. This was really an imposing building, constructed in solid materials, and in the finest stone and marbles of the country. In style, it was of the latter part of the XVIth century, of which the most perfect example is to be found in the *Hotel de Ville*, at Antwerp, but it was not a simple reproduction of that, or of any other actual building, but a fresh composition in that style. A great gate formed the center of this *façade*, above which rose a rich *pignon* with pyramidal superpositions. On the keystone of the main arch were carved the

Belgium.

LA RUE DES NATIONS. CHAMP DE MARS.

[Page 152, vol. II.]

armorial bearings of the provinces, and above, two Belgian lions supported the royal shield; on one side was a salon with a covered balcony, on the other a belfry terminating in an octagonal lantern. All this was worked out with colored marbles, and stone, and brick, and bronze, with snow-like columns, so as to be very effective. *Rue des Nations.*

England did not confine herself to one great building, but erected several in different styles. One of these was the pavilion of the Prince of Wales in the Elizabethan order, constructed in brick and terra cotta, with imitation stone-work and faïence applications, which had nothing special to recommend it as characteristic or original. Besides this there were three houses—one designed by Mr. Norman Shaw, one by Mr. Gilbert R. Redgrave, and one by Messrs. Collinson & Locke, all of them interesting specimens of early English houses. Especially simple and pleasing was the last mentioned. It was a cottage constructed of beams of wood with intervals of rough-cast plaster painted white, roofed with red tiles, with a jutting porch supporting a bay window, and pierced with low, broad windows with diamonded panes. The interior was quite as attractive as the exterior. The cottage by Mr. Redgrave was more elaborate, with carved beams and rosetted woodwork under which the plaster shows, one high peaked central roof, flanked by two smaller ones, and low rows of continuous congregated windows. Messrs. Doulton & Co. also exhibited a square building, two stories high, constructed in brick, with columns, friezes, cornices, etc., in colored terra cotta, and adorned with enameled tiles, which deserves to be noted. England.

Sweden and Norway were both represented by constructions in wood, which were national, characteristic, and striking. They were rustic houses of ancient style, massive in character, with broad projecting eaves and narrow windows to protect them from the snow and icy gales of winter, a covered gallery, and a clock beneath it, and heavy hewn posts. The architect was M. Thrap Meyer, of Christiania. Of the two houses, preference may be given to that of Norway, but both were interesting. Sweden and Norway.

After these came the *Loggia* of Italy, in which the architect cannot be said to have been happily inspired. With all the noble *loggie* of Italy before him, it is difficult to see how he could have gone so astray. This *loggia* is divided into five arches, the central one of which, rising higher than the others, breaks the line of cornice, disturbs the seriousness of the effect, and rounds itself into a cylindrical cupola. These arches are supported by columns of imitation *cipollino*. The Italy.

Rue des Nations. *entablement* is ornamented with poor mosaic and *terra-cotta*, and imitation marbles, out of harmony in color and pretentious in effect. The whole design indicates the same restlessness and want of seriousness which is seen in their sculpture. *Voila des nouveautés.*

Japan. Japan came next, and here we had something peculiar and original, and striking for its bold primitiveness of character. Two great beams of natural wood and traverses support and cover a great door; the ends are finished and protected against the assaults of the weather by capsules of green bronze. On the right and left, in a frame-work of wood, were two great colored maps, one of Tokio, and the other of Japan, and on either side the door was a fountain of ornamented work surrounded by bamboo, and picturesque inscriptions in Japanese served as ornaments to the whole, somewhat after the manner of the Arabian architecture.

China. The Chinese *façade* was insignificant and *bizarre*. The walls were covered with lozenges and octagons of a gray slate color on a ground of green, crowned with a double frieze of angles. The door was of a bright vermilion, and above it was a shield defended by grinning dragons, and groups of diminutive warriors were figured on the wall with sabres and lances.

Spain. Spain came next, and erected a *façade* in the Moorish style, consisting of a central pavilion with lateral walls ending on either side in smaller pavilions. The central pavilion is copied from that of the Palace of Alhamar at Grenada, decorated with details from the principal ancient monuments at Cordova, Grenada, and Seville, with painting and gilding and *faïences* and enamels. The two pavilions at each extremity were more sober in style, and ornamented also with selected details. There was too much decoration, and the eye was fatigued by the want of any repose of simple surfaces to give it relief.

Austria-Hungary. Next came Hungary and Austria (Germany was not represented). This *façade* was a succession of arcades supported by coupled columns of the Doric order, and on the *tympani* and friezes were *graffiti* designs after the manner of the late Munich school, consisting of griffins, garlands, vases, cornucopiæ, cartouches, inscriptions, candelabræ, etc. Below on the bases were diamonded and pointed bosses.

Russia. The Russian, which was next in order, was of an entirely opposite character. The Austrian was composite, and in measure a reminiscence of early Italian, but the Russian was national, affected rudeness and massiveness, and took the theme of her *façade* from old Russian edifices, and particularly from the palace of Kolonera near Moscow, the birth place of Peter the Great. There were three great pavilions with picturesque roofs, connected together by a covered gallery on one side, and an exterior staircase on the other. The heavy woodwork was carved and decorated, and the friezes, cornices, and window frames were cut into various ornamental forms The whole was impressive and had a barbaric character which was not without its charm. *Rue des Nations.*

If from the Swiss Confederation one might have expected a *chalet* as being especially characteristic, he would have been entirely disappointed. Instead of this, we had a massive construction of quite a different style and character. Above a great arch was a balustrade, forming a terrace surmounted by a convex roof, out of character with the rest of the edifice. Above this rose a peaked belfry, and under the open arch were two figures of Burgundians on either side the bell, who struck on it the hours. Right and left of the main door were large shields with the arms of the Confederation in colors, supported by purely heraldic lions, while the frieze under the roof on the lateral parts were adorned with a series of cantonal escutcheons painted in color. It cannot be said on the whole that this was a harmonious structure or particularly happy in its conception. Switzerland.

Greece was particularly unfortunate. It was represented by an *ædiculum* without grace, grandeur, or proportion, with enormous Roman *modillons*, and crude effects of *polychromie*. Greece.

Denmark had a modest *façade* in the style of the Belgian *Renaissance*, but with no specialty of national character. Denmark.

Portugal reproduced in her *façade* the Cloister of Belem near Lisbon. In architecture it was a curious mixture of many styles. Gothic and *Renaissance*, Moorish and Roman, with flat round arches, slender twisted columns, heavy pilasters, Gothic statuettes, and Arabian and Roman ornaments. Portugal.

The States of South and Central America had a structure in the style imported from Spain in the sixteenth century, and modified so as to adapt it to the climate and the customs of the people. It was taken chiefly from a palace at Lima, called La Casa Marques de Torre Tagle, with an inclosed balcony, studded with windows and overhanging a triple-arched portico. The upper part of the balcony was ornamented with the shields of each of the South American republics. South and Central America.

Morocco, Tunis, Siam, and Persia erected small lodges of no importance and scarcely demanding notice. Morocco, Tunis, Siam, Persia.

Holland distinguished herself by a structure in brick and stone of good taste and moderated ornament, which favora- Holland.

Rue des Nations. bly compared with that of Belgium and had more restraint and distinction of style.

United States. I prefer to say nothing about the *façade* of the United States on my own account, but will merely cite the judgment of two or three of the ablest critics:

"La façade des États Unis," says M. Charles Blanc, "est sans caractère et ne manifeste pas même un sóupçon d'art. Quelque chose de sauvage perce encore a travers cette architecture, parfaitement convenable d'ailleurs pour un café de New York, Philadelphie, ou de Chicago." Mons. Paul Sedille, after commenting on the structures of Great Britain, says of them: "Quelle contraste avec le Pavillon des États Unis! Qu'est il? Une gare—un établissement de bains—un poste de police? Cela est difficile à dire. D'ailleurs cette construction, encore en bois, ne pretend pas aux formes solides et durables du monument. Elle semble plutôt offrir un échantillon de des carcasses de bois faciles a démontér et à transporter, destinées à la création instantanée de quelque ville nouvelle sur le bord d'un lac encore inconnu, Ce n'est pas même de la charpente, c'est plutôt une boite en menuiserie, n'expriment qu' un seul désir, faire vite et enconomiquement."

The responsibility of this is not, however, to be thrown solely on the shoulders of the architect, nor indeed upon any of the commissioners. There was neither time nor money to enable us to erect a proper structure, conformable to the wealth or the dignity of our country, and the consequence was precisely what M. Sedille says, that the commissioner-general and his subordinates were forced to have but one aim—to build cheaply and rapidly; to save time and money at any risk. We did save money; we did save time; but we lost credit. We went to a great international reception in our shirt-sleeves.

On the whole the effect of the *Rue des Nations* was very picturesque and varied, and it was thronged by a constant crowd. The idea of this street was Mr. Berger's, and we congratulate him on its happiness and on the success with which it was carried out.

Architectural Designs.

FRANCE.

Architectural designs.

FRANCE.

In the pavilion of the Ville de Paris were exhibited in drawing and in models a number of buildings lately erected or still to be erected, the models of which were carefully executed in plaster of Paris. It is quite impossible to review all these, but among the best in style and design may be mentioned the *Bibliotéque de l'École de Droit*, by M. L. Heureux, architect, and M. Cheville, sculptor. The *Collége Rollin*, by M. Roger, and some of the *Mairies*, which are well designed and effective, specially those of the eleventh and twelfth arrondissements, the former by M. Hénard and the latter by M. Gancel. One room in the main building was devoted to restorations from the antique by the French students at Rome, all well done. Among them we may specially note the restoration of the "Tomb of Mausolus," by Louis Bernier, which is harmonious and effective, and closely conforms to the description of this splendid mausoleum by Pliny; "The Baths of Titus," by M. Leclerc; the "Palestra Palatina" and "Temple of the Sun," by M. Gerhardt; the "Forum of Augustus," by M. Noguet; the "Forum of Trajan," by M. Guadet, and the "Villa Madama," by M. Bénard.

FRANCE. Heureux. Cheville. Roger et al. Restoration from the antique. Bernier. Leclerc. Gerhardt. Noguet. Guadet. Bénard.

There were also a great number of restorations of ancient, mediæval, and *Renaissance* buildings and historical monuments in the French department of architecture, such as the restoration of "*Mont St. Michel*," by M. Corroyer, and the "*Chateau de Pau*," by M. Lafollye, and many of the old abbeys, cloisters, churches, fortifications, castles, tombs, hospices, amphitheatres—all exceedingly interesting, and under the special charge of the *Commission des Monuments Historique*. Besides these were a considerable variety of plans for new buildings of every kind, with their decorations and details, which would merit attention, but as there were nearly 400 different works, it will at once be seen that it is impossible here to do more than simply to refer to them *en masse*, without even attempting to particularize.

Restoration of the mediæval and rennaissance builders and monuments. Corroyer. Lafollye.

ENGLAND.

England also sent a considerable number of architectural designs, chiefly of buildings lately erected. In most of these designs good taste and knowledge of styles and details was shown. The chief fault to be found with them is quite apart from their mere architectural merit, and it is that English architects do not ordinarily take into consideration the dull character of their climate, and rather affect styles which would be better fitted for a bright and sunny atmosphere. As a rule the windows are small and the ornamentation massive and inclined to be heavy, and the *façades* crowded. Among these designs are to be noted specially those by Mr. Charles Barry of "Alleyn's College," at Dulwich, exterior and interior. This building, which is in

ENGLAND. C. Barry.

ENGLAND.

E. M. Barry.

red brick, is handsome and effective. "Stevenstone House," by the same architect, seems in the drawing a little heavy and overweighted by the upper part. Mr. E. M. Barry sent some restorations and additions to "Crewe Hall," also of red brick, well-windowed, surmounted by a balustrade, and plans for the "New National Gallery," which is in the old, well-known style of a central mass with dome and lateral wings. The interior is handsome in itself, but, as far as one can judge from the drawings, the artist seems to have thought of everything rather than the purpose and object of the building, which is to exhibit pictures and statues, and to which it seems little adapted. Mr. Norman Shaw sent drawings of "Pierrepoint," which is a good specimen of old English with gables. Mr. Street sent several drawings, among which is particularly to be noticed the bird's-eye view of the "New Palace of Justice," London, which is admirable. Mr. Wyatt sent drawings of a house in Park Lane in red brick, which is spirited, and of the "New Exchange" at Liverpool, in which there is nothing special or new. Messrs. George & Peto sent drawings of an "Old Manor House" at Rousden with towers and a sloping roof, which is simple, broad in effect, and well designed. We must also note some admirable drawings for the church of "St. Augustine's," Kilburn, London, by Mr. Pearson; the "Exterior of a House" and the "Interior of a Church" by Mr. Plumbe; an "Entresol" by Mr. Plumbe, which is very good; some admirable designs by Mr. Waterhouse; and a "Country House" by Mr. Young, which is pretty and varied in composition.

Shaw. Street. Wyatt. George & Peto. Pearson. Plumbe. Waterhouse. Young.

ITALY.

ITALY.

Italy sent a few architectural drawings, but they are not specially distinguished. The most important was the design for the *façade* of the cathedral at Florence, now in execution.

AUSTRIA-HUNGARY.

AUSTRIA-HUNGARY.

Austria sent 78 architectural designs, some of which are important and admirable. "The Hotel de Ville at Vienna," by Herr Schmidt, has much that is original and striking, and rich in its open-work decoration. The tower seems a little too narrow for the rest of the building, but, worked out, it may be different. His design of the "Post-office at Bâle" is also out of the common, and exhibits much talent. Herr Wurm's project for the "Hotel de Ville at Hamburg" is rich and varied, and very effective in its perfections of light and dark. Herr Ferstel also sent some admirable designs for

Schmidt. Wurm. Ferstel.

a "Votive Church at Vienna," the "Royal Museum of Art at Vienna," and the "University at Vienna." Herr Hansen some very clever designs for the "New Parliament House," the "Academy of the Fine Arts," the "New Exchange," all at Vienna, and the "Academy of Sciences," at Athens, the last especially to be noted for its merit. Herr Hasenauer's designs are also worthy of much praise, and we must also note those of Herr C. Köning, Herr F. Neumann, and Herr A. Wielemans. On the whole, these designs reflect great credit upon the Vienna architects. They are not tame or common, but spirited, clever, and at times original.

{ AUSTRIA-HUNGARY.

Hansen.

Hasenauer.

Köning. Neumann. Wielemans.

In architecture America sent nothing, and there was little to detain us in the other countries.

ENGRAVINGS.

Engravings.

There was a very considerable number of engravings in this Exposition, but we can but give a glance at them. The art of line engraving has of late years counted but few ardent disciples, and Photography has struck at it a severe blow. But there are still eminent engravers who cling to the old and classical style, and from time to time present admirable works to the public.

FRANCE.

Among the French may be named, for instance, Bertinot, Blanchard, Salmon, Huot, Daugnin, Didier, Waltner, Jacquet, and Gaillard, who were all represented here. Most of the engravers, however, have of late rather given themselves to etching and engraving in *aqua-fortis*, and some of these productions have shown great talent, and the comparative freedom and facility of this method of engraving has induced many painters to try their hand at it, with very considerable success, and often with masterly effects. Among engravers and painters who have devoted themselves to this branch may be specially mentioned as in the front line those of M. Jacquemart, who sent a number of spirited and powerful engravings, chiefly from the Dutch and Flemish masters. M. Leopold Fleming has abandoned the burin and acquired a high reputation as an aqua-fortist. He sent 22 specimens of his art. Among others also must be specially noticed as distinguished in this art, Mills, Rajon, Chauvel, Boilvin, Gilbert, Monziès, Milins, and Greux. M. Rajon has, among other works, reproduced with spirit the pictures of Meissonier, Brion, and Alma-Tadema, and particularly a very clever portrait of Darwin, which is admirably rendered; M. Chauvel the landscapes of Diaz, Corot,

FRANCE.

Bertinot, Blanchard, Salmon *et al.*

Jacquemart.

Fleming.

Mills, Rajon *et al.*

Chauvel.

FRANCE. Boilvin. Milius. Gilbert. Monziès. Courtry. Laguillermie. Brunet-Debaines. Nicolle. Hédouin.

Daubigny, Dupré. M. Boilvin has treated a number of his own designs, representing the adventures of Pantagruel, Gargantua, and Panurge. M. Milius has rendered with spirit "*Les Fauconniers*" of Fromentin, the "Cats" of Lambert, and a painting of Goya. M. Gilbert has in some cases adopted another style, touching with the burin after biting with aqua-fortis, as in the portrait of a lady from Henner. So also has M. Monziès in the portrait of "M. Coquelin" after Vibert. Mr. Courtry sent 13 engravings from contemporary painters, such as Troyon and Van Marcke, Delacroix, Gérôme, Meissonier, and Munkacsy. M. Monziès had engravings from Vibert, Goupil, Meissonier, Brion, and Wauters. Among other engravings in the French section should also be noted those by Laguillermie; the ancient "Hotel de Ville," at Paris, by Brunet-Debaines; four engravings of streets and buildings, by M. Nicolle; and a series of illustrations of "*Manon Lescaut*," Sterne's "Sentimental Journey," and the "*Voyage autour de ma Chambre*," composed by the engraver, M. Hédouin.

ENGLAND.

ENGLAND. Herkomer. Palmer. Macbeth. Edwards. Doo. Atkinson. Heseltine. Stacpoole. Evershed. Faed. Haden. Richeton.

England also sent 36 engravings on wood, steel, copper, and aqua fortis. Among these were several by the painters themselves, of their own pictures. M. Herkomer sent two, a souvenir of Rembrandt, and a Welsh Woman; Mr. Palmer his "Early Ploughman" and "Morning of Life"; Mr. Macbeth, aqua-fortes of three of his pictures; Mr. Edwards two pictures of "London from the Observatory," and "Blackfriar's Bridge"; Mr. Doo sent three portraits, one from Sir Thomas Lawrence; Mr. Atkinson three engravings, two from paintings by M. Millais; Mr. Heseltine some aqua-fortes; Mr. Stacpoole sent three—the "Roll Call" of Miss Thompson, "The Palm Offering" by F. Goodall, "Circe and the Companions of Ulysses" by Mr. Briton Rivière; Mr. Evershed "*Sur la Tamise*" and "*Pointes Sèches*"; Mr. Faed two portraits after Sir Daniel Macnee; Mr. Haden the "Pier of Calais," after Turner, and "The Breaking up of the Agamemnon"; Mr. Richeton a portrait of "Richard Wagner" and "William III" after Rembrandt. Messrs. Dalziel Bros. sent some proofs of engravings on wood from their own designs for "The Pilgrim's Progress," and from Mr. Barnard's designs in illustration of some of Dickens' novels.

ITALY.

ITALY. Bartolo.

Italy sent 13 engravings, all of which have merit. Among the best we may note five acqua-fortis portraits and studies of animals by Sig. di Bartolo, and "The Sacred and Profane

Love," by Titian, engraved with the burin. The "Daughter of Tintoretto," by Sig. Pagliano, and the "Arch of Titus," by Sig. Beltrami, and the "Court of the Palazzo Marino" at Milan, by Sig. L. Conconi, and the "Remorse" of Sig. Gilli. Sig. Danele had a "Cleopatra" engraved with the burin, and Sig. Turletti a "Virgin in the Catacombs" and the "Death of Boniface," in aqua-fortis. ITALY.

SPAIN.

Spain sent 52 engravings and chromo-lithographs and lithographs; 24 in aqua-fortis were from the frescoes of "St. Antonio de la Floridas" (by Goya), and engraved by Sig. Galban y Candela; Sen. Rossel y Torres sent also 20 engravings in aqua-fortis, and Sen. Navarrete y Jos a portrait by Goya, engraved with the burin. The remainder were lithographs and sketches for the "*Illustration Espagnole et Americaine.*" SPAIN.

AUSTRIA-HUNGARY.

Austria sent 18 engravings; among which are to be specially noted five in aqua-fortis, by Herr W. Unger, after Rembrandt, Rubens, and Snyders; four by Herr Sonnenleitner (*en taille douce*), after Rubens, Knaus, and Defregger; and eight by Herr Klaus, after L'Allemand, Velasquez, and Müller. AUSTRIA-HUNGARY.

SWITZERLAND.

Switzerland sent 10 engravings, among which are to be noted those by M. F. Weber, of the "Sacred and Profane Love," by Titian, a "Madonna," by Luini, and "Amerbach," by Holbein. M. Girardet sent three after M. Bonheur and M. Baron. SWITZERLAND.

BELGIUM.

Belgium sent 19, of which particularly are to be mentioned three by M. Biot, engravings on steel, representing the "Triumph of Galatea," and portraits of "M. Sanford" and of "the Emperor of Austria," and three engravings on wood by M. Pannemaker. BELGIUM.

RUSSIA.

Russia sent 26, of which ten were in aqua-fortis, by M. Schichkine. M. Redlich sent an engraving on copper, after a picture by Meteiko, representing Pierre Skarga preaching before Sigismond III, for which he received the medal of honor. RUSSIA.

UNITED STATES.

America sent 12 etchings and engravings on wood, of which six by Mr. Henry Marsh, two by Mr. J. A. Mitchell, UNITED STATES.

UNITED STATES. one by Mr. Fred. Moller are specially to be noted. In wood-engraving America distinguishes herself, and we cannot refrain, in passing, from referring to the admirable specimens to be seen lately in "Scribner's" and "Harper's Magazines," in which not only the design is at times to be highly commended but also the engraving. It is greatly to be regretted that in this branch we were not more largely represented in the Exposition.

Scribner's Magazine. Harper's Magazine.

Repoussée Chasings.

Repoussée. Tiffany & Co.

In engraving, laminated metals, *repoussée* work, niello, and chasing, Messrs. Tiffany & Co. eminently distinguished themselves, and for the admirable work they displayed justly received one of the three *grandes medailles*. Not only for mere workmanship are they to be highly commended, but also for the good taste displayed in the designs, many of which were as beautiful in form and outline as in the refined delicacy of their execution. The copies of the gold ornaments of the Cesnola collection were wonderful specimens of elaborate and almost deceptive imitation of the antique originals, even to their defects and imperfections, while the cups, vases, bowls, pictures they exhibited might challenge comparison with the best work of Europe or Japan.

Medals.

Medals.

In medals, America is peculiarly weak, if one may judge from the national coins, which are inferior to the coins of almost every other country, not only in the tastefulness of the design, but in the quality of the workmanship. So far from improving, the later coinage, as far as design and die-work goes, are even worse than those of an early day. They are, in a word, for the most part, vulgar. While in the fine engraving of bank-notes we have risen to excellence, in our coins we have scarcely achieved respectability. On the contrary, the medals here exhibited by France and England are admirable, and the late coinage of England is specially to be commended. Nothing in any coinage can compare to the best antique coins of Greece, at least so far as beauty of design in their ideal heads; but in workmanship the coinage and medals of Europe, and especially of France and England, have been carried to a high point of excellence. Among the medals and coins to be noted are those executed by Messrs. Dubois, Merley, Degeorge, Lagrange, Dupuis, Oudiné, Ponscarme, and Chaplain.

American compared with French and English. Greek coins.

NATIONAL ART EDUCATION.

National Art Education.

I have already occupied too much space and must hurry to a conclusion. But before doing so a few statistics seem to be demanded, in regard to the national encouragement of the fine arts in Europe. There is scarcely a country, however small, that has not national museums and academies devoted to the fine arts, to which an annual sum, and often a very considerable one, is inscribed in the budget, and that does not seek in various ways to honor and encourage art and artists. As a nation we may be almost said to stand alone in our rejection of their claims. Not only painting, sculpture, and architecture are under supervision in England and on the Continent, but music has also its claims and its appropriations of no inconsiderable sums.

ENGLAND.

ENGLAND.

Beginning with England, the sum inscribed in the budget for 1878, for education, science, and art, was £3,847,390, which included the following:

Government aid to science and art.

Museum and galleries.

1st. For the department of science and art		£307,414
For the purchase of works of art	£6,000	
For the reproduction of works of art	1,500	
Making photographs, and engravings in aqua-fortis	750	
Purchase of oil pictures and aquarelles	1,000	
Exchange of reproductions	200	
Library of arts	2,000	
Purchase for museum, Jermyn street	500	
Museum, Edinburgh	2,500	
Museum, Dublin	1,000	
2d. The British Museum		112,990
For the purchase of manuscripts	2,500	
For the purchase of oriental antiquities	250	
Excavations in Assyria	2,000	
Purchase of national antiquities, objects of art of the middle ages, and ethnography	500	
Purchase of Greek and Roman antiquities	2,500	
Purchase of medals and silver coin	1,000	
3d. The National Gallery		11,983
Purchase of pictures and drawings	5,000	
4th. Gallery of National Portraits		2,000
Purchase of pictures, busts, &c	750	
5th. National Gallery of Scotland at Edinburgh		2,100
6th. National Gallery of Ireland at Dublin		2,389
For purchase of pictures	1,000	

This does not take into account special appropriations for accidental purchases, such as, for instance, occurred in 1871, upon the sale of Sir Robert Beal's collection, at which the

ENGLAND.

Royal Academy. National Gallery. British Museum. South Kensington Museum. Gallery of National Portraits. Liverpool Museum and Library.

English Government expended £75,000 for the purchase of 77 pictures, chiefly of the Dutch and Flemish schools, nor of the annual purchases of the Royal Academy. During the year 1878, there were added to the National Gallery by purchase, eight pictures of foreign schools, by Raffaelle (?) Botticelli, Fr. Bigio, Girard Horebout, Paul Veronese, Jean Jerome Savoldo, Catherine Van Hemessen, and Lippi, and six pictures of the English school. A very considerable number of works of various kinds were purchased for the British Museum, from the Italian, French, German, and English schools. The Assyrian department was enriched by a number of ancient relics of art, and by a variety of ancient coins of rarity and value. The museum of South Kensington made very considerable purchases, and acquired by gift or purchase 2,044 rare objects of art, among which were a work by L. Penicaud *dit* Nardon, and an oval portrait of Charles de Guise, Cardinal of Lorraine, surrounded by enamel plaques, attributed to Léonard Limousin, for which £4,000 were paid. The Gallery of National Portraits added greatly to its interesting collection. Besides these the museum, library, and galleries of art at Liverpool expend annually £12,000, in purchases, and new museums of art have been founded at Manchester and at Nottingham.

Prices paid by English government for pictures.

The prices paid in England for some of the pictures of the English school, sold at auction during the year 1878, may also be noted as showing the encouragement there afforded to artists: a portrait of "Lady Smith and Child," by Reynolds, 32,800 francs; portrait of "Madame Stanhope," by Reynolds, 78,750 francs; a "Fish-market" and "Grand Canal at Venice," by Bonnington, 78,750 francs each; "Boats," by Stanfield, 36,750 francs; a picture by Landseer, 42,000 francs; two pictures by Turner, 31,500 francs each; "St. Joseph," by Millais, 11,812 francs; "The Scapegoat," by Holman Hunt, 12,600 francs; portrait by Raeburn, 16,012 francs; "Crossing," by H. Thompson, 20,475 francs; a Landscape, by Gainsborough, 13,125 francs, etc.

The pictures by old masters of the "Gallery Novar" were also sold at auction, and the "Madonna del Candelabri," by Raffaelle, was withdrawn after an offer of 487,500 francs. "*La Vierge de la Legende*," also by Raffaelle, was sold for 78,750 francs; a Seaport, by Claude, at the same price; a Landscape, by Hobbema, at 52,760 francs; a "St. Antonio," by Murillo, 59,062 francs; "*Les deux Marquises*," by Watteau, 59,062 francs; "A Glass of Lemonade," by Terburg, 48,560 francs. "The Vision of St. Helena," by Paul Veronese, was bought by the National Gallery at 86,625 francs.

FRANCE.

FRANCE.

Let us now pass to France. The budget for the fine arts for 1878 amounted to 7,434,830 francs, and this has been vehemently complained of and reported upon by the commission as being altogether too small to meet the requirements of the nation. There is every reason, therefore, to suppose that the recommendations contained in the report of the director and commission for the fine arts will be complied with, and that this sum will be increased very materially.

Budget for the Fine Arts.

This sum was apportioned as follows:

Appropriation of money.

	Francs.
Administration Centrale (personel)	197,000
Administration Centrale (matériel)	40,000
Etablissement des Beaux Arts	597,510
Ouvrages d'art et decoration d'edifices publics	787,140
Exposition des artistes vivants	502,300
Theatres nationaux, Conservatoire de Musique	1,850,500
Souscription aux ouvrages d'art	90,000
Encouragement et secours (Beaux Arts)	140,000
Encouragement et secours (Theatres)	140,000
Monuments historiques	1,335,000
Musées Nationaux	762,000
Palais de Luxembourg	82,000
Manufactures Nationales	883,800
Manufactures Nationales (Exposition)	25,000
	7,434,830

In the annual budget of 698,275 francs accorded to the *Academie des Beaux Arts*, 15,000 are given to the preparation of the "*Dictionnaire des Beaux Arts*," 6,000 for the cost of medals for the *Grand Prix de Rome*, and the execution of cantatas. Every year the *Academie* distributes prizes to young artists at a solemn public meeting. Besides the *Grand Prix de Rome*, and those instituted by the government, the Academy also distributes a series of prizes established by private gift and bequest. The academy at Rome and the school of Athens are also supported by a credit of 144,200 francs. Each pensioner receives an annual pension of 3,510 francs, and the director a salary of 8,000 francs. In the *École des Beaux Arts*, by the last official report, there were 994 pupils, of whom 274 were painters, 146 sculptors, and 574 architects. An annual competition takes place, and prizes of importance are adjudged. Besides this there are the *École des Arts Decorative*, *l'École Nationale de Dessin pour les Jeunes Filles*, and the National Manufactures at Sèvres, Gobelins, and Beauvais, which give much occupation to decorative artists. Besides this the municipality of Paris disposes

Academie des Beaux Arts.

Dictionnaire des Beaux Arts.

Prix de Rome.

Academy at Rome and at Athens.

École des Beaux Arts.

École des Arts Decorative, &c.

Sèvres.

Gobelins.

Beauvais.

FRANCE. of a credit of 300,000 francs in works of art, which is distributed among the best artists of France. Within the year 1878, 52,000 francs were expended in sculpture, and the remainder in other works of decoration, and of painting.

Salon. The government annually purchases from the *Salon*, and from distinguished living artists, a very considerable number of works which are given a permanent place in their noble galleries; and the great national collections are constantly enriched by the purchase of valuable works of antiquity and of the past. In the provinces also art is encouraged by public academies and societies, independently of the government.

Sales at the Hotel Drouot. At the Hotel Drouot, sales of works of art take place, and here, by the prices paid, one can judge of the patronage of art and the interest it arouses in France. It would be quite impossible here to go through the lists of their sales during the year 1878, but we may note a few of the highest prices for works of contemporary artists. "*Le Liseur*," one of the most celebrated pictures of Meissonier, was sold at 27,100 francs; "The two Van der Veldes," by the same artist, at 57,100 francs; "*Reverie*," by Madrago, 4,010 francs; "*Antechambre au Vatican*," by Fortuny, 6,000 francs; "*Le Taureau en Liberté*," by Brácassat, 19,000 francs; "*La Méridienne*," by Jules Dupré, 20,700 francs; "*Le Matin*," by Rousseau, 27,000 francs; "*Les Couturiéres*," by Millet, 10,700 francs; "*Animaux en Pâturages*," by Troyon, 46,000 francs; "*Berger gardant ses Moutons*," by the same, 30,000 francs; "*Le Giaour et le Pacha*," by E. Delacroix, 27,000 francs.

GERMANY.

GERMANY. Budget for the fine arts. In Germany, the budget allowed to the department of the fine arts amounted to 2,438,230 marks, equivalent to 3,047,782 francs, the main part of which was thus distributed:

Sums afforded.

	Marks.
Traitements	156,000
Employés, &c	56,614
Entretien des collections et achats	448,375
Entretien des Batiments	56,620
Frais divers	215,783

National galleries. Great reforms were proposed in this department during the year 1878, and a larger sum was demanded for purchases to enrich the various museums and galleries, and this will, in all probability, be allowed for the future. There are the great galleries of Berlin, of Munich, of Dresden, of Frankfort, and of Cassel, rich in works of eminent masters, and to which constant additions are made. For the Berlin galleries the chefs d'œuvres of the Stroggi collection in Florence were purchased in 1878, for which 180,000 francs were paid. These consisted of 3 pictures—a portrait by Titian, a portrait by Botticelli, and a portrait by Bronzino; one statue and two busts, one of Niccolo Strozzi, by Nieno de Fiesole, and one of Marietta Strozzi, by Desiderio de Settignano. The cabinet of engravings was enriched in 1867 by many prints, among which were more than 40 by Albert Dürer, so that it may now be said to hold the first place after that of the Collection Albertine, at Vienna, in prints by this master. The sum expended on these was 100,000 francs.

FRANCE.

Gallery of Berlin.

The new gallery at Cassel was opened in 1877, and contains among other valuable works the interesting collection of the Dutch masters, formerly belonging to the Electors of Hesse. On this gallery the government expended 1,200,000 marks.

Gallery of Cassel.

Another new gallery has been just opened at Frankfort in which has been placed a very fine collection of pictures and engravings.

Frankfort Gallery.

In the magnificent collection well-known at Dresden 462,972 marks were expended on new purchases in 1874–'75, during which time 49 works of ancient masters were purchased at 257,000 marks, as well as twelve modern pictures.

Dresden Gallery.

Besides this, archæological and artistic societies are established in Rome and Athens, and a considerable number of distinguished archæologists are there supported by the government. The works on art published by these and others in Germany are very important and valuable. Among these may be specified: the "History of Painting in the Middle Ages," by Professor Waltman; the "History of Painting from the IV to the XVI Centuries;" the "General History of the Fine Arts," by Professor Lübec; the "Monograph on Jules Signorelli and the *Renaissance*," by Dr. Visscher; and the "Dictionary of Artists," by Dr. Julius Meyer, which is now in course of publication. In addition to this, large excavations are carried on by the government in Greece, which have resulted in the remarkable discoveries by Dr. Schliemann and others, well-known now throughout the artistic world.

Societies at Rome and Athens.

Histories and Dictionaries of Painting and Artists.

Dr. Schliemann.

ITALY.

In Italy, restricted as are its finances at present, a lively interest is felt in all that appertains to the fine arts. The government is the head of all the academies at Milan, Turin, Florence, Naples, Venice, Bologna, Parma, Modena, Pavia, Lucca, Massa, and Reggio Emelia. In Genoa, Bergamo,

ITALY.

National academies.

ITALY.

Verona, Urbino, Siena, Pisa, Perugia, and Ravenna, the chief burden of the expenses is borne by the provinces and municipalities.

Budget for the fine arts.

The budget gives to the state for the fine arts 1,970,179 francs, thus distributed:

	Francs.
Personnel des Academies, Instituts, et Pinacotheques	697,435
Matériel	451,898
Depense divers	58,289
Personnel des Musées, des Fouilles, Conservation des Antiquités	313,382
Matériel	449,175

Excavations at Pompeii, Rome, etc.

Excavations are now being made in various quarters, and specially at Pompeii, Palestina, Sipontum, and Rome. The Tiber has not as yet yielded any great number of objects, at least as far as they have been exhibited, and questions have raised made as to those which have been discovered, and explanations demanded as to their non-appearance. The result of the excavations during the last few years has been very satisfactory, and a large number of statues and some remarkable wall paintings of great interest and importance have been unearthed. New museums have also been constructed for their exhibition, and the government has now founded a new museum of art applied to industry.

Gallery at Florence.

The gallery at Florence has been enriched by 50 works, chiefly of the science school. Unfortunately the government is too poor to secure for its national collections all the important works which from time to time are sold from private galleries. Many of these have of late gone into the possession of foreign countries, for the weight of taxation and the cost of retaining such works brings about forced sales. Among other things lately sold may be mentioned two bronzes attributed to Michel Angelo (?), which were bought at Venice by Madame le Barronne de Rothschild for 350,000 francs; two busts purchased for the Berlin Gallery for 100,000 francs; 350 pieces of ceramics sold to Paris by Sig. Castellani; and a number of pictures purchased by England.

Monuments to Victor Emanuel.

But, notwithstanding the unfortunate financial condition of Italy at the present moment, conspicuous sums were voted within the year 1878 for the erection in the various cities of monuments in honor of Victor Emanuel, amounting to over 13,000,000 of francs. Of this sum 10,000,000 have been appropriated by the government to the monument in Rome, 1,000,000 to that in Turin, 400,000 to that in Milan, 250,000 to that in Venice, and so on. These were voted within a year of the King's death, while America, as a nation, has as yet, after the lapse of nearly a century, erected no national monument to Washington, and still seems to grudge the outlay necessary to complete one worthy of the country and of its great leader in the path of liberty.

ITALY.

AUSTRIA-HUNGARY.

AUSTRIA-HUNGARY.

Austria also is devoting large sums to the development of art. I have not been able to obtain the amount attributed to her in the budget to this purpose, but it is large. At present, in addition to the magnificent collections of art, she is engaged in building and adorning the new great National Museum in Vienna, some of the statues for which appeared at the Exposition and have already been spoken of. Besides this, there is the Academy of Vienna and the Hotel of the Kunstler Verein at Vienna, now in execution, and the great monument to Beethoven. A glance into the catalogue of architectural places at her section at the Exposition of Paris, as well as of statues and pictures, will show the great works on which she is engaged, all giving work to artists and tending to develop art.

National Museum of Vienna.

Academies at Vienna.

Here I must pause, passing over with merely general remarks the encouragement given by the other nations of Europe to the fine arts. In a word, let it be said that Russia, Spain, Belgium, Holland, Sweden, Norway, Denmark—all, in fact, show a national pride in art, all have their great national galleries, museums, and academies, and all give largely of their means to support them. Nowhere are they neglected by any nation as a nation. Nowhere are they left solely to private patronage or special municipalities. Nowhere are artists without public rewards and honors and distinctions. Nowhere does any nation neglect their claims and deny them their honors, save in America.

National encouragement to fine arts in Europe generally.

We as a nation have built our house. It is useful. It is commodious. To its practical departments we have given much thought. But art as yet has no place in it. We claim to be a practical people. We insist that use is better than beauty; that if our national house is not decorated and beautified, it is because beauty is of no practical benefit to men. We talk perpetually of our being a new country, whose business it is to fell forests, open new paths, plant sawmills, build towns and railways, and attend to business. Undoubtedly this is our duty, but not all our duty, nor the highest and best part of it. A new country, forsooth! As if any people of Anglo-Saxon origin—with all its world of inherited literature behind it and Shakespeare for an an-

None in America.

UNITED STATES.

cestor; with all its history stretching back in direct line two thousand years; with all its religion and law derived from the past—could possibly be called young! As if the mere facts of place made a people young! As if we should all be old if we were on European soil, and are only young because we are on American soil! Do we plead ignorance of finance, of war, of trade, of commerce, of mechanics, on that score? Is there any nation that stands more forward than we in these departments? Why, then, should we excuse ourselves for deficiencies in higher culture by such a plea? We know that it is false. We know that it is only an excuse. So far from this being the case, we are one of the most luxurious nations in the world; one of the most developed in all that relates to convenience and the practical requirements of life, one of the most accomplished in all the so-called useful and mechanical arts; but in the ideal spheres of art we have accomplished little, because we have desired little; our needs and necessities have been amply supplied, but the heart and soul have been fed upon husks. Use has its buildings and habitations, but beauty has not yet its temple.

Plea for a better appreciation of a higher culture.

W. W. STORY,
Additional Commissioner.

[NOTE.—Appended hereto are lists of the jurors of the several classes comprised in the First Group (Works of Art), also of the exhibitors in those classes to whom awards were decreed.]

APPENDIX.

FIRST GROUP—WORKS OF ART.

PRESIDENT AND VICE-PRESIDENTS OF THE JURIES OF THE FIRST GROUP.

TULLO MASSARANI, Senator, President .... Italy.
MEISSONIER, First Vice-President .... France.
GUDE, Second Vice-President .... Sweden and Norway.

JURY ON CLASSES 1 AND 2 (PAINTINGS AND DESIGNS).

ARMITAGE .... England.
LEIGHTON .... England.
DOBSON .... England.
MILLET .... United States.
DARDEL .... Sweden and Norway.
DIETRICHSON .... Sweden and Norway.
PAGLIANO .... Italy.
PONTE DE LA HOZ .... Spain.
PASSINI .... Austria-Hungary.
HARKANYI .... Austria-Hungary.
BOGOLUBOFF .... Russia.
JACOBY .... Russia.
SAUSSURE .... Switzerland.
DELIN .... Belgium.
SLINGENEYER .... Belgium.
DE LAVELEYE .... Belgium.
FRŒLICH .... Denmark.
Marquis of PENAFIEL .... Portugal.
RŒLEFS .... Netherlands.
STORTENBECKER .... Netherlands.
BAUDRY .... France.
HEBERT .... France.
ROBERT-FLEURY .... France.
BONNAT .... France.
BRETON .... France.
DELAUNAY .... France.
JALABERT .... France.
COTTIER .... France.
LAURENS .... France.
REISET .... France.
HESSE .... France.
Vicomte DE TAUZIA .... France.
GRUYER .... France.

AWARDS IN CLASSES 1 AND 2 (PAINTINGS AND DESIGNS).

Of the Grand Prizes given to the Section on Painting, five were given to France, three to Austria-Hungary, two to England, one to Italy, one to Spain, one to Russia, one to Belgium; as follows:

GRAND PRIZES.

"Rappels" (confirmation of previous Medals of Honor, 1867).

Cabanel .... France.
Gérôme .... France.
Meissonier .... France.

Medals of Honor.

Bouguereau .... France.
Français .... France.
Herkonner, H .... Great Britain.
Makart .... Austria-Hungary.
Matejko .... Austria-Hungary.
Millais, J. E .... Great Britain.
Munkacsy, M .... Austria-Hungary.
Pasini, A .... Italy.
Pradilla, F .... Spain.
Siemiradski .... Russia.
Wauters .... Belgium.

MEDALS OF THE FIRST CLASS.

"Rappels" (confirmation of previous Medals of the First Class, 1867).

Bida .... France.
Calderon, P. H .... Great Britain.
Grant, Sir Francis .... Great Britain.
Madrazo, Frédéric .... Spain.
Stevens, Alfred .... Belgium.
Willems, F .... Belgium.

Medals.

Alma Tadema .... Great Britain.
Bloch .... Denmark.
Breton, Émile .... France.
Busson .... France.
Delaunay .... France.
Dubois, Paul .... France.
Glaize, Léon .... France.
Henner .... France.
Israels, J .... Holland.
Lefebvre, Jules .... France.
Lévy, Émile .... France.
Lévy, Henri .... France.
Madrazo, R .... Spain.
Munthe .... Norway.
Nittis, G. de .... Italy.
Robert-Fleury, Tony .. France.
Rousseau, Philippe .... France.
Van-Marcke .... France.
Vautier, B .... Switzerland.
Verlat .... Belgium.
Vollon .... France.
Wahlberg, A .... Sweden.
Watts, G. F .... Great Britain.
Winne, De .... Belgium.

MEDALS OF THE SECOND CLASS.

Bernier, Camille ..... France.
Bisschop .... Holland.
Blanc, P. J .... France.
Boulanger, G .... France.
Bridgman .... United States.
Canon .... Austria-Hungary.
Cederström, Baron G.. Sweden.
Clays .... Belgium.
Cluysenaar .... Belgium.
Cor .... France.
Curzon, De .... France.
Dominguez, D. Manuel, Spain.
Dubufe, Édouard ..... France.
Duran, Carolus .... France.

Goupil, J .... France.
Haanen, C. H. van ... Holland.
Harlamoff .... Russia.
Harpignies .... France.
Jacquemart, Mlle N .... France.
Koller, R .... Switzerland.
Kovalevski .... Russia.
L'Allemand .... Austria-Hungary.
Leloir, Louis .... France.
Machard .... France.
Moreau, Gustave ...... France.
Ouless, W. W......... Great Britain.
Pagliano, E............ Italy.
Pelouse................ France.
Pettersen...... ...... Norway
Thirion, E............ France.

MEDALS OF THE THIRD CLASS.

Angeli, V .... Austria.
Bastien-Lepage........ France.
Benezur Cyula......... Hungary.
Berchère .... France.
Berne-Bellecour ...... France.
Bertrand, J........... France.
Collart, Mme M .... Belgium.
Constant, B .... France.
Cormon .... France.
Dana.................. United States.
Defregger .... Austria.
Gilbert, Sir John ..... Great Britain.
Guillaumet............ France.
Gyzis .... Greece.
Heyerdahl............ Norway.
Humbert .... France.
Induno, Girolamo..... Italy.
Jacquet, G............ France.
Kramskoï .... Russia.
Lambert, Eugène ..... France.
Lamorinière, F .... Belgium.
Le Roux, Hector...... France.
Lupi .... Portugal.
Mesdag, H. W .... Holland.
Orchardson, W. Q .... Great Britain.
Parrot................ France.
Plasencia, C .... Spain.
Protais............... France.
Ribot .... France.
Rico, M .... Spain.
Rivière, B .... Great Britain.
Rotta, A .... Italy.
Santai .... France.
Segé .... France.
Toulmouche .... France.
Verwée .... Belgium.
Vibert .... France.
Worms .... France.

HONORABLE MENTIONS.

Alt.................... Austria-Hungary.
Becker .... France.
Becker, A. von .... Russia.
Blanchard, E .... France.
Braekeleer, H. de..... Belgium.
Claude, J. M .... France.
Desgoffe, Blaise....... France.
Dupain................ France.
Durand, Simon .... Switzerland.
Ferrier................ France.
Feyen-Perrin .... France.
Gaillard.............. France.
Giacomotti .... France.
Girard, Firmin .... France.
Green, C.............. Great Britain.
Hanoteau .... France.
Herpin .... France.
Hennebicq, A......... Belgium.
Jerndorff............. Denmark.
Keil.................. Portugal.
Lafarge .... United States.
Lecomte du Nouy..... France.
Lematte .... France.
Leslie, G. D.......... Great Britain.
Maignan .... France.
Maris, J .... Holland.
Moreau, Adrien....... France.
Pàl, L................ Austria-Hungary.
Perrault.............. France.
Pettie, J............. Great Britain.
Ribera, P............. Spain.
Robert, L. P.......... Switzerland.
Roll.................. France.
Saintin, J. E .... France.
Salmson .... Sweden.
Shirlaw .... United States.
Sinding .... Norway.
Vertunni, A.......... Italy.

DIPLOMAS TO THE MEMORY OF DECEASED ARTISTS.

Belly.................. France.
Corot.................. France.
Daubigny.............. France.
Diaz.................. France.
Fromentin............. France.
Millet................ France.
Pils.................. France.
Régnault.............. France.
Ricard................ France.
Rousseau, Théodore.... France.
Landseer, Sir Edwin.. Great Britain.
Lewis, J. F........... Great Britain.
Mason, G. H........... Great Britain.
Phillip, J............ Great Britain.
Walker, F............. Great Britain.
Čermak................ Austria-Hungary.
Fuhrich, Von.......... Austria.
Leys, Baron........... Belgium.
Madou, J. B........... Belgium.
Wappers, Baron........ Belgium.
Fortuny, M............ Spain.
Rosales, E............ Spain.
Zamacois, E........... Spain.
Meyer, L.............. Holland.
Veroeer, L............ Holland.
Waldorp, A............ Holland
Tideman............... Norway.
Faruffini............. Italy.
Fracassini............ Italy.
Bruni................. Russia.
Gleyre................ Switzerland.

JURY ON CLASS 3 (SCULPTURE AND DIE-SINKING).

MARSHALL, W. CALDER.................. Great Britain.
KUNDMANN, C.......................... Austria-Hungary.
MONTEVERDE, Le Commandeur............ Italy.
FRAIKIN.............................. Belgium.
CHAPU................................ France.
CAVELIER............................. France.
MILLET, A............................ France.

AWARDS IN CLASS 3.

GRAND PRIZE.

"Rappel" (confirmation of previous Medal of Honor, 1867).

Guillaume, Eugène.................... France.

Medals of Honor.

Antokolski............ Russia.
Dubois, Paul.......... France.
Hiolle................ France.
Mercié, A............. France.
Monteverde, G......... Italy.

MEDALS OF THE FIRST CLASS.

"Rappels" (confirmation of previous Medals of the First Class, 1867).

Crauk................. France.
Falguière............. France.
Millet, Aimé.......... France.
Ponscarme, N., graveur en médailles........ France.
Thomas, G. J.......... France.

Medals.

Allar................. France.
Barrias, E............ France.
Chaplain.............. France.
Civiletti, B.......... Italy.
Delaplanche........... France.
De Vigne.............. Belgium.
Lafrance.............. France.
Leighton, Sir F....... Great Britain.

Moreau, Mathurin .... France.
Schœnewerk .... France.
Zumbusch .... Austria-Hungary.

MEDALS OF THE SECOND CLASS.

Aizelin .... France.
Bocquet, J .... France.
Belliazzi, R .... Italy.
Boehm .... Great Britain.
Cain .... France.
Degorge .... France.
Gérôme, J. P .... France.
Ginotti, G .... Italy.
Lenoir, Alfred .... France.
Lepère .... France.
Leroux, Étienne ...... France.
Marqueste .... France.
Mignon, L .... Belgium.
Noël, Tony .... France.
Sanson .... France.
Tautenhayn .... Austria-Hungary.
Tilgner .... Austria-Hungary.
Tournois .... France.

MEDALS OF THE THIRD CLASS.

Aubé .... France.
Banjault .... France.
Borghi, A .... Italy.
Bortone, A .... Italy.
Bourgeois, Baron Ch. A. France.
Caillé .... France.
Cattier, A .... Belgium.
Damé .... France.
Dupuis, D., graveur en médailles .... France.
Gautherin .... France.
Gandarias, J .... Spain.
Hove, B. van .... Holland.
Moreau-Vauthier ..... France.
Morice .... France.
Moulin .... France.
Simoes d'Almeida ..... Portugal.
Tchijoff .... Russia.
Vingtrie, P. A. Bayard de la .... France.
Wagner .... Austria-Hungary.

HONORABLE MENTIONS.

Ahlborn, Mme L. ..... Sweden.
Barthélemy .... France.
Berg, O .... Sweden.
Bertaux, Mme L. ...... France.
Borjesson .... Sweden.
Comein, P .... Belgium.
Corbel .... France.
Doré, Gustave .... France.
Ferrari, E .... Italy.
François, graveur en pierres fines .... France.
Idrac .... France.
Maccagnani, E .... Italy.
Runeberg .... Russia.
Scharff .... Austria-Hungary.
Schmidgruber .... Austria-Hungary.
Smith .... Denmark.
Soares dos Reis .... Portugal.
Tabbachi, D .... Italy.
Wiener .... Belgium.

DIPLOMAS TO THE MEMORY OF DECEASED ARTISTS.

Barye .... France.
Cabet .... France.
Carpeaux .... France.
Perraud .... France.
Rochet, Louis .... France.

JURY ON CLASS 4 (ARCHITECTURAL DRAWINGS AND MODELS).

Barry, M. C. .... Great Britain.
Basile, Le Commandeur .... Italy.
De Fertel, Le Chevalier .... Austria-Hungary.
Mariette-Bey .... Egypt.
De Stuers, Le Chevalier .... Holland.
Ballu .... France.
Duc .... France
Lefuel .... France.
Boeswillwald .... France.
Vaudremer .... France.
Ginain .... France.

AWARDS IN CLASS 4.

GRAND PRIZES.

"*Rappels*" (*confirmation of previous Medals of Honor*, 1867).

Ferstel, Ch. de .... Austria.
Waterhouse, A. F. .... Great Britain.

Medals of Honor.

Paris, Exposition d'Architecture de la Ville de .... France.
Minister of Public Instruction, Public Worship, and Fine Arts (works of the Roman and Historical Monument Commissions) .. France.
Barry, E. M .... Great Britain.
Schmidt .... Austria.

MEDALS OF THE FIRST CLASS.

Chardon, E., and Lambert, M .... France.
École Royale d'Architecture .... Spain.
Hansen, Chevalier T. de .... Austria-Hungary.
Hasenauer, Baron C. de .... Austria-Hungary.
Pearson, J. L .... Great Britain.
Street, G. E .... Great Britain.

Awarded ex æquo to the Architects of the City of Paris.

Bailly, A. N. (diploma). France.
Baltart, V., deceased (diploma) .... France.
Diet, A. S. (diploma).. France.
Godeboeuf, E. (diploma) France.
Hermant, P. A. A. (diploma) .... France.
Janvier, L. J. (diploma) .... France.
Lheureux (diploma) .. France.
Magne, A. J. (diploma) France.

Awarded ex æquo to the works of the Roman Commission.

Bernier, S. L. (diploma) .... France.
Dutert, C. L. F. (diploma) .... France.

Guadet, J. (diploma) .. France.
Leclerc, C. A. (diploma) France.
Noguet, L. (diploma) . France.
Pascal, J. L. (diploma) France.

Awarded ex æquo to the works of the Historical Monument Commission.

Bruyerre, L. C. (diploma) .... France.
Corroyer, E. (diploma) France.
Darcy, D. (diploma) .. France.
Duthoit, C. M. (diploma) .... France.
Lafollye, J. A. (diploma) .... France.
Lisch, J. J. (diploma). France.
Millet, E. L. (diploma) France.
Ruprich-Robert (diploma) .... France.
Sauvageot, L. C. (diploma) .... France.
Simil, A. P. (diploma). France.
Violet-le-Duc, E. E. (diploma) .... France.

MEDALS OF THE SECOND CLASS.

Amador de los Rios, R. Spain.
Aguado, M .... Spain.
Boudier, A .... France.
Cuypers, P. J. H...... Holland.
Guillaume, Edmond and Renaud .... France.
Normand, A. N .... France.
Schmoranz, F., and Machytka, J........... Austria-Hungary.
Shaw, R. N .... Great Britain.
Trèves, M .... Italy.
Wolemans, A .... Austria-Hungary
Wyatt, J .... Great Britain.

Awarded ex æquo to the Architects of the City of Paris.

Aldrophe, A. P. (diploma) .... France.
Bonnet, P. E. (diploma) .... France.
Constant Dufeux, deceased (diploma).... France.
Daumet, P. J. H. (diploma) .... France.
Davioud, G. J. A. (diploma) .... France.
Deperthes, P. J. E. (diploma) .... France.
Devrez, D. H. L. (diploma) .... France.
Hénard, A. J. (diploma) .... France.
Lavezzari, E. (diploma) .... France.
Lebouteux, D. (diploma) .... France.
Roger, N. A. (diploma) France.
Roguet, F. (diploma).. France.
Salleron, C. A. L. (diploma) .... France.
Uchard, T. F. J. (diploma)..... .... France.

Awarded ex æquo to the Commissioners of Rome.

Chabrol, W. F. (diploma) .... France.
Dutert, deceased (diploma) .... France.
Gerhardt, C. A. (diploma) .... France.
Thomas, A. T. F. (diploma) .... France.

Awarded ex æquo to the works of the Historical Monument Commission.

Baudot, J. E. A. de (diploma) .... France.
Bérard, E. (diploma).. France.
Bœswillwald, fils, P. L. (diploma) .... France.
Bourmancé, J. P. (diploma) .... France.
Brune, E. (diploma) .. France.
Bruneau, E. (diploma) France.
Danjoy, G. E. E. (diploma) .... France.
Darcy, fils (diploma).. France.
Formigé, J. C. (diploma). .... France.

Hügelin, V. F. (diploma) .... France.
Ouradon (diploma).... France.
Schuersheim, P. (diploma) .... France.
Suisse, C. L. (diploma) France.

MEDALS OF THE THIRD CLASS.

Ballu, A., fils .... France.
Baudry, A .... France.
Bourgeois, A .... France.
Carpentier .... Belgium.
Fellner & Heimer .... Austria-Hungary.
Ferrario, C .... Italy.
Geymüller, H. A. de... Switzerland.
Guérinot, A. G .... France.
Jones, H .... Great Britain.
Reboul, A. C. J .... France.
Seddon .... Great Britain.
Steindl .... Austria-Hungary.

Awarded ex æquo to Architects of the City of Paris.

Billon, E. M. (diploma) France.
Bourdais, J. (diploma) France.
Calliat, P. V. (diploma) France.
Chat, J. E. A. (diploma) France.
Deconchy, J. J. (diploma) .... France.
Gancel, A. F. (diploma) France.
Hédin, A. (diploma)... France.
Héret, L. A. J. (diploma) .... France
Huillard, C. G. (diploma) .... France.
Train, E. (diploma)... France.
Varcollier, M. F. (diploma) .... France.

HONORABLE MENTIONS.

Arendt, C .... Luxemburg.
Benonville, P. L. A.. . France.
Boffi, L .... Italy.
Busiri, A .... Italy.
Cazaux, C. H .... France.
Coisel, A .... France.
Dartein, M. F. de.. .. France.
Hermain, J. A .... France.
Jackson, T. G .... Great Britain.
Köning, C .... Austria-Hungary.
Muller, A., & Ulrich, C. C .... Switzerland.
Neumann, F. .... Austria-Hungary.
Rumeny Guarini, H... Spain.
Sédille, P .... France.
Weber, A .... Austria-Hungary.

Awarded ex æquo to Architects of the City of Paris.

Cordier, E. (diploma). France.
Maréchal, H. (diploma) .... France.
Narjoux, F. (diploma). France.
Sondée, A. (diploma).. France.
Villain, deceased (diploma) .... France.

JURY ON CLASS 5 (ENGRAVINGS AND LITHOGRAPHS)

CRAIG, GIBSON .... Great Britain.
RICH .... United States.
BURGERS .... Holland.
DELABORDE, Vte .... France.
GATTEAUX .... France.
HENRIQUEL .... France.
CHAUVEL .... France.

AWARDS IN CLASS 5.

GRAND PRIZES.

Medals of Honor.

Huot	France.	Redlich	Russia.
Jacquemart, Jules	France.		

MEDALS OF THE FIRST CLASS.

"Rappel" (confirmation of previous Medal of Honor, 1867).

BERTINOT	France.

Medals.

Biot, G	Belgium.	Didier, A	France.
Danguin	France.	Gaillard	France.

MEDALS OF THE SECOND CLASS.

Blanchard	France.	Rajon	France.
Chauvel	France.	Sonnenleitner	Austria-Hungary.
Levasseur	France.	Weber, F	Switzerland.

MEDALS OF THE THIRD CLASS.

Bour	France.	Klaus	Austria-Hungary.
Flameng	France.	Unger	Austria-Hungary.
Gilbert	France.	Waltner	France.

HONORABLE MENTIONS.

Gilli, A	Italy.	Mitchell	United States.
Greux	France.	Morse	France.
Jacquet, J	France.	Pannemaker, St	Belgium.

This, summarized, shows that in the first and second classes, relating to paintings, there were 14 *grand prizes* or medals of honor, 30 medals of the first class, 30 medals of the second class, 38 of the third class, 38 honorable mentions, and 31 diplomas of deceased artists, making in all 181 prizes and honorable mentions. Of these, there were awarded to the United States 1 medal of the second class, to Mr. Bridgman; 1 medal of the third class, to Mr. Dana; and 2 honorable mentions, one to Mr. Lafarge and one to Mr. Shirlaw.

Of the third class, relating to sculpture and engraving on medals, there were 6 medals of honor (grand prizes), 16 medals of first class, 18 of second class, 19 of third class, 19 honorable mentions, 5 diplomas to deceased artists, making in all 83 medals, none of which were given to America.

Of the fourth class, relating to designs and models of architecture, there were five medals of honor (grand prizes), 31 medals of first-class, 42 medals of second class, 23 of third class, and 15 honorable mentions, making in all 116 medals, none of which were given to America.

Of the fifth class, of engravings and lithographs, there were 3 medals of honor, 5 medals of first class, 6 of second class, 6 of third class, and 6 honorable mentions, making in all 26 medals, of which there was awarded to the United States 1 honorable mention, to Mr. Mitchell.

www.ingramcontent.com/pod-product-compliance
Lightning Source LLC
Chambersburg PA
CBHW020536270326
41927CB00006B/609

* 9 7 8 3 3 3 7 3 1 1 0 1 8 *